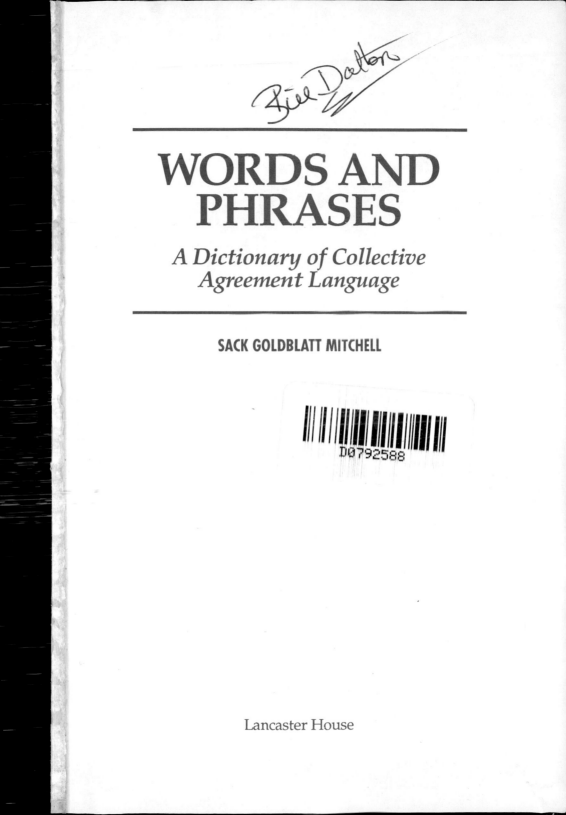

WORDS AND PHRASES

A Dictionary of Collective Agreement Language

SACK GOLDBLATT MITCHELL

Lancaster House

Lancaster House
20 Dundas Street West, Suite 1135
Toronto, Canada
M5G 2G8
©1993

All rights reserved. No part of this publication may be reproduced or
transmitted in any form or by any means, electronic or mechanical, including
photocopy, recording, or any information storage system, without
permission in writing from the publisher.

Canadian Cataloguing in Publication Data

Words and phrases

ISBN 0-920450-07-5

1. Collective labor agreements — Canada — Terms and
phrases — Dictionaries.   I. Sack Goldblatt Mitchell
(Firm).

KE3193.A57S34 1993   344.71'0189   C93-094279-5
KF3408.A35S34 1993

PREFACE

This dictionary contains definitions of words and phrases used in collective agreements in Canada. The definitions are those of arbitrators, as enunciated in awards reported in the series *Labour Arbitration Cases*, primarily during the 10-year period between 1980 and 1990.

An effort has been made to include only those cases where the definition of a term is apparent from the plain meaning of the language itself. However, readers are cautioned that the meaning of a term frequently depends on the context in which it appears and, if the language is ambiguous, on the past practice and negotiating history of the parties.

It is true, of course, that arbitrators are not always agreed on the meaning of certain terms, and occasionally distinct schools of interpretation spring up, espousing conflicting views. More often, however, a consistent pattern of interpretation emerges, which eventually attracts the adherence of a majority of arbitrators. In this manner, a "climate of collective bargaining" develops that invests collective agreement language with a commonly accepted meaning.

As Arbitrator Kevin Burkett has stated (*Macotta*, 1985): "Collective agreements are negotiated in the shadow of the arbitral jurisprudence; the parties look to the jurisprudence for the meaning of the words, phrases and clauses used in collective agreements."

PRINCIPLES OF INTERPRETATION

Generally, arbitrators interpret the provisions of a collective agreement in light of the plain meaning of the language and the purpose of the parties as evidenced in the overall context of the collective agreement. In this task, arbitrators rely upon their knowledge of industrial relations practice, and upon previous arbitration awards. Arbitrators may also use dictionaries and texts as reference sources, and take into consideration the use of the same or similar words in statutes as an aid in construction.

If there is ambiguity in the collective agreement, or an argument of fairness or estoppel is raised, the arbitrator will take into account the past practice and negotiating history of the parties. Subject to this, arbitrators will give primacy to the specific language in the collective agreement under consideration. However, the task of elucidation is not easy, especially when a literal interpretation would undermine the apparent purpose of the parties. Moreover, when they negotiate, the parties will sometimes disagree on the meaning of language, and leave it to an arbitrator to decide what it means. Since the parties have no common understanding, the task of divining their intention is somewhat artificial.

Arbitrators frequently resort to so-called rules of construction to assist them in ascertaining the negotiators' intent. Thus, for example, while the collective agreement must be read as a whole, arbitrators will try to give all words some meaning, and render all clauses operative. An attempt will be made to give the same words the same meaning, and different words different meanings, but an effort will also be made to avoid inconsistency, as well as impractical or

5

absurd results. Specific terms are usually treated as overriding general terms. For example, where management rights are stated in broad terms, they will generally be considered subject to particular provisions found elsewhere in the collective agreement.

The words "shall" and "may" are often the subject of interpretation. Ordinarily, "shall" is imperative, i.e. it means that a party must do something, while "may" is permissive, i.e. it means that a party has a discretion as to whether to do something or not, but this is not invariably the case. Sometimes, as in determining whether a time limit is mandatory or merely directory, the word "shall" is interpreted to mean "may", and *vice versa*. Much depends on the context in which the words appear.

Notwithstanding its ancient lineage, the *"ejusdem generis"* rule is very much alive as a rule of construction. Translated literally as "of the same class", the expression means that, where particular items having a common characteristic are followed by general words, the items encompassed by these general words are to be limited to items of the same type as those previously specified. Take, for example, a clause requiring the supply of shoes, jackets and trousers, and "anything else needed by the employees". The concluding words are likely to be interpreted by an arbitrator, in light of the *"ejusdem generis"* rule, as being limited to items of clothing.

Some examples may be instructive. In one case, where an agreement provided that seniority did not have to be applied on temporary layoffs resulting from an interruption due to breakdowns "or other causes beyond the company's control", the quoted words were held not to include an interruption due to inability of employees to do the job assigned. On an application of the *"ejusdem generis"* rule, the general words were limited by the previous words specifying a breakdown. Similarly, a clause providing for leave of absence to attend "union conventions, seminars, educational classes or other union business" was held not to include attendance at arbitration.

However, the courts have warned against extending the "*ejusdem generis*" rule too far, and have said that care must always be taken that the application of the rule does not defeat the true intention of the parties. If you wish to avoid application of the "*ejusdem generis*" rule, it is advisable, when drafting the collective agreement, to use general words only or to itemize everything intended to be covered.

"*Expressio unius est exclusio alterius*" is another venerable Latin maxim. Literally, it means that the expression of one thing is the exclusion of the other. The maxim has been applied to be the interpretation of contracts and statutes. In this context, it means that the express mention of one matter implies the exclusion of related matters. Take the following case. A clause in a collective agreement specifies that a doctor's certificate must be obtained after three days' absence due to illness. Does this mean that the employer cannot automatically require a certificate before three days have elapsed? If so, it is because of the application of the "*expressio unius*" rule.

How has the "*expressio unius*" rule been applied by arbitrators? In one case, where the contract expressly provided that seniority applied on promotion, it was held that it did not apply on layoff. In another case, where a letter of understanding expressly provided for bereavement leave when a death occurred in the immediate family during an employee's scheduled vacation, it was held that the grievor was not entitled to leave when the death occurred while he was on sick leave. In a third case, where the contract expressly imposed a duty on the company to meet with the union "in the event of a change in the shift arrangements as a result of a loss of volume or reduction in hours", it was held that there was no obligation to meet in other situations not mentioned, although a change in shift arrangements was involved. In a fourth case, where the contract provided for a procedure for scrutinizing sick leave claims, it was held that, by implication, the parties had excluded other techniques such as a home visitation program.

Some arbitrators have refused to apply the *"expressio unius"* rule on the ground that it is "a valuable servant, but a dangerous master", or that it is "continually relied on by despairing counsel, but very rarely applied by a court". However, despite repeated judicial cautions, arbitrators are occasionally persuaded by the *"expressio unius"* rule. Moreover, even where the maxim is not explicitly relied upon, the process of reasoning represented by it is often employed. In short, be careful that specific reference to one matter does not lead to a conclusion that other matters are excluded. Such a result can be avoided by using general language or by indicating that the specific reference is not intended to be exhaustive.

Sometimes these devices can be of assistance, but it is dangerous to apply them slavishly, and indeed more often than not, they are cited merely to support conclusions that have already been reached by the arbitrator on other grounds. Moreover, common law rules applicable to the construction of commercial contracts do not necessarily apply, and where they do apply, they should be applied with caution. Thus, the common law doctrine of frustration, which relieves a party of its contractual obligations where unforeseeable circumstances occur, is not applicable to collective agreement interpretation.

Indeed, arbitrators have developed an approach to construction based on the unique nature of collective agreements. Thus, in some cases, terms may be implied by arbitrators, such as an obligation to act fairly. In other cases, so-called presumptions may be invoked. There is a presumption, for example, that, in the absence of language to the contrary, premiums of the same kind ought not to be pyramided, contracting out will not be restricted, seniority will be applied plant-wide, statutory holiday pay will be considered as an earned benefit, monetary improvements are retroactive to the effective date of the contract, seniority is to be given special importance, etc.

Finally, it is important to note that the law of collective agreement administration has been characterized by a tension between two schools of interpretation, one insisting upon a strict construction of the literal terms of the document that reserves to management all rights not expressly taken away by the collective agreement, the other supportive of a broad reading of the agreement based on the premise that it is a bargain struck by two equal parties. The attitudes of arbitrators vary, but the courts have come down on the side of the view that collective agreements should be interpreted so as to require the parties to act reasonably, fairly, in good faith, and in a manner consistent with the collective agreement as a whole. It is important to remember that collective agreements are long-term arrangements, designed to govern an on-going relationship, and they should be interpreted in that light.

CASE CITATION

Labour Arbitration Cases, published by Canada Law Book, is presently in its fourth series. Several volumes appear per year. It contains awards from across Canada on all arbitration topics. The volumes are indexed, and a cumulative index is published periodically. Each award is reproduced verbatim and is prefaced by a listing of the issues involved in the award. A case citation is illustrated below.

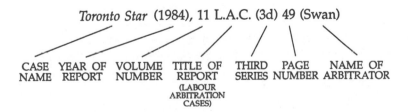

Toronto Star (1984), 11 L.A.C. (3d) 49 (Swan)

| CASE NAME | YEAR OF REPORT | VOLUME NUMBER | TITLE OF REPORT (LABOUR ARBITRATION CASES) | THIRD SERIES | PAGE NUMBER | NAME OF ARBITRATOR |

A

ABILITY, see also SKILL AND ABILITY

CONTRACT
TERM

Employees shall be selected for positions on the basis of their skill, *ability*, experience and qualifications. Where these factors are relatively equal, seniority shall govern provided the successful applicant is qualified to perform the available work within an appropriate familiarization period.

ARBITRATOR'S
RULING

While they are not distinct, and there is considerable overlap, "skill" is competence in particular tasks; "qualifications" refers to possession of necessary education, training and certification; "ability" relates to overall qualities of an employee with respect to the work to be done; and "experience" refers to the breadth and length of actual experience. Relative equality involves a determination of whether one employee is more qualified than another by a substantial and demonstrable margin in relation to the relevant circumstances. The employer cannot seize on minor differences between candidates to defeat the application of seniority.

Wellesley Hospital (1989), 5 L.A.C. (4th) 55 (Weatherill)

▼

CONTRACT
TERM

Applications for a bulletined position shall be given preference in accordance with seniority where *ability*, skill and merit are equal.

ARBITRATOR'S
RULING

Depending on the job, ability may include interpersonal skills.

Grace Maternity Hospital (1986), 27 L.A.C. (3d) 204 (DeMont).

▼

CONTRACT TERM	Selection of the qualified candidate shall be made by the department head on the basis of each candidate's *ability*, seniority and suitability for the position.
ARBITRATOR'S RULING	Ability may include the ability to communicate effectively in the English language if that is a necessary requirement of the job.

Metropolitan Toronto (1986), 26 L.A.C. (3d) 333 (Burkett).

▼

CONTRACT TERM	Layoff and recall will be based on seniority provided qualifications and *ability* are relatively equal.
ARBITRATOR'S RULING	Subject to a familiarization period in the case of an ordinary job that is not highly technical, "ability" means immediate and present ability to perform the work or, if a trial or training period is provided for under the collective agreement, sufficient potential ability to be able to perform the job satisfactorily at the conclusion of the period.

Lennox Industries (1983), 12 L.A.C. (3d) 241 (Kennedy).

▼

CONTRACT TERM	Seniority shall be the governing factor regarding promotion, where *ability* and qualifications are relatively equal among employees.
ARBITRATOR'S RULING	Ability refers to an employee's inherent capacities whereas qualifications refer to some form of training or experience.

Dominion Stores (1983), 9 L.A.C. (3d) 47 (Saltman).

▼

CONTRACT TERM	Selection to a posted position shall be made on the basis of seniority provided the employee has the *ability* to do the job.
ARBITRATOR'S RULING	"Ability to do the job" includes availability of the applicant to perform the work. An employee on vacation for a week when the job is scheduled to commence may nonetheless be available, depending on the job requirements and the facts of the case.

Seaway/Midwest (1982), 6 L.A.C. (3d) 295 (Devlin).

ABLE

CONTRACT
TERM

Seniority governs on layoff and recall; on layoff the employee must be *able* to fulfill the normal requirements of the job.

ARBITRATOR'S
RULING

The phrase requires present ability, without training, not just potential ability. In the absence of a trial period, the employer is not required to grant the employee an opportunity to demonstrate his or her skills before making an assessment of the employee's ability; however, a short familiarization period is permitted to become familiar with the routine and details of the job.

Denison Mines (1986), 25 L.A.C. (3d) 230 (Springate).

ABSENCE WITHOUT CAUSE

CONTRACT
TERM

To be eligible for holiday pay, an employee, unless *absent due to justifiable cause*, must have been present on the work-day immediately preceding and following such a holiday.

ARBITRATOR'S
RULING

Employees who leave work on illegal strike before completing at least half the required shift on the day before a statutory holiday are not in substantial compliance with the agreement and are therefore not entitled to holiday pay. However, employees who work two-thirds of the shift, on the day the illegal strike ends, are in substantial compliance, and are entitled to holiday pay.

Rothesay Paper Ltd. (1989), 5 L.A.C. (4th) 103 (MacLean).

ABSENCE WITHOUT LEAVE

CONTRACT
TERM

Plant holidays shall be recognized with pay provided the employee is not *absent without leave* on the working days immediately preceding and following the holiday.

ARBITRATOR'S
RULING

Absence on disciplinary suspension is not an absence with leave, since "leave" involves an application to be absent for which permission is granted, which does not occur where an employee is suspended for misconduct.

13

Canadian Timken Ltd. (1989), 8 L.A.C. (4th) 193 (Little).

▼

CONTRACT TERM

Seniority rights shall be terminated if the employee is *absent* from work for 3 consecutive days *without a satisfactory reason.*

ARBITRATOR'S RULING

Management must exercise its discretion by balancing its interests against those of the employee, and each application for leave of absence must be given fair and proper consideration. Here, the company based its decision on the application of a fixed policy of limiting the number of employees absent within each zone, as opposed to the required balancing of interests. In the contemporary industrial context, an employee is assumed to have a life outside and opportunities can occur which constitute a satisfactory reason, especially where the employer is not taken by surprise and has an opportunity to deal with the grievor's absence in advance. *Mack Canada Inc.* (1988), 33 L.A.C. (3d) 320 (Kennedy).

▼

CONTRACT TERM

An employee *absent from duty without written authority* in excess of 5 working days shall be considered to have left the services of the employer.

ARBITRATOR'S RULING

This language contemplates a requirement that the employer will act reasonably in invoking its discretion to terminate employees. *B.C. Rail* (1985), 21 L.A.C. (3d) 257 (Hope).

▼

CONTRACT TERM

An employee shall lose seniority status if he is *absent from work* for 5 consecutive working days without leave or notice unless in the opinion of the company there was reasonable justification.

ARBITRATOR'S RULING

Unauthorized absence does not reduce an employee to probationary status, but rather renders him an employee with zero seniority who is nonetheless entitled to the full protection of the "just cause" clause of the collective agreement. *Arrowhead Metals* (1984), 19 L.A.C. (3d) 59 (Hinnegan).

▼

CONTRACT
TERM
An employee shall lose seniority and be deemed to have terminated her employment if she is *absent from work without permission,* unless she furnishes a reason satisfactory to the employer.

ARBITRATOR'S
RULING
Under this language, the issue is not whether the employee's explanation would be accepted by an arbitrator; the question is whether the employer's decision is arbitrary, discriminatory or in bad faith.

Guelph General Hospital (1982), 5 L.A.C. (3d) 289 (Saltman).

▼

CONTRACT
TERM
An employee's service shall be considered broken if *absent* from work for 3 consecutive days *without permission* unless he furnishes a satisfactory reason upon his return.

ARBITRATOR'S
RULING
A loss of seniority does not result in a reversion to probationary status. The employee is not a new hire, and is protected against discharge without just cause.

Collingwood Shipyards (1982), 4 L.A.C. (3d) 132 (Carter).

▼

CONTRACT
TERM
Continuity of service shall be considered broken and employment terminated when an employee is *absent from work* without a satisfactory reason or without consent.

ARBITRATOR'S
RULING
This clause (which applies to all absences, however brief) operates where the predominant motive for the employer's decision is the seriousness of the absence; otherwise, an employee could be terminated for being 15 minutes late. Where the predominant motive for the employer's action is an illegal strike, it is a disciplinary discharge, and subject to just cause.

McKellar General Hospital (1981), 30 L.A.C. (2d) 229 (Prichard).

▼

CONTRACT
TERM
Failure to notify the company when *absent from work* for 7 consecutive days shall terminate all seniority rights.

ARBITRATOR'S
RULING
Under this clause, while the employee loses seniority rights, he does not revert to probationary status, and cannot be discharged without just cause.

Firestone Canada (1980), 28 L.A.C. (2d) 119 (Brunner).

▼

CONTRACT TERM An employee shall lose seniority and be deemed to have quit if he is *absent* for 3 consecutive working days without notifying the Personnel Office unless a *reason satisfactory to the company is given.*

ARBITRATOR'S RULING While the clause gives the company the initial right to assess the validity of the reasons given, the company must do so reasonably, and cannot act in an arbitrary or capricious manner; the company cannot refuse to accept a valid reason.

Welmet Industries (1980), 28 L.A.C. (2d) 84 (Rayner).

ABSENT

CONTRACT TERM Holiday pay is payable provided the employee is not *absent* from his last scheduled shift before such holiday or his first scheduled shift after such holiday without a doctor's certificate.

ARBITRATOR'S RULING Substantial compliance is the test; an employee who reports for work on a qualifying day, but leaves mid-way through the shift without permission, may be subject to discipline, but he has completed a substantial portion of the shift, and is entitled to holiday pay.

Stran-Steel (1980), 28 L.A.C. (2d) 153 (Betcherman).

ACCIDENT

CONTRACT TERM Weekly indemnity insurance benefits include sickness and accident insurance up to 66-2/3% of basic weekly earnings, for a maximum period of 32 weeks on the fourth day of sickness, on the first day for hospitalization or *accident.*

ARBITRATOR'S RULING An accident is an injury that is the fortuitous and unexpected result of natural causes; an injury to the back while bending over to put on one's socks qualifies as an accident. By contrast, sickness is a disability arising from the operation of natural causes such as old age, congenital or insidious disease, or the natural progression of some constitutional, physical or mental defect.

Long Manufacturing (1987), 30 L.A.C. (3d) 156 (Swan).

▼

CONTRACT
TERM

The welfare plan includes coverage for an off-duty *accident,* defined as a disability which is the result of an external force or is of an unexpected or uncommon nature.

ARBITRATOR'S
RULING

Accident does not include injury sustained off work while practising karate, since disabilities are normal for this activity, which was voluntarily undertaken by the employee.

Lear Siegler Industries (1977), 17 L.A.C. (2d) 168 (Palmer).

ACCUMULATED SICK LEAVE

CONTRACT
TERM

Permanent employees will be granted sick leave of 12 days for each calendar year. At the end of each calendar year, employees will be paid for unused days at their straight-time hourly rate, but may elect to accumulate 3 unused sick days. Unused sick days that are *accumulated* will be paid for at the rate the employee was making at the time he elected to accumulate said days.

ARBITRATOR'S
RULING

"Accumulation" implies credit for time worked, here one day's credit for each month worked; therefore, sick leave does not accumulate during a strike.

Consolidated Aviation Fueling Services (Pacific) Ltd. (1987), 30 L.A.C. (3d) 130 (Greyell).

▼

CONTRACT
TERM

A retiring employee is entitled to a cash payment equivalent to 50% of his *accumulated sick leave credit.*

ARBITRATOR'S
RULING

Where an employee's period of service is broken by resignation and subsequent return as a new employee, the employee is not entitled to sick leave credits accumulated prior to resignation.

B.C. Government (1985), 19 L.A.C. (3d) 347 (Thompson).

ACTIVE EMPLOYMENT/PAYROLL

CONTRACT
TERM

Probationary employees shall be required to complete 6 months of *active employment* to attain seniority.

17

ARBITRATOR'S RULING For the purposes of a probation clause, absence due to a compensable accident interrupts the period of active employment, given the employer's need to observe the employee's performance.

Algonquin College (1986), 22 L.A.C. (3d) 129 (Brent).

▼

CONTRACT TERM The company will provide health and welfare benefits to all *active employees.*

ARBITRATOR'S RULING Phrase includes ill or injured employees, e.g. those on Workers' Compensation, but does not include employees on indefinite layoff.

United Tire (1979), 23 L.A.C. (2d) 434 (Haladner). Contrast *Toronto General Hospital,* below.

▼

CONTRACT TERM Vacations and health benefits are based on months of *active employment.*

ARBITRATOR'S RULING Term does not include period off work on Workers' Compensation.

Toronto General Hospital (1977), 16 L.A.C. (2d) 113 (Brown). Contrast *United Tire,* above.

▼

CONTRACT TERM A cost of living bonus is payable to employees on the *active payroll* of the employer.

ARBITRATOR'S RULING Phrase includes employees on unpaid sick leave even though they are not in receipt of wages from the employer.

Metro Toronto (1977), 14 L.A.C. (2d) 395 (Brent).

ACTIVITY, see **UNION ACTIVITY**

ACTUAL WORK, see also **TIME WORKED, WORK**

CONTRACT TERM For the purposes of calculating vacation pay and vacation bonus, where an employee has been absent on WCB benefits, such time will be considered as time worked, provided that such employee *actually worked* for some period during the vacation eligibility period in question.

18

ARBITRATOR'S RULING An employee absent on WCB who shows up to work on only one day during the year, without authorization by the employer, is not entitled to vacation monies for the year in question. He cannot be said to have actually worked, since he was not directed or assigned work by the employer. One cannot establish a claim to vacation and bonus pay simply by volunteering for work or by assigning oneself to perform work.

Rio Algom Ltd. (1988), 2 L.A.C. (4th) 151 (O'Shea).

AGE, *see also* DISCRIMINATION

CONTRACT TERM There shall be no *discrimination* on the basis of *age*, sex, etc.

ARBITRATOR'S RULING This clause prohibits mandatory retirement at age 65. The definition of age in Ontario human rights legislation, which ends protection at age 65, is not to be read into the word "age" in the collective agreement, unless the parties so provide.

O.P.E.I.U. (1982), 8 L.A.C. (3d) 71 (Swan). Contrast *Canadian Porcelain,* below.

▼

CONTRACT TERM There shall be no *discrimination* because of *age*.

ARBITRATOR'S RULING "Age" is to be defined in accordance with the definition in Ontario human rights legislation, which ends protection against age discrimination in employment at age 65. Thus, the clause is not violated by company policy, enshrined in an optional company pension plan, of mandatory retirement at age 65. However, "discrimination", a word of very wide import, means differential or unequal treatment, and a company practice of continuing some employees beyond age 65, but not others, without standards or reasons, constitutes discrimination.

Canadian Porcelain (1981), 30 L.A.C. (2d) 40 (Brunner). Contrast *O.P.E.I.U.,* above.

AS FAR AS POSSIBLE, *see* POSSIBLE

ASSESSMENTS

CONTRACT TERM The employer agrees to the monthly check-off of all union dues, *assessments*, initiation fees and written assignments of amounts equal to union dues.

19

ARBITRATOR'S RULING	Term includes assessments of 100% of gross wages imposed by the union on members who crossed the picket line during a legal strike. *Windermere Central Park Lodge* (1983), 12 L.A.C. (3d) 9 (Getz).

ASSIGN

CONTRACT TERM	It is the exclusive function of the employer to transfer and *assign* employees provided that a claim for discriminatory transfer may be the subject of a grievance.
ARBITRATOR'S RULING	The term "transfer" means to move from one job to another. The move may be within a classification, or across classification lines. The essential element of a transfer is that the new job and the old must be distinctly different. The term "assign" means the general deployment of the workforce including organization of shift schedules and matters of a similar kind. Here, a move from the recreation department to the custodial shift, in a corrections institution, constitutes a transfer, not an assignment, since the jobs are different. The term "discriminatory" involves drawing a distinction for reasons that are illegal, arbitrary or unreasonable. Here, the transfer was not discriminatory, since the reason was that it was less costly to cover the grievor's absences from work on the custodial shift. *Metropolitan Authority* (1983), 10 L.A.C. (3d) 265 (Outhouse).

AUTHORIZED ABSENCE/LEAVE OF ABSENCE

CONTRACT TERM	To be eligible for holiday pay, an employee must work the full scheduled work day immediately preceding and following such holiday, unless absent on *authorized leave of absence*, layoff or proven illness or injury.
ARBITRATOR'S RULING	An employee who misses the first hour of work the day following a holiday, and telephones his employer to advise that he will be late, is entitled to a full day's pay for the holiday, where the absence would ordinarily have been authorized by the company after the fact, or where the company would have been obliged to grant a leave of absence for the time involved. Here, the employee's absence would have been considered authorized since he was obliged to deal with his child's recurrent medical problems.

Union Felt Products (Ont.) Ltd. (1988), 1 L.A.C. (4th) 148 (Kennedy).

▼

CONTRACT
TERM

Employees are entitled to holiday pay despite absence from work on the day before or after the holiday if the absence is due to *specific authorized absence*.

ARBITRATOR'S
RULING

While employees on layoff remain employees, a layoff is not a specific authorized absence so as to entitle employees laid off for 3 months to 5 holidays occurring during that period.

Baie Verte Mines (1986), 27 L.A.C. (3d) 135 (Easton).

AUTHORIZED OVERTIME WORKED, see also
OVERTIME, WORK

CONTRACT
TERM

A premium is payable for all *authorized overtime worked*.

ARBITRATOR'S
RULING

Travel required by the employer constitutes "work", and travel time is authorized overtime worked.

Alberta Housing Corp. (1982), 4 L.A.C. (3d) 228 (Taylor).

B

BARGAINING UNIT WORK, *see* **CONTRACTING OUT**

BEREAVEMENT LEAVE

CONTRACT TERM — "Immediate family" for the purposes of *bereavement leave* shall mean brother-in-law, etc.

ARBITRATOR'S RULING — "Brother-in-law" includes only the brother of one's husband or wife, and not a spouse's sister's spouse, because of the restriction in the definition of leave to "immediate family", which is a narrower concept than "family", and includes only the employee's close relatives, not those of his or her spouse.

Greater Niagara General Hospital (1989), 4 L.A.C. (4th) 283 (McLaren).

▼

CONTRACT TERM — An employee who suffers the death of his/her mother, father, husband, wife, mother-in-law, father-in-law, etc. will be granted 3 consecutive working days' *leave of absence*.

ARBITRATOR'S RULING — In the absence of words of general application, such as "immediate family", "father-in-law" does not include the father of a common law spouse.

Hermes Electronics Ltd. (1989), 4 L.A.C. (4th) 257 (Kydd).

▼

CONTRACT TERM — Employees attending the funeral of a near relative shall be granted 5 days' paid *leave of absence* if the funeral is outside the city.

ARBITRATOR'S RULING — Bereavement leave is not restricted to situations where the employee is at work; employees can take a leave of absence from a vacation. An employee whose sister dies while he is on vacation is therefore entitled to paid leave to attend the funeral.

Calgary Roman Catholic Separate School District No. 1 (1989), 3 L.A.C. (4th) 385 (Ponak).

▼

CONTRACT TERM
The purpose of *bereavement leave* is to reimburse active, permanent employees for wage loss in the event of death in the immediate family, defined to include grandparents, grandparents-in-law, etc.

ARBITRATOR'S RULING
The term "grandparents-in-law" does not include the grandfather of a common law spouse.

MacMillan Bathurst Inc. (1988), 35 L.A.C. (3d) 415 (H.D. Brown).

▼

CONTRACT TERM
Employees shall be allowed one day to attend the employee's grandparents' or brother- or sister-in-law's *funeral*.

ARBITRATOR'S RULING
"Grandparent" does not include the grandmother of an employee's spouse.

Windsor Star (1988), 34 L.A.C (3d) 438 (Roberts).

▼

CONTRACT TERM
Employees who suffer *bereavement* within the immediate family will be granted 3 days' leave of absence; immediate family includes grandparents.

ARBITRATOR'S RULING
"Grandparents" includes spousal grandparents, since a broad interpretation of "immediate family" is warranted in the absence of restrictive language.

Associated Freezers of Canada (1987), 32 L.A.C. (3d) 79 (Kilgour).

▼

CONTRACT TERM
When the current spouse, mother-in-law, etc. dies, the employee will be excused for a period not exceeding 3 days.

ARBITRATOR'S RULING
Mother-in-law includes the mother of an employee's common law spouse.

Lakeview Development (1987), 31 L.A.C. (3d) 85 (Haefling).

▼

CONTRACT TERM
In the event of the death of an employee's immediate relative, an employee will be granted *leave of absence* with pay; immediate relative shall mean: wife, mother-in-law, etc.

ARBITRATOR'S
RULING
Mother-in-law includes mother of common law wife.

Genaire Ltd. (1987), 27 L.A.C. (3d) 188 (Weatherill).

▼

CONTRACT
TERM
Bereavement leave of up to 5 days to be granted upon request with maximum of 3 days' bereavement pay.

ARBITRATOR'S
RULING
Since the purpose of bereavement pay is to provide time off work without loss of pay, an employee on layoff has no entitlement. However, an employee who does not return to work because of bereavement is not on layoff, but on bereavement leave.

Northern Telecom (1986), 25 L.A.C. (3d) 193 (Springate).

▼

CONTRACT
TERM
Where *bereavement leave* falls on a scheduled working day for the employee, he shall be paid a bereavement allowance.

ARBITRATOR'S
RULING
Where entitlement to bereavement leave is unrestricted, it is payable regardless whether the individual is on vacation; but where it is restricted to attendance at the funeral on scheduled working days, it is not payable when the employee is on vacation at the time of death.

Rio Algom (1986), 24 L.A.C. (3d) 194 (Tacon).

▼

CONTRACT
TERM
In the case of death in the immediate family (defined to include spouse, common law spouse, father-in-law, mother-in-law, etc.) of an employee, up to 3 days' *bereavement leave* allowed.

ARBITRATOR'S
RULING
Where "immediate family" is not defined, or the definition includes certain persons, but is not an exhaustive list, the family of a common law spouse might be covered. However, where "immediate family" is defined, the father or other family of a common law spouse is not covered unless specifically mentioned.

Alberta Wheat Pool (1986), 23 L.A.C. (3d) 316 (Kelleher).

▼

CONTRACT TERM

In the event of a death in the immediate family, employees shall be given a *leave of absence* for 5 calendar days and shall not suffer any loss of regular pay and benefits as a result of the leave of absence.

ARBITRATOR'S RULING

Where vacation falls during bereavement leave, an employee is entitled to a vacation day in addition to bereavement.

Halifax Infirmary (1985), 20 L.A.C. (3d) 123 (Darby).

▼

CONTRACT TERM

When death occurs to a member of a regular full-time employee's immediate family, the employee will be granted an appropriate *leave of absence*; immediate family is defined as the employee's spouse, grandparents, etc.

ARBITRATOR'S RULING

Bereavement leave clauses should be read broadly to advance their purpose, which is to accommodate grief, and immediate family includes the grandparents of an employee's spouse.

North Cariboo Labour Relations Association (1985), 19 L.A.C. (3d) 115 (Hope).

▼

CONTRACT TERM

In the event of the death of an employee's grandparent, etc., the employer will grant *leave of absence* with pay.

ARBITRATOR'S RULING

The word "grandparent" designates an employee's own grandparents; a spouse's grandparents are not included.

Beer Precast Concrete (1984), 15 L.A.C. (3d) 107 (Swan).

▼

CONTRACT TERM

A *bereaved* employee is entitled to four consecutive days leave.

ARBITRATOR'S RULING

Saturday and Sunday must be counted toward leave entitlement, since use of the word "days" means a reference to calendar days, rather than working days.

City of Hamilton Board of Education (1983), 10 L.A.C. (3d) 126 (Kennedy).

▼

CONTRACT TERM	In the event of the death of a nurse's spouse, mother-in-law, etc., 3 working days' *leave of absence* shall be granted with pay.
ARBITRATOR'S RULING	"Mother-in-law" does not include the mother of an employee's common law spouse.

Peel Board of Health (1983), 9 L.A.C. (3d) 94 (Shime).

▼

CONTRACT TERM	In the case of death in the immediate family of an employee, the company will grant three days *leave of absence* with pay.
ARBITRATOR'S RULING	Vacation and bereavement leave are separate benefits, that address different circumstances, and an employee who suffers a bereavement during vacation is entitled to additional time.

Alcan Smelters (1982), 5 L.A.C. (3d) 83 (Hope).

▼

CONTRACT TERM	*Bereavement leave* with pay shall be available in the event of the critical illness or death of any of the following relatives of the employee or his spouse, child, etc.
ARBITRATOR'S RULING	The clause covers not just blood relationships but relationships through marriage, including a spouse's stepchild, where there has been a real life relationship.

Southern Alberta School Authorities Assn. (1981), 5 L.A.C. (3d) 351 (Mason).

▼

CONTRACT TERM	Employees *absent due to death* of [specified relatives] will be compensated for time lost from their regular schedule to a maximum of 3 working days.
ARBITRATOR'S RULING	Where bereavement leave occurs during vacation, no compensation is due, since there is no loss of time from the regular schedule, and the employee is not entitled to reschedule the vacation.

City of Toronto (1981), 2 L.A.C. (3d) 61 (Beatty).

▼

CONTRACT TERM	*In the event of a death* in his immediate family, 3 days off work will be paid for by the company.
ARBITRATOR'S RULING	An employee on vacation at the time of bereavement remains eligible for bereavement leave at the conclusion of his vacation.

Lafarge Concrete (1980), 27 L.A.C. (2d) 429 (Mc-Coll).

▼

CONTRACT TERM

In the event of death in the immediate family of an employee, the company shall grant a paid *leave of absence* not exceeding three days for the purpose of attending the funeral and/or making funeral arrangements.

ARBITRATOR'S RULING

An employee whose father dies while the employee is on vacation is not entitled to an additional three days of vacation. The clause is not operative while an employee is on vacation since the purpose of bereavement leave, to grieve and make funeral arrangements with no loss of pay, has been satisfied. Also, the concept of "leave" implies that an employee is working in the first place, so there is no need to grant leave to an employee already on vacation.

Gray Forging Limited (1980), 27 L.A.C. (2d) 61 (Shime). Contrast *Alcan Smelters*, above.

BEYOND THE EMPLOYER'S CONTROL

CONTRACT TERM

Employees reporting for work for whom no work is available will be paid 4 hours' pay unless the lack of work is caused by strike, machinery breakdown, fire, flood, power failure or other like cause *beyond the control of the company.*

ARBITRATOR'S RULING

A chemical spill caused by employee negligence was beyond the control of the company. The test is whether it could have been avoided with the exercise of reasonable care. Since the procedure to prevent spills had been successfully followed for 14 years, it was not reasonably foreseeable that the procedure would not be followed by an employee.

Robertshaw Controls Canada Inc. (1989), 5 L.A.C. (4th) 124 (Saltman).

▼

CONTRACT TERM

A premium will be payable in the event of a change of shift schedule on short notice, unless the change is caused by events *beyond the (employer's) control.*

ARBITRATOR'S
RULING

The death of an employee's relative, requiring bereavement leave, does not fall within the exemption, since management had an alternative method of filling the vacancy, besides changing the shift schedule.

Re Charlebois (1981), 27 L.A.C. (2d) 316 (Swan).

▼

CONTRACT
TERM

Shift schedules shall be posted not less than 15 days in advance and there shall be no change in the schedule unless 72 hours' notice is given. If the employee is not notified 72 hours in advance, he shall be paid time and a half, provided that no premium shall be paid where the change of schedule is caused by events *beyond the (employer's) control.*

ARBITRATOR'S
RULING

Events which are foreseeable are not beyond an employer's control since they may be provided against. Therefore, absences arising out of bereavement leave that require a shift change are not due to circumstances beyond an employer's control, and a shift premium must be paid.

Crown in Right of Ontario (Ministry of Correctional Services) (1980), 27 L.A.C. (2d) 316 (Swan).

▼

CONTRACT
TERM

A reporting allowance is payable except where an employee is prevented from working because of a power shortage, power failure or any circumstance *beyond the control of the company.*

ARBITRATOR'S
RULING

Such phrases are strictly construed, since their clear purpose is to protect employees against loss of pay. Frigid conditions preventing employees from working are not beyond the control of the company, although the weather itself may have been cold, since the company could have taken a number of measures to ensure adequate heating.

Sasco Tubes (1977), 15 L.A.C. (2d) 99 (Linden).

BREADWINNER

CONTRACT
TERM

Employees established as *breadwinners* in a family shall be covered [by group insurance] on a family basis.

ARBITRATOR'S RULING The breadwinner in the family is the partner whose income is higher, and includes a married woman whose husband is on unemployment insurance.

T.R.E. Inc. (1983), 10 L.A.C. (3d) 295 (Brent).

BROTHER-IN-LAW, *see also* BEREAVEMENT LEAVE

CONTRACT TERM "Immediate family" for the purposes of bereavement leave shall mean *brother-in-law*, etc.

ARBITRATOR'S RULING "Brother-in-law" includes only the brother of one's husband or wife, and not a spouse's sister's spouse, because of the restriction in the definition of leave to "immediate family", which is a narrower concept than "family", and includes only the employee's close relatives, not those of his or her spouse.

Greater Niagara General Hospital (1989), 4 L.A.C. (4th) 283 (McLaren).

BULLETIN BOARD, *see* UNION ACTIVITY

BUMPING, *see* LAYOFF

C

CALL-BACK/CALL-IN/CALL-OUT

CONTRACT
TERM

An employee, if *called out* or scheduled to work overtime, shall receive compensation for a minimum of three hours at the applicable overtime rate provided that the period of overtime worked by the employee is not contiguous to his scheduled working hours.

ARBITRATOR'S
RULING

Work involves providing a service to clients, and it is not necessary to leave home to do so, provided the service is an integral part of the employee's job. Employees who receive telephone calls at home from clients are therefore entitled to call-out pay.

Queen in Right of Manitoba (1987), 28 L.A.C. (3d) 241 (Freedman).

▼

CONTRACT
TERM

Stand-by pay is payable (1/2 hour's pay for 4 hours on stand-by) when an employee is designated to be immediately available to return to work during a period he is not on regular duty. *Call-back pay* is payable (at the overtime rate) when an employee is called back to work for a period in excess of 2 hours.

ARBITRATOR'S
RULING

Stand-by pay and call-back pay are both payable, and pyramiding of benefits is not involved, since the purpose of stand-by pay is to compensate an employee for the inconvenience of arranging his life to be able to respond to a call-back, whereas the purpose of call-back pay is to compensate the employee for the actual work done once the employee is called back.

Crown in Right of Alberta (1986), 25 L.A.C. (3d) 276 (Elliott).

▼

="66

CONTRACT TERM An employee *called in* outside his standard hours shall be paid a minimum of 4 hours.

ARBITRATOR'S RULING An employee answering a call-in would normally expect not to work and has no obligation to hold himself ready whereas an on-call employee is obliged to respond to emergency calls; thus, where the collective agreement provides separately for on-call status, and pay rates for hours worked by an on-call employee, an on-call employee is not entitled also to call-in pay.

Regional Municipality of Niagara (1986), 23 L.A.C. (3d) 190 (Egan).

▼

CONTRACT TERM A minimum of 4 hours' work is required where an employee is *called in* to work outside of his normal hours of work.

ARBITRATOR'S RULING "Call-in" refers to call-in of an employee from home, without prior warning, to work outside the normal hours of work, whether or not an extra trip is involved and whether or not a break occurs before or after the regular shift.

Ontario Hydro (1984), 16 L.A.C. (3d) 207 (Tacon). Contrast *City of Toronto* and *Kent County*, below.

▼

CONTRACT TERM Employees who have left the building and are *called back* shall be paid for time worked, but not less than 4 hours plus all travel time, all at the overtime rate.

ARBITRATOR'S RULING Call-back pay is intended to provide payment to employees who are called in without sufficient notice after they have left the premises; thus, it applies where the employee is telephoned at his or her home only hours prior to the regular shift requiring him or her, without prior notice, to report for work in an emergency situation.

Pacific Press (1983), 13 L.A.C. (3d) 238 (McColl). Contrast *City of Toronto* and *Kent County*, below.

▼

CONTRACT TERM A minimum guarantee of 3 hours' work at overtime rate is payable where an employee who has completed the regular day's work has left the workplace and is *called out* for overtime work.

ARBITRATOR'S RULING
Call-out pay involves work scheduled at a time that is not contiguous with the employee's regular work schedule, thus normally necessitating an extra trip by the employee.

City of Toronto (1983), 12 L.A.C. (3d) 232 (P.C. Picher). Contrast *Ontario Hydro* and *Pacific Press,* above.

▼

CONTRACT TERM
An employee who has left the work premises, but is *called back* to work outside his regular hours shall be paid a minimum of 3 hours' pay at time and a half.

ARBITRATOR'S RULING
Call-out is intended to compensate employees for the inconvenience and expense of being called back to work, and to discourage the employer from calling employees back unless there is a serious need. Call-out is not applicable where employees work continuously up to the start of their shift or from the end of their shift since they are then not required to make an extra trip.

County of Kent (1982), 8 L.A.C. (3d) 188 (Swinton). Contrast *Ontario Hydro* and *Pacific Press,* above.

▼

CONTRACT TERM
Should the company *call out* any employee to work he shall be paid at a rate of one and a half times the applicable hourly rate for time worked.

ARBITRATOR'S RULING
A call-out occurs when work is required, outside an employee's regular hours, that is not planned overtime but is required as a result of an emergency. An emergency occurs when an unforeseen occurrence requires immediate attention. Contacting an employee on Saturday evening to come into work the next day to do emergency repair work on his day off entitles him to call-out pay.

Falconbridge Nickel Mines Ltd. (1980), 26 L.A.C. (2d) 338 (H.D. Brown).

CAPABILITY, see SKILL AND ABILITY

CASUAL EMPLOYEE/CASUAL EMPLOYMENT

CONTRACT TERM
Casual employee means any employee hired for a specific period of time or on a casual basis or as a temporary or spare employee.

ARBITRATOR'S RULING   Trainees hired by the employer in preparation for an expected strike, to undertake bargaining unit functions, are casual employees during their period of training, since they are hired for a specific period to perform a bargaining unit function.
Canada Post Corp. (1987), 31 L.A.C. (3d) 211 (Burkett).

▼

CONTRACT TERM   There are two categories of employees: permanent employees and *casual employees.*

ARBITRATOR'S RULING   The term "casual employment" means employment at uncertain times or irregular intervals; it lacks continuity and has reference to the nature of the employment and not to its duration.
Town of Dieppe (1982), 9 L.A.C. (3d) 76 (Stanley).

▼

CONTRACT TERM   A *casual employee* is a person employed to perform services for which no regular position exists or to perform services where the incumbent of a regular position is temporarily unable to do so.

ARBITRATOR'S RULING   Under this definition a casual employee does not become a regular employee unless appointed by the employer to a regular position.
Board of School Trustees (1981), 2 L.A.C. (3d) 221 (Borowicz).

CHARGE PAY ✳

CONTRACT TERM   *Charge pay:* when an employee who holds the position of a staff nurse is designated *in charge of* a ward or unit, such employee shall be paid an additional $1.00 per hour.

ARBITRATOR'S RULING   The sole employee working in a unit over the weekend is considered to be "in charge of" the unit where she is in fact responsible for its administration, whether or not she has been formally designated in charge.
Metro Edmonton Hospital District No. 106 (1989), 4 L.A.C. (4th) 330 (Thomas).

CHILD, *see also* BEREAVEMENT LEAVE

CONTRACT TERM   Bereavement leave with pay shall be available in the event of the critical illness or death of any of the following relatives of the employee or his spouse, *child*, etc.

ARBITRATOR'S
RULING
The clause covers not just blood relationships but relationships through marriage, including a spouse's stepchild, where there has been a real life relationship.

Southern Alberta School Authorities Assn. (1981), 5 L.A.C. (3d) 351 (Mason).

CLOSURE

CONTRACT
TERM
A part-time employee may elect to transfer to another store in the event of a permanent store *closure*.

ARBITRATOR'S
RULING
Franchising of a store does not amount to closure, even though the transaction may be considered a sale for successor rights purposes under labour relations legislation.

Oshawa Foods (1987), 27 L.A.C. (3d) 105 (Joyce).

COMMON LAW SPOUSE, *see* BEREAVEMENT LEAVE

COMPARABLE

CONTRACT
TERM
In making promotions, transfers, and demotions the skill, knowledge and work record of the employee shall be the primary considerations. Where two or more applicants are capable of fulfilling the duties of the position and the aforesaid qualifications are otherwise *comparable*, seniority or years of experience shall be determining factors.

ARBITRATOR'S
RULING
Comparability is defined as "able to be compared, capable of comparison, worthy of comparison", while "equal" denotes possessing a like degree of a quality, on the same level of ability. Relative equality is therefore a higher test than comparability between candidates. A junior employee must be superior to a senior one by a "clear and demonstrable margin".

Board of School Trustees, School District No. 39 (1987), 30 L.A.C. (3d) 257 (Thompson).

COMPASSION/COMPASSIONATE LEAVE

CONTRACT
TERM
Applications for leaves of absence without pay will be adjudicated on the basis of merit, *compassion*, length of service and the operational needs of the store. Leaves of absence shall not be unreasonably withheld.

ARBITRATOR'S
RULING

The employer's policy of refusal to grant extended leaves of absence due to incarceration violates the collective agreement, since it is based on an automatic, rigid policy, and the agreement requires each application to be considered on its own merits. The grievor's application for leave had "merit" since he was attempting to protect his employment status following incarceration, and he had been regarded as a worthy employee. Also, "compassion" can be interpreted to extend beyond family or marital circumstances, and is not precluded by criminal conduct.

Canada Safeway Ltd. (1988), 1 L.A.C. (4th) 435 (McColl).

▼

CONTRACT
TERM

The employer may grant an employee leave of absence with pay for not more than three days in a year upon special or *compassionate grounds*.

ARBITRATOR'S
RULING

Compassionate leave is granted in situations deserving of sympathetic treatment, including emergencies beyond the control of the employee, and should not be confined to planned events, such as a spouse's major surgery or a child's court date. Compassionate leave is therefore warranted for an employee who wishes to visit another city where her son's wife has been seriously injured in a car accident.

Crown in Right of Ontario (Ministry of Health) (1980), 27 L.A.C. (2d) 283 (Swinton).

COMPETENCY

CONTRACT
TERM

Following a layoff, an employee shall be recalled in order of seniority, subject to *competency*.

ARBITRATOR'S
RULING

An employee's competency cannot be determined on the basis of assumptions about strength and ability to do a job based on his or her age or sex, but must be determined through an objective, non-discriminatory assessment relating to the employee's work habits and experience.

Pelton Reforestation Ltd. (1988) 33 L.A.C. (3d) 40 (Kelleher).

CONDITIONS OF EMPLOYMENT

CONTRACT
TERM

New employees shall be on a probationary period normally not exceeding 6 consecutive calendar months. All vacancies and new positions of a permanent nature shall be posted. Any general *conditions of employment* not specifically mentioned in this agreement and not contrary to its intent shall continue in force and effect.

ARBITRATOR'S
RULING

Temporary employment on fixed term contracts does not prevent the accumulation of seniority where there is no provision for temporary employees in the collective agreement. Allowing non-permanent vacancies to be filled without posting does not give an employer the right to employ people on temporary contracts. A practice of hiring employees on temporary contracts does not make it a general condition where there is no evidence the union acquiesced in the practice and it has applied only to a transitory 5% of the bargaining unit; such a practice is contrary to the intent of the agreement, since it denies rights set out in the agreement; and it is immaterial that individual employees accepted the contracts.

Ottawa-Carleton (1981), 4 L.A.C. (3d) 77 (Swan).

CONFERRING OVER GRIEVANCES

CONTRACT
TERM

Union representatives shall not lose regular wages while *conferring with employees over grievances* and while attending grievance meetings with the company.

ARBITRATOR'S
RULING

"Grievance meetings" does not include arbitration hearing, but "conferring with employees over grievances" does, although payment is only an indemnity for actual lost earnings.

Ross Laboratories (1981), 30 L.A.C. (2d) 125 (Kennedy).

CONSIDER

CONTRACT
TERM

In filling vacancies, the company will give *consideration* to seniority and ability.

ARBITRATOR'S RULING — "Consideration" requires the company to put its collective mind to certain criteria, but the final evaluation is left largely to the discretion of the company, and it may not be interfered with in the absence of evidence of arbitrariness or discrimination.

Partek Insulations Ltd. (1989), 5 L.A.C. (4th) 253 (Palmer).

▼

CONTRACT TERM — Subject to the operating needs of the business, management will *consider* senior employees with respect to assignment of shifts and hours.

ARBITRATOR'S RULING — "Operating needs" means *bona fide* business reasons, whether or not wise, and "consider" means only to take into consideration, or be aware of; where the employer satisfies this requirement, it can institute rotating shifts.

Arbutus Club (1986), 23 L.A.C. (3d) 241 (MacIntyre).

▼

CONTRACT TERM — The company may grant a leave of absence to an employee for personal reasons. In granting such a leave, the company will *consider* the nature of the personal reasons, seniority, and efficient operation of the plant.

ARBITRATOR'S RULING — To "consider" requires a company to "reckon with" or "make allowances for" an employee's request, i.e. to fairly and reasonably consider the nature of the personal reasons for a request and the effects on other circumstances of the request. A flat denial of a request by the company's most senior employee to add a week's leave of absence to the annual vacation shutdown to visit a sick parent overseas violates the collective agreement.

Whitby Boat Works (1980), 27 L.A.C. (2d) 269 (O'Shea).

CONSULTATION

CONTRACT TERM — The company shall allow disciplined or discharged employees to *consult* with a shop steward, prior to the recorded discharge or recorded discipline.

ARBITRATOR'S
RULING

The presence of a union steward at a meeting where discipline is handed out satisfies the collective agreement; there is no mandatory obligation on the company to ensure that employees have exercised their right of consultation, and the failure of employees to exercise their right does not void the discipline.

Sunrype Products Ltd. (1988), 4 L.A.C. (4th) 62 (Chertkow).

▼

CONTRACT
TERM

The employer agrees to hold *constructive consultation* with the union prior to having the work usually done by the employees of the bargaining unit given outside.

ARBITRATOR'S
RULING

Constructive consultation concerning the contracting out of work in the form of a franchise requires the union to be given an opportunity to have input into a decision to establish a particular franchise, an opportunity to convince the employer that the basic business reasons for contracting out are invalid, and that there is a real reason to change the objectives or a means of achieving them in some other way.

Canada Post Corporation (1988), 34 L.A.C. (3d) 28 (Christie).

CONTINUOUS SERVICE/EMPLOYMENT, *see also* SERVICE

CONTRACT
TERM

Seniority shall mean length of *continuous service* in the employ of the [employer]. Annual leave for all full time professional staff shall accumulate on the following basis: 22 working days per year upon completion of one year of *service*.

ARBITRATOR'S
RULING

Express language is necessary to reduce vacation entitlement for absence due to illness, and there is no evidence that service should be interpreted to mean "active service", nor that service should be given a different meaning than continuous service.

Children's Aid Society of Algoma (1988), 1 L.A.C. (4th) 143 (Brent).

▼

CONTRACT TERM An employee will be considered on probation until he has completed 3 months' *continuous service* or 90 days of intermittent employment within any 12 month period.

ARBITRATOR'S RULING Absence due to strike, layoff, illness, etc., interrupts an employee's continuous service for the purpose of calculating his probationary period, with the result that such an "intermittent employee" must meet the test of working 90 calendar days in a 12-month period to achieve seniority status.

Ferro Industrial Products Ltd. (1988), 35 L.A.C. (3d) 324 (Stanley).

▼

CONTRACT TERM Vacation entitlement is based on years of *continuous service.*

ARBITRATOR'S RULING Period is not broken by absence on long-term disability.

Lethbridge General Hospital (1986), 26 L.A.C. (3d) 372 (Taylor).

▼

CONTRACT TERM The amount of sick pay benefits is based on length of *continuous service.*

ARBITRATOR'S RULING A change of status from part-time to full-time employment does not break service.

Welland County General Hospital (1986), 24 L.A.C. (3d) 421 (T.A.B. Jolliffe).

▼

CONTRACT TERM The amount of sick pay is determined by length of *continuous service.*

ARBITRATOR'S RULING Continuous service includes part-time employment prior to transfer to full-time bargaining unit.

Salvation Army Grace Hospital (1986), 24 L.A.C. (3d) 318 (Roberts).

▼

CONTRACT TERM No employee shall receive holiday pay unless he has been *continuously employed* for a period of 30 calendar days immediately preceding the holiday.

ARBITRATOR'S RULING Even though service or employment has been held, in cases of layoff or legal strike, to mean simply employment status, rather than attendance at work, an illegal strike breaks continuous employment.

City of Penticton (1985), 21 L.A.C. (3d) 233 (MacIntyre).

▼

CONTRACT TERM
Reduction of teaching staff necessary because of redundancy shall be made on the basis of length of *continuous service.*

ARBITRATOR'S RULING
Continuous service refers to continuous employment; thus, the service of part-time teachers is not to be pro-rated on the basis of teaching load.

Sault Ste. Marie Roman Catholic Separate School Board (1985), 21 L.A.C. (3d) 107 (P.C. Picher).

▼

CONTRACT TERM
New employees shall be on a probationary period normally not exceeding 6 consecutive months. Seniority shall mean length of *continuous service.*

ARBITRATOR'S RULING
Successive 3-month terms of employment interrupted by one working day off without pay do not prevent the completion of a continuous probation period.

City of Ottawa (1984), 13 L.A.C. (3d) 293 (Little).

▼

CONTRACT TERM
Employees shall receive 11 statutory holidays. Vacation shall be based on years of *continuous service.* Sick leave credits shall accumulate based on months or years worked.

ARBITRATOR'S RULING
Some benefits accrue by virtue of employment, others depend on the employee's presence at the workplace and performance of work. It all depends on the agreement. Here, in the absence of restrictions, employees absent from work because of a compensable disability are entitled to holiday pay and vacations, since continuous service is synonymous with seniority, but sick leave credits do not accumulate since they are based on months or years worked.

City of Trail (1983), 10 L.A.C. (3d) 251 (Munroe).

▼

CONTRACT TERM
Regular full-time employees having completed 8 years or more of *continuous full-time service* shall be granted 4 weeks' vacation.

ARBITRATOR'S RULING
Service is not broken by maternity leave.

Canada Safeway (1981), 30 L.A.C. (2d) 273 (Brown).

▼

CONTRACT TERM
Maternity leave up to 6 months will be granted upon request. Seniority is based on continuous *service*.

ARBITRATOR'S RULING
Since "service" means "employment", temporary absences such as maternity leave do not cause a break in service, and seniority continues to accumulate.

Toronto Star (1981), 30 L.A.C. (2d) 267 (Weatherill).

▼

CONTRACT TERM
Employees shall be entitled to annual vacations with pay as follows: four weeks' vacation after 10 or more years' *continuous service*. In no circumstances shall an employee who has acquired seniority lose it because of absence due to illness.

ARBITRATOR'S RULING
Employees absent on workers' compensation for most of the year are entitled to full vacation pay, since there is an uninterrupted employment relationship tantamount to continuous service for the period of absence.

Union Gas Limited (1980), 27 L.A.C. (2d) 72 (McLaren).

▼

CONTRACT TERM
Disability retirement plan is based on years of *continuous employment*.

ARBITRATOR'S RULING
Employment is not broken by periods of leave of absence for reasons of illness.

Canadian Johns-Manville (1979), 21 L.A.C. (2d) 226 (Kennedy).

▼

CONTRACT TERM
Vacations are based on years of *continuous service*.

ARBITRATOR'S RULING
Service is not broken by period of maternity leave.

Air Canada (1976), 13 L.A.C. (2d) 225 (Brown).

CONTRACTING OUT, *compare* EMPLOYEES, PERSONS

CONTRACT
TERM

The employer agrees that persons not covered by this agreement will not perform duties normally assigned to persons in the bargaining unit except for purposes of instruction, experimentation, emergency or as may be agreed. In order to provide job security for members of the bargaining unit the employer will not *contract out* work usually performed by members of the bargaining unit if a layoff follows. Nor will an employee remain on layoff if that employee can perform the normal requirements of the work.

ARBITRATOR'S
RULING

The first clause applies to non-bargaining unit employees, the second to contracting out of bargaining unit work. Where the second clause applies (as here), "work" has a broader meaning than "duties", and is the composite of tasks, duties and activities employees are required to perform. The question is whether the outside contractor is doing similar work for the employer. Where this occurs, and probationary employees are on layoff, a violation of the collective agreement results.

Regional Municipality of Ottawa-Carleton (1989), 9 L.A.C. (4th) 201 (Thorne).

▼

CONTRACT
TERM

Management and excluded personnel shall not work on any jobs which are included in the bargaining unit. The employer will give the union two months' notice of its intention to *contract out* work.

ARBITRATOR'S
RULING

"Excluded personnel" is restricted to non-bargaining unit employees. Otherwise, the term "persons" would have been employed. The painting by tenants of their own apartments therefore does not violate the collective agreement. A contracting-out of work requires an assignment of bargaining unit work to an independent contractor and his employees, which did not occur here: no work could be said to have been assigned to tenants, particularly since they had complete discretion whether or not to paint.

Newfoundland and Labrador Housing Corp. (1988), 4 L.A.C. (4th) 89 (Cooper).

▼

CONTRACT
TERM

The employer agrees to hold constructive consultation with the union prior to having the work usually done by the employees of the bargaining unit *given outside.*

ARBITRATOR'S
RULING

Both the conversion of a subpost office to a franchise, and the establishment of a franchise in an area not previously served by a postal facility, constitute contracting out, where they involve work which would have been done by bargaining unit employees if the contracting out or franchising had not occurred.

Canada Post Corp. (1988), 34 L.A.C. (3d) 28 (Christie).

▼

CONTRACT
TERM

The union recognizes the right of the company to contract and subcontract provided bargaining unit employees are not laid off by reason of such *contracting out.*

ARBITRATOR'S
RULING

The transfer of bargaining unit work from one plant, where employees are working at overcapacity, to another does not amount to contracting out, even though it is assigned to employees outside the bargaining unit; contracting out is the practice whereby an employer arranges with a second independent employer to perform work on its behalf, and it does not include the transfer of work within the same company.

SKD Manufacturing Div. (1988), 33 L.A.C. (3d) 381 (Weatherill).

▼

CONTRACT
TERM

The company agrees not to extend present practices with respect to the *contracting out* of work.

ARBITRATOR'S
RULING

Contracting out is generally understood to be the practice whereby one employer arranges to have a second employer perform work on its behalf.

Coca-Cola Ltd. (1983), 11 L.A.C. (3d) 207 (Springate).

▼

CONTRACT
TERM

Contracting out of work is prohibited where it would result in the layoff of bargaining unit employees.

43

ARBITRATOR'S
RULING
The term "layoff" in this clause means initial layoff, not continuing layoff; the clause does not apply to the contracting out of work normally performed by an employee already on layoff, since the layoff precedes and is not caused by the contracting out.

Rockwell International of Canada (1982), 6 L.A.C. (3d) 304 (Rayner).

▼

CONTRACT
TERM
Persons whose regular jobs are not in the bargaining unit shall not work on any jobs which are included in the bargaining unit, except for the purpose of instruction, experimenting or when regular employees are not available. The company shall continue to use *outside contractors* but shall, wherever practicable, have such work performed by employees within the bargaining unit, provided they have the necessary skills.

ARBITRATOR'S
RULING
The first clause is a "working foreman" clause, designed to prevent the assignment of bargaining unit work to supervisory employees; "persons" in this context means employees, and not independent contractors. In the second clause, the word "practicable" means "possible or feasible", whereas the word "practical" means "efficient and workable"; thus, "wherever practicable" does not mean "unless it is more efficient to do otherwise". As a result, where bargaining unit members are capable of doing the work, during regular hours or on overtime, the mere fact that outside contractors are better or faster does not make it impracticable to use bargaining unit employees.

Ivaco Rolling Mills (1981), 1 L.A.C. (3d) 186 (Adell).

▼

CONTRACT
TERM
Contracting out bargaining unit work is restricted except in emergencies when regular employees are not available.

ARBITRATOR'S
RULING
Shortage of nursing staff is not an emergency where it did not arise suddenly and has continued for over two years, and where overtime by regular staff might have sufficed.

Riverdale Hospital (1975), 7 L.A.C. (2d) 40 (Schiff).

CONTROL, see BEYOND THE EMPLOYER'S CONTROL

CONVENIENCE OF MANAGEMENT

CONTRACT TERM
In the event that an employee is assigned temporarily to a job, contrary to his seniority, *at the convenience of management*, he shall receive the established rate of the job. While performing such work, the employee will receive such compensation as may be required to equal the earnings he would otherwise have realized.

ARBITRATOR'S RULING
A transfer of an employee into a lower-paying job because a compassionate leave of absence was granted to the incumbent does not relieve the company of paying the difference in salary. The fact that a transfer occurs for the convenience of an employee does not mean that it is not also for the convenience of the employer. The cause of the grievor's transfer was the company's decision to maintain production schedules.

Armco Canada Ltd. (1980), 25 L.A.C. (2d) 145 (O'Shea).

COST

CONTRACT TERM
The company agrees to assume the *cost* of the welfare plans.

ARBITRATOR'S RULING
The term "cost" has the same meaning as "full cost" or "entire cost" and, unless there is (as here) limiting language in the collective agreement, it includes not just the cost of premiums, but all costs relating to the administration of the welfare plans, such as doctors' fees for medical certificates required by the insurer.

H.J. Heinz (1982), 4 L.A.C. (3d) 1 (Burkett).

D

DAMAGES

CONTRACT
TERM

The employer agrees to indemnify the employees for *damages* or claims for damages or injuries or accidents done or caused by them during the performance of their duties excluding willful and malicious damage.

ARBITRATOR'S
RULING

Clause requires employer to reimburse employee for legal costs in defending criminal negligence charges initiated against him as a result of a motor vehicle accident while performing job duties.

City of Ottawa (1984), 15 L.A.C. (3d) 193 (Kates).

DAY

CONTRACT
TERM

No report may be placed in an employee's file unless it is sent to the employee within 10 *days* after the date of the employee's alleged infraction or of its coming to the attention of the employer.

ARBITRATOR'S
RULING

A "day" is to be interpreted as a calendar day, and not as a working day.

Canada Post Corp. (1989), 3 L.A.C. (4th) 444 (Weatherill).

▼

CONTRACT
TERM

Employees working overtime on *Sundays* shall receive double time; workweek is Monday to Friday starting at 7 a.m. Monday.

ARBITRATOR'S
RULING

If an employee's regular shift commences late on a particular day and overlaps into a second day, as for example a Friday evening into a Saturday morning, the shift worked is viewed as a "day" corresponding to the day on which the shift commenced. Where a 3-shift operation is in effect, and the col-

46

lective agreement provides that the workweek begins at 7 a.m. Monday, work between 5 a.m. and 7 a.m. on Monday is to be treated as work on a Sunday, and double time is payable.

Canron Inc. (1987), 27 I..A.C. (3d) 379 (M.G. Picher).

▼

CONTRACT TERM

A bereaved employee is entitled to not more than 4 *days'* leave.

ARBITRATOR'S RULING

Although "day" generally refers to a calendar day for the purposes of bereavement leave or holiday pay, etc. it means a working day where leave, i.e. authorized absence from duty during regular or normal hours of work, would not be required on non-working days.

Treasury Board (1986), 26 L.A.C. (3d) 187 (Nisbet).

▼

CONTRACT TERM

Time and a half is payable for time worked in excess of 8 hours per *day* or in excess of 8 continuous hours.

ARBITRATOR'S RULING

"Days" means calendar days, not a 24-hour period commencing at the start of an employee's shift.

Chrysler Canada (1985), 22 L.A.C. (3d) 342 (O'Shea).

▼

CONTRACT TERM

An employee shall acquire seniority rights when he has worked 90 *days*; a probationary employee may be separated without reference to seniority, but if he is continued in employment, his seniority shall be accumulated from the original date of his employment.

ARBITRATOR'S RULING

For purposes of probation, which involves assessment of the employee's performance, a "day" means a "working day", but interruption of the probationary period by a brief layoff due to lack of work does not result in termination so as to require a new probation period.

Gainers Inc. (1985), 22 L.A.C. (3d) 214 (Owen).

▼

CONTRACT TERM

A bereaved employee is entitled to four consecutive *days* leave.

ARBITRATOR'S RULING — Saturday and Sunday must be counted toward leave entitlement, since use of the word "days" means a reference to calendar days, rather than working days.

City of Hamilton Board of Education (1983), 10 L.A.C. (3d) 126 (Kennedy).

▼

CONTRACT TERM — Temporary shift procedure is to be used only when such is required for three *days* or more.

ARBITRATOR'S RULING — Term "days" means calendar days, not working days.

City of London (1975), 7 L.A.C. (2d) 46 (Hinnegan).

DAY OF REST

CONTRACT TERM — *Day of rest* means a calendar day on which an employee is not ordinarily required to perform the duties of his position other than a designated holiday and calendar day on which he is on leave of absence. An employee who is required to work on a day off shall be paid time-and-one-half.

ARBITRATOR'S RULING — Where the normal work week is Monday to Friday, employees who are required to work on a Saturday to make up for a day lost through an illegal walkout are required to work on a "day of rest" and are therefore eligible for overtime pay.

Newfoundland Farm Products Corp. (1988), 4 L.A.C. (4th) 343 (Easton).

▼

CONTRACT TERM — Where an employee who is required to travel on behalf of the employer is absent from home on a designated paid holiday or *day of rest* and does not work, he shall receive time and a half or the equivalent leave with pay.

ARBITRATOR'S RULING — Clause does not require absence from home during full day of rest, i.e. for 24 hours; absence from home during normal hours of work is compensable at time and a half.

Commissioner of N.W.T. (1985), 21 L.A.C. (3d) 441 (Chertkow).

DAYS WORKED

CONTRACT
TERM

New employees will be considered probationary employees for the first 45 workdays on the active payroll of the employer. Upon completion of 30 *days worked*, probationary employees shall be entitled to payment for the paid holidays specified.

ARBITRATOR'S
RULING

Because management needs a reasonable opportunity to assess an employee, paid holidays to which a probationer becomes entitled are not counted in calculating the probationary period; "workdays" and "days worked" are synonymous.

General Coach (1988), 35 L.A.C. (3d) 235 (Roberts).

DEEMED

CONTRACT
TERM

Any employee who is absent from work for 3 or more consecutive working days, and cannot prove that a request for authorization was not possible due to circumstances beyond his/her control, may at the employer's discretion be *deemed* to have resigned without notice.

ARBITRATOR'S
RULING

"Deemed" is mandatory in meaning, and does not create a rebuttable presumption, i.e., "deemed until the contrary is proved". Evidence that an employee absent more than 3 days did not intend to resign is irrelevant in the face of a deemed resignation clause.

University of Manitoba (1989), 4 L.A.C. (4th) 249 (Bowman).

DESIGNATED

CONTRACT
TERM

A special allowance will be paid to nurses *designated* in charge of the facility for a specified shift.

ARBITRATOR'S
RULING

Use of the term "designated" does not require a formal act by the employer where the employee in question is placed in charge or given responsibility by the employer as a matter of fact.

Richmond Lions Senior Citizen Housing (1982), 6 L.A.C. (3d) 319 (Hope).

49

DISABILITY/DISABLED, see also ILLNESS, SICK LEAVE, SICKNESS

CONTRACT TERM — Employees who are totally *disabled* are entitled to sick pay benefit for the purposes of sick pay; totally *disabled* means a state of bodily injury or disease which prevents the employee from performing the regular duties of the occupation.

ARBITRATOR'S RULING — Participation in an *in vitro* fertilization program involving medical and surgical treatment qualifies an employee for sick leave benefits, since the grievor's absence results from an underlying diseased condition.

Hamilton Civic Hospitals (1988), 32 L.A.C. (3d) 284 (Saltman).

▼

CONTRACT TERM — Sick pay benefits shall be paid if an employee is totally *disabled*; totally *disabled* means an employee's inability to perform the regular duties pertaining to her occupation due to illness or injury.

ARBITRATOR'S RULING — Participation in an *in vitro* fertilization program, involving medical and surgical procedures to remedy infertility, entitles an employee to short-term sick leave benefits, because it is a recognized medical treatment for a pre-existing abnormal condition, which causes physical incapacity. Infertility itself qualifies as an illness or disease according to worldwide medical standards.

Metropolitan General Hospital (1987), 32 L.A.C. (3d) 10 (H.D. Brown).

▼

CONTRACT TERM — Sick leave plan covers *disability*, defined as inability to perform regular duties due to injury or illness.

ARBITRATOR'S RULING — Inability to work due to pregnancy complication endangering growth of foetus constitutes a disability due to illness. While a normal healthy pregnancy is not an illness, an abnormal unhealthy pregnancy constitutes a disabling illness entitling the employee to sick leave benefits.

Hotel Dieu of St. Joseph Hospital (1985), 20 L.A.C. (3d) 299 (MacDowell).

▼

CONTRACT TERM Insurance coverage depends on whether or not employee is totally *disabled.*

ARBITRATOR'S RULING Clause requires assessment, not just of organic, but also of psychogenic illness.

Dominion Stores (1985), 20 L.A.C. (3d) 97 (Kennedy).

▼

CONTRACT TERM Long-term disability benefits are available in the event of *total disability,* defined to mean the "continuous disability of the employee to engage in each and every gainful occupation or employment for which he is reasonably qualified by education, training or experience".

ARBITRATOR'S RULING Total disability means inability to perform work reasonably comparable to the work previously performed by the employee even though the employee may be capable of marginal employment.

Dominion Stores (1983), 11 L.A.C. (3d) 221 (M.G. Picher).

▼

CONTRACT TERM Sick pay is payable for absence from work due to *disability.*

ARBITRATOR'S RULING Word includes abnormal pregnancy, i.e. where complications or aggravating features exist, by reason of which the employee cannot or reasonably ought not, without endangering her physical or emotional well-being, to continue with her work.

Clinton Public Hospital (1979), 22 L.A.C. (2d) 37 (Brunner).

DISCHARGE/DISMISSAL

CONTRACT TERM The employer has the right to *discharge* for just cause.

ARBITRATOR'S RULING A proviso for loss of seniority on failure to notify the employer of absence and to justify absence constitutes an agreed upon result, not discharge, and in such circumstances the employer is not required to establish just cause.

Stelco (1985), 22 L.A.C. (3d) 65 (McLaren).

▼

51

CONTRACT
TERM

Just cause is required for *dismissal*. An employee absent from duty without written authority for a period in excess of 5 working days shall be considered as having left the service of the employer.

ARBITRATOR'S
RULING

Termination for unauthorized absence, as provided for under the collective agreement, is brought about by operation of the agreement. Even though management cannot act unreasonably or in bad faith, a deemed quit does not amount to dismissal for cause, which is for culpable conduct.

B.C. Rail (1985), 21 L.A.C. (3d) 257 (Hope).

▼

CONTRACT
TERM

Cause shall be required for *discharge*.

ARBITRATOR'S
RULING

Discharge may be for culpable conduct or non-culpable deficiency in job performance. Where discharge occurs for non-culpable deficiency in job performance, the employer must establish (a) the level of performance required; (b) that the standard expected was communicated to the employee; (c) that it gave reasonable supervision and instruction to the employee and afforded the employee a reasonable opportunity to meet the standard; (d) inability to meet the standard to an extent that renders the employee incapable of performing the job, together with reasonable efforts to find alternative work the employee can do; (e) reasonable warnings.

Edith Cavell Private Hospital (1982), 6 L.A.C. (3d) 229 (Hope).

▼

CONTRACT
TERM

There shall be no discrimination in the matter of *discharge* by reason of age, etc.

ARBITRATOR'S
RULING

The term "discharge" does not include retirement, so that the clause does not prohibit mandatory retirement at age 65.

Prince Rupert Fishermen's Co-op (1980), 29 L.A.C. (2d) 69 (Larson).

DISCIPLINE/DISCIPLINARY

CONTRACT
TERM

If an employee is *disciplined*, he shall be advised of the reasons for the *discipline* in writing.

ARBITRATOR'S RULING

The requirement to give reasons for discipline requires that sufficient information be given to permit an employee to know the basis on which discipline is being imposed, and whether he or she should grieve the discipline.

City of Calgary (1989), 9 L.A.C. (4th) 1 (Rooke).

▼

CONTRACT TERM

At the time formal *discipline* is imposed or at any stage of the grievance procedure, including the complaint stage, an employee is entitled to be represented by her representative.

ARBITRATOR'S RULING

The right to union representation arises from the point at which the disciplinary process is invoked, but before the employer has made up its mind to impose discipline. The clause does not require union representation at a meeting where a matter is discussed that *might* ultimately lead to discipline. The right to union representation does not apply to a meeting to discuss a patient complaint. A request that the grievor meet with her supervisor to explore a patient complaint, when discipline was not yet in issue, did not trigger the clause.

Montfort Hospital (1988), 3 L.A.C. (4th) 244 (Adell).

▼

CONTRACT TERM

Just cause is required for *discipline*.

ARBITRATOR'S RULING

A letter criticizing an employee is not a grievable disciplinary warning, where there is no indication that dismissal might follow in the event of further accidents, and it is not intended to have a prejudicial effect on the employee's position in future disciplinary proceedings.

City of Cornerbrook (1986), 27 L.A.C. (3d) 439 (Roberts).

▼

CONTRACT TERM

In the event of sick leave abuse, the employer shall *discipline* the employee as follows — first case: warning with memo to the employee's personnel file.

ARBITRATOR'S RULING   A letter from the employer advising employees of their poor attendance record and expressing the hope that it can be corrected, but without threatening future action, is not a grievable warning, since a warning must have a prejudicial effect upon an employee's position in future grievance arbitrations.

The Queen in Right of Nfld. (1986), 27 L.A.C. (3d) 284 (Easton).

▼

CONTRACT TERM   An employee is entitled to have a shop steward present as an observer at a *disciplinary* discussion with supervisory personnel.

ARBITRATOR'S RULING   Discipline includes discharge, so that the requirement applies where the meeting is to notify the employee of discharge.

City of Toronto (1986), 24 L.A.C. (3d) 115 (T.A.B. Jolliffe).

▼

CONTRACT TERM   Just cause is required for *discipline*.

ARBITRATOR'S RULING   A letter of dissatisfaction is grievable as discipline where it alleges misconduct and could support disciplinary action, despite the fact that the collective agreement also allows the employee to put a reply on record.

Pacific Press (1986), 23 L.A.C. (3d) 251 (McColl).

▼

CONTRACT TERM   A written *disciplinary* notice shall be given to employees.

ARBITRATOR'S RULING   Performance evaluations do not constitute discipline and, except for limited purposes, cannot be used as evidence to support just cause for discharge unless they form part of the employee's record, are communicated to the employee, contain critical comment that relates to specific incidents, are accompanied by a sanction such as a warning, and are grievable.

Calgary General Hospital (1986), 23 L.A.C. (3d) 25 (Beattie).

▼

CONTRACT TERM

No employee shall be *disciplined* or discharged except for just and sufficient cause.

ARBITRATOR'S RULING

A letter of criticism from an official in another ministry with no authority over the employee, which cannot be used against him, is not discipline and is therefore not grievable, although it would be if it were a reprimand from a superior.

Government of Nova Scotia (1985), 23 L.A.C. (3d) 58 (Veniot).

▼

CONTRACT TERM

Employees must be advised they may have a union representative in attendance if management proposes taking any *disciplinary* action.

ARBITRATOR'S RULING

A warning letter is not disciplinary where the employer files a notation with it that it is not disciplinary and will not be used as evidence in any future grievance proceeding except to rebut a claim by the grievor that he was unaware of management's concerns.

Metropolitan Transit Commission of Halifax (1985), 20 L.A.C. (3d) 203 (Darby).

▼

CONTRACT TERM

The company agrees that when an employee is to be *disciplined* a local union official shall be present.

ARBITRATOR'S RULING

Discipline is a generic term, and may, depending on the context, include discharge; here, it does, because it would be absurd to require union representation for minor discipline, but not for discharge. Since the right to union representation is a substantive right of basic importance, the absence of a union steward renders the discharge void.

Saville Food Products (1985), 20 L.A.C. (3d) 114 (Brandt).

▼

CONTRACT TERM

Accidents for which the employee is at fault will result in *disciplinary* action which may range from reprimand to suspension to dismissal.

ARBITRATOR'S RULING

Collective agreement language that provides for a range of penalties or states that an offence is subject to dismissal does not constitute a specific penalty within the meaning of labour legislation that permits an arbitrator to modify discipline except where the collective agreement contains a specific penalty for the infraction.

55

Essex Terminal Railway Co. (1985), 20 L.A.C. (3d) 1 (MacDowell).

▼

CONTRACT TERM
Employees are entitled to access to their file in order to review evaluations or *disciplinary* notations.

ARBITRATOR'S RULING
The term includes adverse performance notations where the employer may rely on them in the future to justify a change in status or to implement a decision involving monetary loss to the employee.

City of Toronto (1984), 16 L.A.C. (3d) 384 (M.G. Picher).

▼

CONTRACT TERM
There shall be no *discipline* except where there is just and reasonable cause.

ARBITRATOR'S RULING
An adverse performance appraisal is not grievable discipline where the employer undertakes that it will not be used in disciplinary proceedings.

Lake Cowichan Credit Union (1984), 15 L.A.C. (3d) 248 (Bluman).

▼

CONTRACT TERM
The arbitrator is empowered to substitute a penalty for *discipline* imposed by the employer.

ARBITRATOR'S RULING
A demotion may be disciplinary or non-disciplinary. A disciplinary demotion is to be distinguished from a "pure" or non-disciplinary demotion. The former is a form of corrective discipline based on culpable behaviour, and hence cannot be imposed permanently. The latter involves the transfer of an employee whose conduct is non-culpable but who is nevertheless incapable of meeting and maintaining a proper standard of work performance.

Wire Rope Industries (1983), 13 L.A.C. (3d) 261 (Hope).

▼

CONTRACT TERM
The company has the right to *discipline* employees for just cause.

ARBITRATOR'S RULING
Discipline does not include a non-disciplinary warning letter for innocent absenteeism, which is therefore not arbitrable. If the warning is unjustified, a reply can be sent to the company; moreover, if the warning letter is subsequently relied on by the company, it will have to be justified at that time.

Denison Mines (1983), 12 L.A.C. (3d) 364 (Adams).

▼

CONTRACT TERM
The employer may discharge or *discipline* only for just cause.

ARBITRATOR'S RULING
An adverse letter of reference is not grievable discipline since it aims to evaluate an employee for future employers.

New Orchard Lodge (1983), 12 L.A.C. (3d) 221 (Swinton).

▼

CONTRACT TERM
Any adverse document relating to a *disciplinary* matter, other than an employee performance appraisal, shall be removed from the personnel file after 2 years.

ARBITRATOR'S RULING
A performance appraisal is grievable where it could be the basis for future action of a disciplinary nature or could prejudice the employee in subsequent proceedings.

B.C. Workers' Compensation Board (1982), 7 L.A.C. (3d) 92 (Ladner).

DISCRETION

CONTRACT TERM
There may, in the *discretion* of the employer, be no payment [of sick pay] for the first 2 days of absence in the fourth and succeeding periods of leave due to sickness in each calendar year.

ARBITRATOR'S RULING
Discretion requires a genuine, good faith exercise, not merely the application of a rigid policy. The merits of each case must be considered, together with all relevant factors, and extraneous or irrelevant considerations may not be taken into account. The exercise of discretion must not be so unreasonable that no reasonable employer could have ever come to the decision in dispute.

Meadow Park Nursing Home (1983), 9 L.A.C. (3d) 137 (Swan).

DISCRIMINATION/DISCRIMINATORY

CONTRACT TERM
The parties agree that there shall be no *discrimination* with respect to terms or conditions of employment on the grounds of union membership or non-membership or activity or lack of activity.

57

ARBITRATOR'S
RULING

"Discrimination" for the purposes of the collective agreement refers only to distinctions made in relation to persons covered by the collective agreement, not in relation to excluded personnel. All employees covered by the agreement must be treated equally with regard to benefits under the agreement. The fact that a dental plan is made available to excluded personnel does not violate the agreement.

Major Foods Ltd. (1989), 7 L.A.C. (4th) 129 (Stanley).

▼

CONTRACT
TERM

The employer and union agree that there shall be no *discrimination* in any relationship with employees by reason of political affiliation.

ARBITRATOR'S
RULING

"Discrimination" encompasses an act based on prejudice, i.e. bias or a preconceived preference or idea; "by reason of" means "because of", and does not imply that prejudice was the *sole* reason for the employer's action; it may have been a main reason or only one incidental to it. In this case, the employer discriminated on the basis of political affiliation against an employee who was on the executive of the local NDP, when it withdrew a work assignment from him after pressure from the Conservative Party was brought to bear. Even if there were other legitimate reasons for withdrawing the assignment, discrimination had occurred.

Government of Nova Scotia (Department of Transport) (1989), 2 L.A.C. (4th) 115 (Veniot).

▼

CONTRACT
TERM

It is agreed that there will be no *discrimination* by either party on the basis of sexual orientation in relation to salary or fringe benefits. Spouse designates a husband or wife in law or in common law.

ARBITRATOR'S
RULING

The restriction of certain fringe benefits (free tuition, bereavement leave) to partners of the opposite sex does not constitute discrimination on the basis of sexual orientation, since even the *Human Rights Code*, which prohibits sexual orientation discrimination, defines spouse to mean, not a same-sex partner, but a person of the opposite sex who is either married or living in a common law relationship.

Carleton University (1988), 35 L.A.C. (3d) 96 (Wright).

▼

CONTRACT TERM
The collective agreement confirms company policy against *discrimination.*

ARBITRATOR'S RULING
Discrimination includes adverse effect discrimination, i.e. conduct that results in discrimination although there is no intent to discriminate. The obligation not to discriminate includes a duty to accommodate (here, employee's religion which prohibits work on Saturday) without undue expense or hardship.

Chrysler Canada (1986), 23 L.A.C. (3d) 366 (Kennedy).

▼

CONTRACT TERM
The company shall not *discriminate* against or discharge any employee for refusing to work overtime.

ARBITRATOR'S RULING
Discrimination means making a difference in treatment or favour on a class or categorical basis, and differs from discipline, which means punishment by one in authority, especially with a view to correct. Thus, the company can suspend the least senior employee for refusal to work overtime.

Sealy (1985), 20 L.A.C. (3d) 45 (Wakeling).

▼

CONTRACT TERM
A claim of *discriminatory* transfer may be the subject of a grievance.

ARBITRATOR'S RULING
The term "discriminatory" means the application of rules to distinguish between individuals or groups on grounds that are illegal, arbitrary or unreasonable.

Metropolitan Authority (1983), 10 L.A.C. (3d) 265 (Outhouse).

▼

CONTRACT TERM
There shall be no *discrimination* on the basis of age, sex, etc.

ARBITRATOR'S RULING
This clause prohibits mandatory retirement at age 65. The definition of age in Ontario human rights legislation, which ends protection at age 65, is not to be read into the word "age" in the collective agreement, unless the parties so provide.

59

O.P.E.I.U. (1982), 8 L.A.C. (3d) 71 (Swan). Contrast *Canadian Porcelain*, below.

▼

CONTRACT TERM

There shall be no *discrimination* because of *age*.

ARBITRATOR'S RULING

"Age" is to be defined in accordance with the definition in Ontario human rights legislation, which ends protection against age discrimination in employment at age 65. Thus, the clause is not violated by company policy, enshrined in an optional company pension plan, of mandatory retirement at age 65. However, "discrimination", a word of very wide import, means differential or unequal treatment, and company practice of continuing some employees beyond age 65, but not others, without standards or reasons, constitutes discrimination.

Canadian Porcelain (1981), 30 L.A.C. (2d) 40 (Brunner). Contrast *O.P.E.I.U.*, above.

▼

CONTRACT TERM

In the event that an employee feels that a job posting has been applied in a *discriminatory* manner, it may be the subject of a grievance.

ARBITRATOR'S RULING

When the person making a selection among applicants takes irrelevant matters into consideration and makes the decision on the basis thereof, the job posting has been applied in a discriminatory manner. In this case, rejecting an applicant for a job on the basis that he was already in a higher job classification, without inquiring into his qualifications and abilities, was discriminatory and violated the collective agreement.

Consolidated-Bathurst Packaging Ltd. (1980), 25 L.A.C. (2d) 229 (Brunner).

DISPLACE

CONTRACT TERM

Employees with more than one year's service who are *displaced* and for whom no job is available due to permanent reduction in the number of employees will be entitled to severance pay.

ARBITRATOR'S RULING

Displacement embraces a layoff. Permanent reduction means a reduction of the employee complement due to lack of work, with no fixed date for recall, that is not part of the usual cyclical pattern of layoffs, and lasts for the period during which recall rights may be exercised.

Council of Marine Canners (1983), 10 L.A.C. (3d) 375 (Munroe).

▼

CONTRACT
TERM

The company agrees not to hire freelancers for the purpose of eliminating or *displacing* regular full time employees or to avoid hiring regular or full-time employees.

ARBITRATOR'S
RULING

For an employee to be displaced, he or she must be scheduled or normally scheduled to work, and someone must have taken his or her place or he or she must have been put out of place for some reason.

CFTO-TV (1983), 10 L.A.C. (3d) 233 (Kennedy).

DUE

CONTRACT
TERM

Employees are entitled to pay for absence *due* to illness.

ARBITRATOR'S
RULING

Term "due" means that illness must be the effective or proximate cause of absence and cannot be just an originating or remote cause, as where absence is due to incarceration in a psychiatric institution resulting from offences committed under the influence of mental illness.

Etobicoke Board of Education (1984), 17 L.A.C. (3d) 40 (Brunner).

E

EFFICIENCY, see SKILL AND ABILITY

EMERGENCY

CONTRACT
TERM

To qualify for statutory holidays with pay, an employee must work the last scheduled shift before and the first scheduled after the holiday, unless absent through *emergency* in the employee's family.

ARBITRATOR'S
RULING

An emergency is an unusual and sudden happening. A child's adverse reaction to an immunization shot qualifies as an emergency especially since the child was generally healthy and the physician had told the employee that the adverse reaction could occur any time within a 3-month period.

Simmons Ltd. (1989), 7 L.A.C. (4th) 252 (Barton).

▼

CONTRACT
TERM

A layoff may be implemented without regard to seniority, for a period of 5 working days, where a reduction of forces is caused by *emergency* conditions.

ARBITRATOR'S
RULING

"Emergency" refers to a sudden, unexpected occasion or combination of events calling for immediate action (here, equipment breakdown).

B.C. Forest Products Ltd. (1984), 16 L.A.C. (3d) 147 (McKee).

▼

CONTRACT
TERM

Where a reduction of forces is caused by *emergency* conditions the application of plant seniority may be postponed for up to 5 working days; if the company decides to exercise its right under this provision it shall notify the shop committee as soon as possible.

ARBITRATOR'S RULING An emergency is "a sudden juncture demanding immediate action" and therefore includes burnout of a motor, since although this was anticipated there was no way of anticipating when it would happen. However, although no special words are required, notice must be given to a representative of the shop committee as soon as possible that the company intends to invoke the emergency clause; it cannot be given after the layoff is over.

Gregory Manufacturing (1981), 30 L.A.C. (2d) 427 (Bird).

▼

CONTRACT TERM Contracting out bargaining unit work is restricted except in *emergencies* when regular employees are not available.

ARBITRATOR'S RULING Shortage of nursing staff is not an emergency where it did not arise suddenly and had continued for over two years, and where overtime by regular staff might have sufficed.

Riverdale Hospital (1975), 7 L.A.C. (2d) 40 (Schiff).

▼

CONTRACT TERM A premium is payable for shift change on short notice except if such change of shift is caused by illness or *emergency*.

ARBITRATOR'S RULING An "emergency" is "a condition of things causing a reasonable apprehension of the near approach of danger", and need not be sudden or unanticipated. The term would thus include the accumulation of garbage during a strike, even though this was not unanticipated and the recall of workers in such circumstances had been planned when the strike began.

City of Toronto (1973), 2 L.A.C. (2d) 199 (O'Shea).

EMPLOYEES, *see also* **PERSONS,** *compare* **CONTRACTING OUT**

CONTRACT TERM In job postings, the employer shall first consider all applications received from present *employees*.

ARBITRATOR'S RULING "Employees" refers only to employees in the same bargaining unit, not all employees of the company. The word "present" may have a temporal limitation, but it does not expand the meaning to include non-bargaining unit employees. Thus, persons excluded from the bargaining unit, such as part-time employees, may not be considered on the same footing in a job posting competition as bargaining unit employees, in the absence of express language.

Religious Hospitallers of Hotel Dieu (1989), 9 L.A.C. (4th) 296 (Palmer).

▼

CONTRACT TERM Supervisors and other *employees* outside the scope of this agreement shall not perform the regular duties of *employees* within the bargaining unit unless training or instructing an employee during the performance of his duties.

ARBITRATOR'S RULING "Employees" means only employees of the company, not third parties, i.e. employees of other companies or "persons" in general. Engaging outside trucking firms for single trips when company personnel are unavailable does not violate the agreement, since the agreement does not prohibit contracting-out, and the persons hired do not fall within the category of employees of the company.

White Pass Transportation Ltd. (1989), 3 L.A.C. (4th) 301 (MacIntyre).

▼

CONTRACT TERM All penalties and reprimands must be issued to the *employee* within 72 hours from the time the infraction became known, with a copy to the local union.

ARBITRATOR'S RULING Notice to the union alone, on the basis that it is the agent for the employee, does not satisfy the requirement of notice to the grievor, where there is no evidence that the union is the agent for employees who have been disciplined, or that the grievor consented to the union receiving such notice on his behalf.

Trans Western Express Ltd. (1988), 33 L.A.C. (3d) 188 (Brunner).

▼

CONTRACT TERM	The company recognizes the union as bargaining agent for its *employees*.
ARBITRATOR'S RULING	Term does not include employees of independent contractors; test is not who directs or controls the persons alleged to be employees, but rather who pays their wages.

Liquid Carbonic (1986), 25 L.A.C. (3d) 309 (Melnyk). Contrast *Maple Leaf Mills*, below.

▼

CONTRACT TERM	*Employees* whenever mentioned in the agreement shall not be deemed to include foremen; seniority shall be broken by resignation, discharge, or long-term sickness or disability.
ARBITRATOR'S RULING	Clause entitles returning supervisor to retain bargaining unit seniority but not to accumulate seniority while a foreman.

Pacific Truck (1986), 24 L.A.C. (3d) 299 (Munroe).

▼

CONTRACT TERM	The employer agrees to bargain with the union with respect to *employees* in the bargaining unit, i.e. security personnel.
ARBITRATOR'S RULING	Term includes temporary employees, i.e. employees whose employment is limited in time, where they perform the same type of work and their inclusion does not compromise the majority status of the permanent employees.

Ottawa-Carleton Transit Commission (1986), 24 L.A.C. (3d) 48 (Foisy).

▼

CONTRACT TERM	The provisions of this agreement apply to all *employees*.
ARBITRATOR'S RULING	Where the work of watchman is assigned to a private security firm, the determination of the identity of the employer depends upon which company controls how the work is done (the control test), and whether the work is an integral part of the employer's organization rather than merely an accessory to it (the organization test).

Maple Leaf Mills (1986), 24 L.A.C. (3d) 16 (Devlin).

▼

CONTRACT TERM
The company may retire an *employee* at age 65 or older because of inability to properly perform his regularly assigned work; weekly disability benefits are not payable during any period following an employee's resignation/termination.

ARBITRATOR'S RULING
The term "employee" is not restricted to active employees; the company can retire employees who are absent due to disability and in receipt of weekly disability benefits.

Hussman Store Equipment (1986), 23 L.A.C. (3d) 442 (H.D. Brown).

▼

CONTRACT TERM
A full-time *employee* who has 9 or more years of continuous service is entitled to severance pay equal to a maximum of 20 weeks.

ARBITRATOR'S RULING
The provision applies to persons employed on or after the effective date of the collective agreement, not just to those who happen to be employed at the time the agreement is signed or ratified.

Bonavista School Board (1985), 22 L.A.C. (3d) 430 (Easton).

▼

CONTRACT TERM
Life insurance coverage shall be increased for all full-time seniority *employees*.

ARBITRATOR'S RULING
An employee on long-term disability benefits, even though not actively employed, is nonetheless a full-time employee, and so entitled to increased insurance coverage.

Somerville Belkin (1985), 21 L.A.C. (3d) 358 (Hinnegan).

▼

CONTRACT TERM
An *employee* shall not be eligible for holiday pay if he is absent on the scheduled workday immediately preceding or next following the holiday; *employees* on the payroll as of November 1st in each year are entitled and shall be granted an additional holiday.

ARBITRATOR'S
RULING

An extended layoff during plant renovations does not disentitle employees to holiday pay where they were not scheduled to work during layoff. Use of the word "the" does not mean that grievors become disentitled when some employees are recalled early and plant is again in operation, because the objective/subjective distinction between "his" and "the" is a sterile distinction, and anyway the use of the phrase "absent on the scheduled workday" requires that employees themselves be scheduled to work. Workers remain "employees" as long as they retain seniority for purposes of recall, but qualification "on the payroll" requires active employment around the date specified and continuing beyond it.

Canada Packers (1985), 21 L.A.C. (3d) 289 (Swan).

▼

CONTRACT
TERM

The union holds bargaining rights for *employees* (health care aides, housekeeping, and maintenance staff).

ARBITRATOR'S
RULING

In determining whether workers supplied by an outside agency are employees, the tests are: the *"Montreal Locomotive"* test (control or supervision on a day-to-day basis over what the workers do and how they do it; the *"York Condominium"* tests (set out in *Ford Motor Co.,* below); and the *"Co-operators Insurance"* test (integration as part of the organization). Here, where the entire function of the bargaining unit was contracted out, the workers supplied to a home for the aged were determined to be employees of the home.

Don Mills Foundation (1984), 14 L.A.C. (3d) 385 (P.C. Picher).

▼

CONTRACT
TERM

The collective agreement applies to *employees* for whom the union is the certified bargaining agent.

ARBITRATOR'S
RULING

The term employee includes a handicapped student employed on a summer work experience program, even though wages are paid by the federal government, where the work performed is normally done by bargaining unit employees, and the employer has the right to control the method of doing the work.

University of Manitoba (1983), 10 L.A.C. (3d) 413 (Freedman).

▼

CONTRACT TERM
Employees have the right to continue to be covered by welfare plans by paying premiums.

ARBITRATOR'S RULING
Plant closure does not put an end to the company's obligation as long as it remains in existence; employees' entitlement continues as long as the collective agreement continues.

Hyde Spring & Wire (1983), 8 L.A.C. (3d) 442 (McLaren).

▼

CONTRACT TERM
A written grievance shall be signed by the employee filing the grievance.

ARBITRATOR'S RULING
An employee can authorize a union official to sign the grievance as agent.

Crossley Kerastan Carpet Mills (1982), 6 L.A.C. (3d) 282 (MacDougall).

▼

CONTRACT TERM
Persons employed outside the bargaining unit shall not perform work of union members except in an emergency.

ARBITRATOR'S RULING
This clause prevents non-bargaining unit personnel of the company from doing bargaining unit work except in emergencies. It does not prevent contracting out.

Nabob Foods (1982), 5 L.A.C. (3d) 256 (Munroe).

▼

CONTRACT TERM
The collective agreement applies to all employees at designated company facilities.

ARBITRATOR'S RULING
Where the work is purportedly contracted out, the test of who is an employee involves a consideration of a variety of factors including (1) the party exercising the direction and control over the employees performing the work; (2) the party bearing the burden of remuneration; (3) the party imposing discipline; (4) the party hiring the employees; (5) the party with the authority to dismiss the employees; (6) the party which is perceived to be the employer by the employees; and (7) the existence of an intention to create the relationship of employer-employee.

Ford Motor Co. (1981), 1 L.A.C. (3d) 141 (Mac-Dowell).

▼

CONTRACT
TERM

Full-time *employees* in the bargaining unit employed on the date of the signing of the collective agreement, and on December 11, are entitled to settlement pay.

ARBITRATOR'S
RULING

Where full-time employees were actively employed in the bargaining unit on the date the collective agreement was signed, but had been laid off prior to December 11, such persons were still accumulating seniority pursuant to the collective agreement and were therefore full-time employees in the bargaining unit on December 11, entitled to settlement pay.

National Dry Co. Ltd. (1981), 30 L.A.C. (2d) 53 (Weatherill).

▼

CONTRACT
TERM

Where a vacancy exists other than entry positions, the employer shall post notice of the initial vacancy on the bulletin board for a period of five consecutive days in order that the *employees* may make written application for such job vacancies.

ARBITRATOR'S
RULING

"Employees" means only bargaining unit employees, since these are the only individuals regarded as acquiring rights and obligations under the collective agreement. Bargaining unit employees are therefore to be considered first before the employer can exercise its discretion to fill the job from outside the bargaining unit.

Scarborough General Hospital (1980), 26 L.A.C. (2d) 28 (Brent).

▼

CONTRACT
TERM

The collective agreement applies to *employees* for whom the union is the certified bargaining agent. *Employees* whose jobs are not in the bargaining unit shall not work on any jobs which are included in the bargaining unit, except for purposes of instruction, experimenting or emergencies.

ARBITRATOR'S RULING Temporary staff supplied and paid by an employment agency are not employees, but unless the work is contracted out, the employer must be taken to have agreed with the union to engage them on the terms of the collective agreement, including the stipulated wage rate. "Employees whose jobs are not in the bargaining unit" refers to supervisors and does not restrict contracting out to an independent contractor.

City of Kelowna (1980), 25 L.A.C. (2d) 314 (Larson).

EMPLOYMENT

CONTRACT TERM No regular employees who attain 2 years of regular service will lose their *employment* as a result of technological change.

ARBITRATOR'S RULING Relocation to another geographical area, made necessary by declining demand, constitutes a loss of employment, triggering the employment guarantee, but the relocation must be due to a technological change, and here it was not, since closure of the employer's office was due to economic reasons, i.e. failure to achieve growth.

British Columbia Telephone Co. (1989), 7 L.A.C. (4th) 75 (Kelleher).

▼

CONTRACT TERM Where an employee is made party to criminal, civil or quasi-judicial proceedings, by reason of conduct within the scope of his *employment*, the employer agrees to retain and pay counsel the legal fees incurred in defending the employee.

ARBITRATOR'S RULING Term refers to conduct occurring in the course of employment, or arising out of the employer's enterprise, whether or not it involves an excess of actual authority, or actions which the employer could reasonably be expected to approve.

Ottawa-Carleton Treatment Centre (1985), 18 L.A.C. (3d) 350 (Weatherill).

EQUAL

CONTRACT TERM Seniority shall govern in all cases of promotions, transfers and demotions when the qualifications and ability of the applicants concerned are *equal*.

ARBITRATOR'S RULING The word "equal" is not an invitation to consider insignificant differences between applicants, but to determine whether one employee is more qualified than another by a "substantial and demonstrable margin", having regard to the particular job in question.

Board of School Trustees, School District #88 (Terrace) (1989), 9 L.A.C. (4th) 432 (Kelleher).

▼

CONTRACT TERM In the filling of vacancies, new positions, transfers or promotions, appointments shall be made to the employee with the required qualifications, and level of competency and efficiency, and where such requirements are *equal*, seniority shall be the determining factor.

ARBITRATOR'S RULING Under this clause, the junior applicant must be better by a substantial and demonstrable margin; there must be a discernible, material difference. Management must reach a decision fairly, on the basis of relevant factors.

Princeton General Hospital (1987), 32 L.A.C. (3d) 35 (Hope)

▼

CONTRACT TERM In making staff changes, transfers or promotions, where efficiency, work history and qualifications are judged to be *equal*, seniority shall be the determining factor.

ARBITRATOR'S RULING Absolute equality is a futile concept. Applicants are equal unless there is a discernible, material difference around which a reasonable and objective employer might pivot his decision.

University of British Columbia (1982), 5 L.A.C. (3d) 69 (Munroe).

EQUALLY RATED

CONTRACT TERM When selecting an applicant for a regular vacancy or newly created position, seniority, qualifications, ability, service requirements and acceptable performance will be considered. Seniority shall be the governing factor in the case of *equally rated* applicants.

ARBITRATOR'S RULING "Equally rated" is a narrower concept than "relatively equal", but still does not require that there be mathematical equality in point scores between competing applicants for a job. However, a 5.5 point difference in scores between two applicants, out of a possible score of 90, is sufficiently significant to reject the assertion that they are equally rated.

Manitoba Telephone System (1988), 2 L.A.C. (4th) 136 (Bowman).

EQUITABLY

CONTRACT TERM The company will attempt to distribute overtime work *equitably* among the employees who normally perform the work.

ARBITRATOR'S RULING "Equitably" does not mean "equally", but rather "fairly"; thus, if two or more employees normally perform similar work, the overtime assigned should be roughly the same.

Worthington Pump Div. (1989), 3 L.A.C. (4th) 399 (Samuels).

EXCUSED

CONTRACT TERM A nurse who is scheduled to work on a holiday and who fails to do so shall forfeit her holiday pay unless her absence is *excused* by the employer.

ARBITRATOR'S RULING An absence is "excused" if it is either recognized as a proper and appropriate reason for absence or if the employer has made a determination to permit the absence. An employee who is absent due to illness is therefore entitled to holiday pay, notwithstanding the fact that no prior decision had been made or discretion exercised to approve the absence.

Temiskaming Hospital (1987), 28 L.A.C. (3d) 178 (Devlin).

EXCLUDED PERSONNEL

CONTRACT TERM Management and *excluded personnel* shall not work on any jobs which are included in the bargaining unit. The employer will give the union two months' notice of its intention to contract out work.

ARBITRATOR'S
RULING

"Excluded personnel" is restricted to non-bargaining unit employees. Otherwise, the term "persons" would have been employed. The painting by tenants of their own apartments therefore does not violate the collective agreement. A contracting-out of work requires an assignment of bargaining unit work to an independent contractor and his employees, which did not occur here: no work could be said to have been assigned to tenants, particularly since they had complete discretion whether or not to paint.

Newfoundland and Labrador Housing Corp. (1988), 4 L.A.C. (4th) 89 (Cooper).

EXPERIENCE, *see* **SKILL AND ABILITY**

F

FAILS TO REPORT

CONTRACT TERM Seniority will be lost if an employee after a layoff *fails to report* for 5 working days after being recalled.

ARBITRATOR'S RULING There is an implied exception for *bona fide* circumstances beyond the employee's control, such as sickness or injury. Sick leave should be granted as a matter of course where there is a *bona fide* reason.

Hudson's Bay Co. (1985), 21 L.A.C. (3d) 407 (Bird).

▼

CONTRACT TERM An employee shall lose his seniority if he *fails to report* for work for 3 consecutive working days without notifying his immediate supervisor during such period, unless the employee provides an acceptable reason to the company.

ARBITRATOR'S RULING Under this clause, the employee loses all seniority, but is not reduced to the status of a probationary employee.

Indalloy (1979), 27 L.A.C. (2d) 35 (Kennedy).

FAILS TO RETURN

CONTRACT TERM An employee shall lose seniority standing if he is laid off and *fails to return* to work within 5 days after he has been notified to do so.

ARBITRATOR'S RULING Where the employee does not fall within the definition of a probationary employee, he loses his seniority, but retains his right to protection against discharge without just cause.

J.C. Hallman Mfg. (1982), 8 L.A.C. (3d) 164 (Brent).

FATHER-IN-LAW, *see also* BEREAVEMENT LEAVE

CONTRACT TERM An employee who suffers the death of his/her mother, father, husband, wife, mother-in-law, *father-in-law*, etc. will be granted 3 consecutive working days' leave of absence.

ARBITRATOR'S RULING In the absence of words of general application, such as "immediate family", "father-in-law" does not include the father of a common law spouse.

Hermes Electronics Ltd. (1989), 4 L.A.C. (4th) 257 (Kydd).

FIRST CONSIDERATION

CONTRACT TERM In filling vacancies, a current regular full-time or regular part-time employee having the required qualifications, experience, skill and ability to do the work will be given *first consideration* over an external applicant.

ARBITRATOR'S RULING "First consideration" means preference; an employee with the required qualifications, experience, skill and ability goes to the top of the list and is to be awarded the job in question, even if an external applicant is demonstrably superior.

Capital Regional District (1989), 8 L.A.C. (4th) 307 (Munroe).

FLOATER HOLIDAY

CONTRACT TERM Two *floater holidays* will be observed between Christmas and New Year's.

ARBITRATOR'S RULING Floating holidays do not fall on a designated date, although a specific time frame or a number of possible dates may be designated; an employer cannot, however, deprive an employee of a day off work by directing that the floating holiday fall on an employee's day off.

Canteen of Canada (1981), 1 L.A.C. (3d) 359 (Gorsky).

FULL-TIME EMPLOYEE

CONTRACT TERM Life insurance coverage shall be increased for all *full-time seniority employees.*

ARBITRATOR'S RULING An employee on long-term disability benefits, even though not actively employed, is nonetheless a full-time employee, and so entitled to increased insurance coverage.

Somerville Belkin (1985), 21 L.A.C. (3d) 358 (Hinnegan).

▼

CONTRACT TERM *Full-time employees* in the bargaining unit employed on the date of the signing of the collective agreement, and on December 11, are entitled to settlement pay.

ARBITRATOR'S RULING Where full-time employees were actively employed in the bargaining unit on the date the collective agreement was signed, but had been laid off prior to December 11, such persons were still accumulating seniority pursuant to the collective agreement and were therefore full-time employees in the bargaining unit on December 11, entitled to settlement pay.

National Dry Co. Ltd. (1981), 30 L.A.C. (2d) 53 (Weatherill).

FULL-TIME POSITION WITH THE UNION

CONTRACT TERM An employee who assumes a *full-time position with the union* or a labour organization with which the union is affiliated shall be granted up to one year's leave of absence.

ARBITRATOR'S RULING Clause is broadly drafted, and includes leave of absence to engage in a Canadian Labour Congress' campaign to support the NDP in a federal election, since that is a union activity within the union's constitution; and a three-week campaign may be considered as full-time since that was the length of the federal campaign.

Borough of Etobicoke (1981), 30 L.A.C. (2d) 289 (McLaren).

FULL WORKING DAY

CONTRACT TERM Statutory holiday pay is conditional upon an employee working the *full working day* preceding and following the holiday.

ARBITRATOR'S
RULING

Condition is satisfied where a part-time employee works as required on both qualifying days though less than an eight-hour shift.

Humpty Dumpty Foods (1983), 11 L.A.C. (3d) 385 (Weatherill).

G

GENERAL CONDITIONS, *see* CONDITIONS OF EMPLOYMENT

GRANDPARENTS, *see also* BEREAVEMENT LEAVE

CONTRACT TERM — Employees shall be allowed one day to attend the employee's *grandparents'* or brother- or sister-in-law's funeral.

ARBITRATOR'S RULING — "Grandparent" does not include the grandmother of an employee's spouse.

Windsor Star (1988), 34 L.A.C (3d) 438 (Roberts).

▼

CONTRACT TERM — Employees who suffer bereavement within the immediate family will be granted 3 days' leave of absence; immediate family includes *grandparents.*

ARBITRATOR'S RULING — "Grandparents" includes spousal grandparents, since a broad interpretation of "immediate family" is warranted in the absence of restrictive language.

Associated Freezers of Canada (1987), 32 L.A.C. (3d) 79 (Kilgour).

▼

CONTRACT TERM — In the event of the death of an employee's *grandparent*, etc., the employer will grant leave of absence with pay.

ARBITRATOR'S RULING — The word "grandparent" designates an employee's own grandparents; a spouse's grandparents are not included.

Beer Precast Concrete (1984), 15 L.A.C. (3d) 107 (Swan).

GRANDPARENTS-IN-LAW, see also BEREAVEMENT LEAVE

CONTRACT TERM
The purpose of bereavement leave is to reimburse active, permanent employees for wage loss in the event of death in the immediate family, defined to include grandparents, *grandparents-in-law*, etc.

ARBITRATOR'S RULING
The term "grandparents-in-law" does not include the grandfather of a common law spouse.

MacMillan Bathurst Inc. (1988), 35 L.A.C. (3d) 415 (H.D. Brown).

GRIEVANCE MEETINGS

CONTRACT TERM
Union representatives shall not lose regular wages while conferring with employees over grievances and while attending *grievance meetings* with the company.

ARBITRATOR'S RULING
"Grievance meetings" does not include arbitration hearing, but "conferring with employees over grievances" does, although payment is only an indemnity for actual lost earnings.

Ross Laboratories (1981), 30 L.A.C. (2d) 125 (Kennedy).

GROSS EARNINGS/GROSS ANNUAL EARNINGS

CONTRACT TERM
Employees shall be entitled to vacation pay accumulated on a percentage of *gross earnings*.

ARBITRATOR'S RULING
Gross earnings are all sums paid to employees as wages or benefits, including vacation pay received by employees in the previous year, but not OHIP premiums since these are not received directly by employees.

St. Joseph Nursing Home (1989), 7 L.A.C. (4th) 187 (Roach).

▼

CONTRACT TERM
An employee shall receive the employee's *gross earnings* for the previous year multiplied by the applicable percentage rate for the employee's vacation entitlement.

ARBITRATOR'S RULING   "Gross earnings" does not include WCB payments nor income continuation benefits for non-occupational illness, since these are insurance benefits and are not paid out by the employer. Long-term disability benefits are also excluded from gross earnings, where the cost of the plan is borne solely by employees. Tool, cleaning and safety shoe allowances are also excluded from gross earnings, since they are reimbursement of expenses, not wage items.

B.C. Transit (1988), 3 L.A.C. (4th) 151 (MacIntyre).

▼

CONTRACT TERM   Vacation pay shall be at the rate of 2% of *gross annual earnings* during the vacation year.

ARBITRATOR'S RULING   The term is broader than "wages", and encompasses workers' compensation benefits and other supplements arising out of the employment relationship.

JBG Management Inc. (1987), 30 L.A.C (3d) 101 (Haefling).

▼

CONTRACT TERM   Vacation pay shall be calculated at the rate of 4% of *gross earnings*.

ARBITRATOR'S RULING   Term includes all earnings without deductions including the previous year's vacation pay.

Apex Metals (1981), 29 L.A.C. (2d) 15 (Brown).

▼

CONTRACT TERM   Vacation pay is based on *gross earnings*.

ARBITRATOR'S RULING   Term includes previous year's vacation and holiday pay.

St. Peter's Hospital (1981), 28 L.A.C. (2d) 284 (O'Connor).

▼

CONTRACT TERM   Pension plan is based on *gross earnings*.

ARBITRATOR'S RULING   Term includes severance payments.

Western-National Drug Services (1978), 20 L.A.C. (2d) 202 (Weiler).

▼

CONTRACT
TERM
Vacation pay is based on *gross earnings*.

ARBITRATOR'S
RULING
Term includes previous year's vacation and holiday pay.

Phoenix Paper (1977), 14 L.A.C. (2d) 201 (O'Shea).

GROSS WEEKLY SALES

CONTRACT
TERM
Wage rates for driver-salesmen are calculated as 14% on the first $1900 *gross weekly sales*, and 8% on *gross weekly sales* over $1900.

ARBITRATOR'S
RULING
"Gross" means an amount in hand representing the total from all sources from which specified deductions are made, and an employer is not justified in calculating commissions by deducting the special discount offered to some customers. "Net" means the result after deductions and is the opposite of "gross".

Hostess Food Products Ltd. (1988), 1 L.A.C. (4th) 173 (H.D. Brown).

H

HANDLING GRIEVANCES

CONTRACT TERM
There shall be no pay deduction for time spent by union stewards in *handling grievances*.

ARBITRATOR'S RULING
Term includes attendance at arbitration hearing.

Leamington District Memorial Hospital (1976), 13 L.A.C. (2d) 30 (Weatherill).

HEADQUARTERS

CONTRACT TERM
An employee has an option to move or decline to do so where the *headquarters* location of a position is moved.

ARBITRATOR'S RULING
The headquarters of an employee is his or her regular place of employment.

CN/CP Telecommunications (1985), 18 L.A.C. (3d) 79 (M.G. Picher).

HIRING

CONTRACT TERM
Seniority shall commence from the date of last *hiring*.

ARBITRATOR'S RULING
Under this clause, previous service with the employer is not included in calculating seniority.

House of Braemore (1984), 14 L.A.C. (3d) 193 (P.C. Picher).

HIS/HER REGULARLY SCHEDULED SHIFT/ WORKDAY

CONTRACT TERM
In order to qualify for payment of statutory holidays, an employee must have worked the whole of *his regularly scheduled shift* prior to and immediately following the holiday; an employee who is absent from his regularly scheduled duties before *or* after the holiday due to an authorized leave of absence shall be entitled to the holiday.

ARBITRATOR'S
RULING

Since the language is personalized, the clause refers to the shift regularly scheduled for the individual claimant, rather than to shifts worked by employees of the plant as a group. Thus, an employee is entitled to pay for a holiday occurring during pregnancy leave, where she works her regularly scheduled shifts before the leave and upon her return, but she is not entitled to pay for a holiday occurring during an extended unpaid pregnancy leave. The word "or", which may be either conjunctive or disjunctive, is here both conjunctive and disjunctive, i.e. it means before, after or before, and after the holiday.

FBI Foods (1986), 22 L.A.C. (3d) 157 (Emrich).

▼

CONTRACT
TERM

An employee is entitled to holiday pay when he has worked *his last scheduled workday* before the holiday and his first scheduled workday following the holiday.

ARBITRATOR'S
RULING

Since the employer has no right to schedule striking employees to work during a legal strike, absence on a qualifying day due to a lawful strike does not disentitle an employee to holiday pay; his last scheduled workday means his last scheduled workday before the strike.

General Refractories (1985), 20 L.A.C. (3d) 380 (Davis).

▼

CONTRACT
TERM

To qualify for holiday pay an employee must work on *his scheduled workday* immediately preceding the holiday and must return to work as scheduled immediately following the holiday.

ARBITRATOR'S
RULING

Where a holiday falls during a strike, employees are not at work so as to qualify for holiday pay, unless the strike settlement provides otherwise.

Abitibi-Price (1981), 1 L.A.C. (3d) 193 (Gorsky).

▼

CONTRACT
TERM

Holiday pay is due only if employees have worked *their last regular full shift* immediately preceding, and the first regular full shift immediately following, any such holiday.

ARBITRATOR'S
RULING
Since the purpose of the clause is to deter absenteeism, involuntary absence caused by a lockout does not detract from entitlement to holiday pay; the employee's last regular shift before the holiday was the shift prior to the lockout.

Township of Muskoka Lakes (1981), 1 L.A.C. (3d) 125 (MacDowell).

HOLIDAY PAY

CONTRACT
TERM
Plant *holidays* shall be recognized with pay provided the employee is not absent without leave on the working days immediately preceding and following the holiday.

ARBITRATOR'S
RULING
Absence on disciplinary suspension is not an absence with leave, since "leave" involves an application to be absent for which permission is granted, which does not occur where an employee is suspended for misconduct.

Canadian Timken Ltd. (1989), 8 L.A.C. (4th) 193 (Little).

▼

CONTRACT
TERM
In order to qualify for a paid *holiday*, an employee must work the full scheduled shift preceding and immediately following the statutory holiday, unless the employee is absent on *one* of the aforementioned days due to illness or injury, or an approved leave of absence.

ARBITRATOR'S
RULING
"One" does not mean only one, but any of the qualifying days; an employee absent on both days due to compensable illness is entitled to holiday pay. Moreover, the employee is entitled under this clause, not just to the first holiday, but to whatever number of holidays occur during the absence, so long as the employer-employee relationship continues.

Chelsey Park Oxford (1989), 8 L.A.C. (4th) 1 (Mitchnick).

▼

CONTRACT
TERM
To be eligible for *holiday pay*, an employee, unless absent due to justifiable cause, must have been present on the work-day immediately preceding and following such a holiday.

ARBITRATOR'S RULING   Employees who leave work on illegal strike before completing at least half the required shift on the day before a statutory holiday are not in substantial compliance with the agreement and are therefore not entitled to holiday pay. However, employees who work two-thirds of the shift, on the day the illegal strike ends, are in substantial compliance, and are entitled to holiday pay.

Rothesay Paper Ltd. (1989), 5 L.A.C. (4th) 103 (MacLean).

▼

CONTRACT TERM   To be eligible for *holiday pay*, an employee must work the full scheduled work day immediately preceding and following such holiday, unless absent on authorized leave of absence, layoff or proven illness or injury.

ARBITRATOR'S RULING   An employee who misses the first hour of work the day following a holiday, and telephones his employer to advise that he will be late, is entitled to a full day's pay for the holiday, where the absence would ordinarily have been authorized by the company after the fact, or where the company would have been obliged to grant a leave of absence for the time involved. Here, the employee's absence would have been considered authorized since he was obliged to deal with his child's recurrent medical problems.

Union Felt Products (Ont.) Ltd. (1988), 1 L.A.C. (4th) 148 (Kennedy).

▼

CONTRACT TERM   In order to qualify for *holiday pay*, an employee must work his last full scheduled shift immediately preceding and his first full scheduled shift immediately following the holiday, unless he is excused because of illness or for other reasonable excuse.

ARBITRATOR'S RULING   Employees on workers' compensation on the qualifying days are entitled to holiday pay for all holidays occurring during the absence. Absence for such a reason, which is beyond the employee's control, is a reasonable excuse. Holiday pay is an earned benefit, not to be taken away without clear language. Moreover, the receipt of holiday pay and workers' compensation is not double payment, since workers' compensation is not provided by the employer, nor does it flow from the collective agreement.

Caressant Care (1987), 29 L.A.C. (3d) 347 (Walters).

▼

CONTRACT TERM

An employee who is scheduled to work on a *holiday* and who fails to do so shall forfeit her holiday pay unless her absence is excused by the employer.

ARBITRATOR'S RULING

An absence is "excused" if it is either recognized as a proper and appropriate reason for absence *or* if the employer has made a determination to permit the absence. An employee who is absent due to illness is therefore entitled to holiday pay, notwithstanding the fact that no prior decision had been made or discretion exercised to approve the absence.

Temiskaming Hospital (1987), 28 L.A.C. (3d) 178 (Devlin).

▼

CONTRACT TERM

Employees are entitled to *holiday pay*.

ARBITRATOR'S RULING

Employees on maternity leave are entitled to holiday pay, which is an earned benefit, provided the holiday is in reasonable proximity to the employee's past work.

City of Timmins (1987), 26 L.A.C. (3d) 444 (Betcherman).

▼

CONTRACT TERM

Overtime at time and a half is payable after 40 hours in a workweek; time and a half is payable for work on a *holiday*.

ARBITRATOR'S RULING

A workweek consists of days and hours spent working within a given time frame, and for purposes of calculating overtime it includes a holiday on which the employee works. No question of pyramiding arises because the purpose of overtime is to compensate for the effort and inconvenience of having to work beyond the normal work schedule, whereas the purpose of holiday pay, an earned benefit, is to ensure enjoyment of a holiday without loss of pay.

J. Xavier Enterprises (1987), 26 L.A.C. (3d) 289 (T.A.B. Jolliffe).

▼

CONTRACT TERM
Each employee shall receive *holiday pay* provided he is at work on the last regular scheduled workday before and the first regular scheduled workday after the holiday.

ARBITRATOR'S RULING
Some arbitrators consider holiday pay as compensation for work done, while others regard it as a consequence of the fact that an employment relationship exists. Here, since the phrase is not personalized by use of the pronoun "his", it is not sufficient that an employee work his last regular scheduled workday; he must work on the regular scheduled workday before and after the holiday. *Browing Harvey Ltd.* (1986), 27 L.A.C. (3d) 239 (Dicks).

▼

CONTRACT TERM
Employees are entitled to *holiday pay* despite absence from work on the day before or after the holiday if the absence is due to specific authorized absence.

ARBITRATOR'S RULING
While employees on layoff remain employees, a layoff is not a specific authorized absence so as to entitle employees laid off for 3 months to 5 holidays occurring during that period. *Baie Verte Mines* (1986), 27 L.A.C. (3d) 135 (Easton).

▼

CONTRACT TERM
To qualify for *holiday pay* an employee must work the full workday immediately preceding and the full workday immediately following the holiday unless absent due to illness, etc.

ARBITRATOR'S RULING
The qualifying days are not the workdays on which employees are personally scheduled to work, but rather the workdays scheduled for employees generally. *Dorr-Oliver Canada* (1986), 23 L.A.C. (3d) 92 (Weatherill).

▼

CONTRACT TERM
In order to qualify for payment of *statutory holidays,* an employee must have worked the whole of his regularly scheduled shift prior to and immediately following the holiday; an employee who is absent from his regularly scheduled duties before *or* after the holiday due to an authorized leave of absence shall be entitled to the holiday.

ARBITRATOR'S RULING Since the language is personalized, the clause refers to the shift regularly scheduled for the individual claimant, rather than to shifts worked by employees of the plant as a group. Thus, an employee is entitled to pay for a holiday occurring during pregnancy leave, where she works her regularly scheduled shifts before the leave and upon her return, but she is not entitled to pay for a holiday occurring during an extended unpaid pregnancy leave. The word "or", which may be either conjunctive or disjunctive, is here both conjunctive and disjunctive, i.e. it means before, after or before, and after the holiday.

FBI Foods (1986), 22 L.A.C. (3d) 157 (Emrich).

▼

CONTRACT TERM In order to qualify for *holiday pay*, an employee must be entitled to wages for at least 12 shifts during the 30 preceding calendar days.

ARBITRATOR'S RULING Phrase requires more than continued employment; absence on workers' compensation disqualifies employee from entitlement.

B.C. Railway Co. (1985), 22 L.A.C. (3d) 299 (Hope).

▼

CONTRACT TERM An employee shall not be eligible for *holiday pay* if he is absent on the scheduled workday immediately preceding or next following the holiday; employees on the payroll as of November 1st in each year are entitled and shall be granted an additional holiday.

ARBITRATOR'S RULING An extended layoff during plant renovations does not disentitle employees to holiday pay where they were not scheduled to work during layoff. Use of the word "the" does not mean that grievors become disentitled when some employees are recalled early and plant is again in operation, because the objective/subjective distinction between "his" and "the" is a sterile distinction, and anyway the use of the phrase "absent on the scheduled workday" requires that employees themselves be scheduled to work. Workers remain "employees" as long as they retain seniority for purposes of recall, but qualification "on the payroll" requires active employment around the date specified and continuing beyond it.

Canada Packers (1985), 21 L.A.C. (3d) 289 (Swan).

▼

CONTRACT TERM
No employee shall receive *holiday pay* unless he has been continuously employed for a period of 30 calendar days immediately preceding the holiday.

ARBITRATOR'S RULING
Even though service or employment has been held, in cases of layoff or legal strike, to mean simply employment status, rather than attendance at work, an illegal strike breaks continuous employment.

City of Penticton (1985), 21 L.A.C. (3d) 233 (MacIntyre).

▼

CONTRACT TERM
An employee is entitled to *holiday pay* when he has worked his last scheduled workday before the holiday and his first scheduled workday following the holiday.

ARBITRATOR'S RULING
Since the employer has no right to schedule striking employees to work during a legal strike, absence on a qualifying day due to a lawful strike does not disentitle an employee to holiday pay; his last scheduled workday means his last scheduled workday before the strike.

General Refractories (1985), 20 L.A.C. (3d) 380 (Davis).

▼

CONTRACT TERM
Statutory holidays shall be observed without deduction of pay.

ARBITRATOR'S RULING
Term guarantees pay only where an employee is otherwise entitled to it, and thus not where the employee is on layoff anyway.

United Co-Operatives of Ontario (1983), 13 L.A.C. (3d) 376 (Weatherill).

▼

CONTRACT TERM
Statutory *holiday pay* is conditional upon an employee working the full working day preceding and following the holiday.

ARBITRATOR'S RULING
Condition is satisfied where a part-time employee works as required on both qualifying days though less than an eight-hour shift.

Humpty Dumpty Foods (1983), 11 L.A.C. (3d) 385 (Weatherill).

▼

CONTRACT TERM

Employees shall receive 11 *statutory holidays*. Vacation shall be based on years of continuous service. Sick leave credits shall accumulate based on months or years worked.

ARBITRATOR'S RULING

Some benefits accrue by virtue of employment, others depend on the employee's presence at the workplace and performance of work. It all depends on the agreement. Here, in the absence of restrictions, employees absent from work because of a compensable disability are entitled to holiday pay and vacations, since continuous service is synonymous with seniority, but sick leave credits do not accumulate since they are based on months or years worked.

City of Trail (1983), 10 L.A.C. (3d) 251 (Munroe).

▼

CONTRACT TERM

Employees must have worked the complete shift before and after the holiday to qualify for *holiday pay*.

ARBITRATOR'S RULING

As a result of the use of the definite article "the", the clause refers to shifts which employees generally are scheduled to work, even if the employee personally is not scheduled to work because of layoff; it would be a different matter if the clause referred to "his scheduled shift".

Hamilton Gear Machine (1982), 6 L.A.C. (3d) 311 (Brown).

▼

CONTRACT TERM

To obtain *holiday pay* employees must work on the last regularly scheduled shift prior to the holiday.

ARBITRATOR'S RULING

A shift may be scheduled prior to a holiday even though employees are on strike; where it is so scheduled, then the last day before the strike is not the last regularly scheduled shift before the holiday. [This ruling must be reconsidered in light of present Ontario legislation which prohibits bargaining unit employees from working during a legal strike.]

3M Canada (1982), 4 L.A.C. (3d) 420 (M.G. Picher).

▼

CONTRACT TERM
To qualify for *holiday pay* an employee must work on his scheduled workday immediately preceding the holiday and must return to work as scheduled immediately following the holiday.

ARBITRATOR'S RULING
Where a holiday falls during a strike, employees are not at work so as to qualify for holiday pay, unless the strike settlement provides otherwise. *Abitibi-Price* (1981), 1 L.A.C. (3d) 193 (Gorsky).

▼

CONTRACT TERM
Holiday pay is due only if employees have worked their last regular full shift immediately preceding, and the last regular full shift immediately following any such holiday.

ARBITRATOR'S RULING
Since the purpose of the clause is to deter absenteeism, involuntary absence caused by a lockout does not detract from entitlement to holiday pay; the employee's last regular shift before the holiday is the shift prior to the lockout. *Township of Muskoka Lakes* (1981), 1 L.A.C. (3d) 125 (MacDowell).

▼

CONTRACT TERM
An employee will qualify for *holiday pay* if he is not employed under an arrangement whereby he may elect to work or not.

ARBITRATOR'S RULING
Casual part-time employees do not qualify for holiday pay where they are on call or attend at work when they wish, since these employees may elect to work or not, as distinct from casual employees who are hired for a fixed although temporary period and are obliged to work according to a schedule. *Belleville General Hospital* (1981), 30 L.A.C. (2d) 323 (M.G. Picher).

▼

CONTRACT TERM
Holiday pay is payable provided the employee is not absent from his last scheduled shift before such holiday or his first scheduled shift after such holiday without a doctor's certificate.

ARBITRATOR'S RULING
Substantial compliance is the test; an employee who reports for work on a qualifying day, but leaves mid-way through the shift without permission, may be subject to discipline, but he has completed a substantial portion of the shift, and is entitled to holiday pay.

Stran-Steel (1980), 28 L.A.C. (2d) 153 (Betcherman).

▼

CONTRACT
TERM

In order to qualify for *holiday pay*, an employee shall work the full shift on each of the working days immediately preceding and following the plant holidays unless the employee is absent due to a leave of absence, etc.

ARBITRATOR'S
RULING

A disciplinary suspension is not a leave of absence.

Thomas Built Buses (1980), 27 L.A.C. (2d) 409 (Weatherill).

▼

CONTRACT
TERM

Pay for sick leave is for the sole and only purpose of protecting the employee against loss of regular income when she is legitimately ill and unable to work. An employee required to work on a designated *holiday* shall be paid at time and a half her regular straight time rate of pay for all hours worked on such holiday, and will receive in addition a lieu day off at her regular straight time rate of pay.

ARBITRATOR'S
RULING

An employee who is scheduled to work on a statutory holiday but is unable to do so because of *bona fide* illness is entitled to both holiday and sick pay, since both are earned benefits. Had she worked on the holiday, the employee would have been entitled to both payments, which are for separate purposes, and are not duplications. Once scheduled to work a statutory holiday, entitlement to holiday pay becomes part of an employee's regular income since the employee is expected to attend work at that time.

North York General Hospital (1980), 27 L.A.C. (2d) 64 (Shime).

▼

CONTRACT
TERM

Employees required to work on a recognized *holiday* shall be paid at the rate of two and a half times the base rate for all hours worked. If hours actually worked are outside of the employee's normal shift hours, he shall also be entitled to the 8 hours recognized holiday pay at his base rate.

ARBITRATOR'S
RULING
Any work outside the normal workweek, and not just the normal workday, is "outside normal shift hours". Employees required to work on a recognized holiday on a scheduled day off are therefore entitled to two and a half times the base rate plus the 8 hours' base pay, whether or not the employees are required to work the same hours they would have worked had they been scheduled to work on the recognized holiday.

Fiberglas Canada Ltd. (1980), 26 L.A.C. (2d) 145 (Sychuk).

▼

CONTRACT
TERM
In order to be entitled to payment for a plant *holiday* an employee must have worked the full working day immediately preceding and following the holiday except where management has given permission to be absent on either of these days.

ARBITRATOR'S
RULING
Because "the" is used, rather than "his", the qualifying days are to be determined objectively for all employees, and not subjectively for individual employees. Where employees are on layoff on the day preceding a holiday, they are not scheduled to work, and are not entitled to holiday pay. A layoff is not synonymous with permission to be absent.

Caravelle Foods (1980), 26 L.A.C. (2d) 1 (O'Shea).

▼

CONTRACT
TERM
An employee will be entitled to payment for specified *holidays* only if he or she has completed the probationary period and attends for the declared working day immediately preceding the holiday and reports back at the start of operations immediately following the holiday.

ARBITRATOR'S
RULING
Exact performance is required, subject to the rule that "minute and unimportant deviations" from exact compliance will be ignored. Although the employer was prepared to excuse lateness of up to 5 minutes, as constituting substantial performance, lateness for longer periods disentitles employees to holiday pay.

Patons & Baldwins (Canada) Ltd. (1980), 25 L.A.C. (2d) 332 (Brunner).

HOSPITALIZED

CONTRACT
TERM

Where it is established by an employee that an illness or accident occurred while on vacation and the employee was *hospitalized* as a result, sick pay shall be substituted for vacation.

ARBITRATOR'S
RULING

"Hospitalization" is confined to in-patient treatment, in order to trigger vacation pay replacement; a visit to an emergency room on an out-patient basis for treatment is not hospitalization for purposes of the agreement.

Public Utilities Commission of City of Scarborough (1989), 6 L.A.C. (4th) 170 (T.A.B. Jolliffe).

HOURS PAID

CONTRACT
TERM

Part-time employees shall receive an additional $0.40 *per hour paid* in lieu of benefits provided in the full-time agreement.

ARBITRATOR'S
RULING

The clause requires additional pay for each hour paid, whether or not worked, and thus would apply to statutory holidays.

Leisure World Nursing Homes (1983), 12 L.A.C. (3d) 345 (Langille).

HOURS WORKED, *see also* TIME WORKED, WORKED

CONTRACT
TERM

For *hours worked* in excess of 45 hours per week, the employees shall receive overtime at the rate of one and a half times their regular rate.

ARBITRATOR'S
RULING

"Hours worked" denotes hours actually worked, and does not include paid sick leave or statutory holidays — "hours worked" and "hours paid" are distinct concepts.

Brookfield Foods Limited (1987), 28 L.A.C. (3d) 1 (Outhouse).

I

ILLNESS, *see also* DISABILITY, SICK LEAVE, SICKNESS

EDITORS' NOTE The Supreme Court of Canada has held that, while pregnancy is not an illness, it is a valid health-related reason for absence, and it is sex-based discrimination, contrary to human rights legislation, to allow paid leave for other health-related absences, but not for pregnancy. In short, a plan which provides benefits for valid health-related absences cannot exclude coverage for absences which are pregnancy-related. See *Brooks v. Canada Safeway Ltd.* (1989), 59 D.L.R. (4th) 321.

CONTRACT TERM Lost time due to injury or accidents occurring while on duty or *illness* shall not be considered as breaking a month's service.

ARBITRATOR'S RULING Absence for illness presupposes an underlying disease. Dental appointments to install a bridge prosthesis do not arise from illness, but are designed to prevent a health problem in the future; moreover, they are too remote from the original extraction to entitle the employee to sick pay.

Municipality of Metropolitan Toronto (1989), 7 L.A.C. (4th) 214 (Davis).

▼

CONTRACT TERM Sick leave with pay shall be granted to those full-time employees who, through *illness*, are unable to perform the duties of their positions.

ARBITRATOR'S RULING Pre-menstrual syndrome is a disability rooted in a recognized medical condition, and discipline for absence without leave due to P.M.S. is without just cause.

Metropolitan Authority (1989), 6 L.A.C. (4th) 371 (Archibald).

▼

CONTRACT TERM — Sick leave benefits are payable for an *illness* which causes an employee to be absent from duty for a period of 3 to 80 consecutive workdays.

ARBITRATOR'S RULING — In general, an employer cannot selectively refuse benefits based on an unusual susceptibility to a particular illness, unless an injury is self-inflicted or acquired while working for another employer. Thus, an allergic reaction to cigarette smoke in the workplace entitles an employee to sick leave benefits, particularly since the presence of tobacco smoke is not essential to the employer's business nor beyond its ability to control.

Government of Province of Alberta (1989), 5 L.A.C. (4th) 68 (McFetridge).

▼

CONTRACT TERM — The employer agrees to continue the current income disability plan, providing for benefits when an employee is incapacitated and unable to work because of *illness*. The employer may require the employee to begin a maternity leave of absence at such time as in its opinion the duties of her position cannot reasonably be performed by a pregnant woman or the performance of her work is materially affected by the pregnancy.

ARBITRATOR'S RULING — Where the disability plan covers only incapacitating disability, a pregnant employee is not entitled to sick leave if she can do light work, despite muscle spasms accompanying the pregnancy. If no light duties are available, and she cannot do her regular job, the employer has the right to place the employee on early maternity leave.

Brantwood Residential Development Centre (1988), 1 L.A.C. (4th) 47 (O'Shea).

▼

CONTRACT TERM — Sick pay benefits shall be paid if an employee is totally disabled; totally disabled means an employee's inability to perform the regular duties pertaining to her occupation due to *illness* or injury.

ARBITRATOR'S RULING — Participation in an *in vitro* fertilization program, involving medical and surgical procedures to remedy infertility, entitles an employee to short-term sick leave benefits, because it is a recognized medical treatment for a pre-existing abnormal condition, which causes physical incapacity. Infertility itself qualifies as an illness or disease according to worldwide medical standards.

Metropolitan General Hospital (1987), 32 L.A.C. (3d) 10 (H.D. Brown).

▼

CONTRACT
TERM

A teacher shall be granted 20 days' [*sick*] leave per teaching year to a maximum of 75 days.

ARBITRATOR'S
RULING

"Sickness" means a condition of ill health preventing an employee from working. While pregnancy itself is not an illness, and a normal pregnancy does not entitle an employee to sick leave, inability to work due to or consequential upon pregnancy does entitle an employee to sick leave, and this includes disability due to pain and discomfort following a caesarean birth.

Agassiz School Division No. 13 (1987), 28 L.A.C. (3d) 420 (Freedman).

▼

CONTRACT
TERM

Sick leave will be provided by the employer for any *illness*, quarantine or because of an accident for which compensation is not payable under the *Workers' Compensation Act*.

ARBITRATOR'S
RULING

Whether an employee suffers from an illness should be based on the symptoms experienced, rather than the causes. A condition involving emotional depression, acute anxiety and "an inability to cope" on learning of her mother's life-threatening illness qualifies as an illness and therefore entitles an employee to sick leave benefits.

St. Joseph's Hospital (1987), 28 L.A.C. (3d) 185 (Ponak).

▼

CONTRACT
TERM

Sick leave plan covers disability, defined as inability to perform regular duties due to injury or *illness*.

ARBITRATOR'S
RULING

Inability to work due to pregnancy complication endangering growth of foetus constitutes a disability due to illness. While a normal healthy pregnancy is not an illness, an abnormal unhealthy pregnancy constitutes a disabling illness entitling the employee to sick leave benefits.

Hotel Dieu of St. Joseph Hospital (1985), 20 L.A.C. (3d) 299 (MacDowell).

▼

CONTRACT TERM
Employees are entitled to pay for absence due to *illness.*

ARBITRATOR'S RULING
Term "due" means that illness must be the effective or proximate cause of absence and cannot be just an originating or remote cause, as where absence is due to incarceration in a psychiatric institution resulting from offences committed under the influence of mental illness.

Etobicoke Board of Education (1984), 17 L.A.C. (3d) 40 (Brunner).

▼

CONTRACT TERM
An employee who is frequently absent on account of pregnancy-related *illness* may be required by the employer to commence her maternity leave.

ARBITRATOR'S RULING
Term does not include pre-existing medical condition of high blood pressure, even though the employee was advised by her doctor to rest at home because medication was restricted by the pregnancy. Alternatively, the clause contravenes the provisions of Ontario's *Employment Standards Act.*

Metropolitan Separate School Board (1984), 16 L.A.C. (3d) 353 (Adams).

▼

CONTRACT TERM
The sick leave plan provides sick pay benefits in the event of disability due to injury or *illness.*

ARBITRATOR'S RULING
Term includes medical complications or pathological conditions related to pregnancy, in this case, threatened premature labour requiring medication and bedrest.

Oshawa General Hospital (1984), 16 L.A.C. (3d) 65 (Swan).

▼

CONTRACT TERM
An employee's earnings will be protected in the event of absence for verified personal *illness.*

ARBITRATOR'S RULING
Absence from work to attend at a physician's office for diagnostic examination of a chronic migraine headache condition is not absence due to illness where the cause of absence is not the condition but the conflict of the physician's schedule with the company's schedule.

General Bakeries (1981), 2 L.A.C. (3d) 444 (Rayner).

IMMEDIATE FAMILY, see also BEREAVEMENT LEAVE

CONTRACT
TERM
Immediate family for the purposes of bereavement leave shall mean brother-in-law, etc.

ARBITRATOR'S
RULING
"Brother-in-law" includes only the brother of one's husband or wife, and not a spouse's sister's spouse, because of the restriction in the definition of leave to "immediate family", which is a narrower concept than "family", and includes only the employee's close relatives, not those of his or her spouse.

Greater Niagara General Hospital (1989), 4 L.A.C. (4th) 283 (McLaren).

▼

CONTRACT
TERM
Employees who suffer bereavement within the *immediate family* will be granted 3 days' leave of absence; immediate family includes grandparents.

ARBITRATOR'S
RULING
"Grandparents" includes spousal grandparents, since a broad interpretation of "immediate family" is warranted in the absence of restrictive language.

Associated Freezers of Canada (1987), 32 L.A.C. (3d) 79 (Kilgour).

▼

CONTRACT
TERM
In the case of death in the *immediate family* (defined to include spouse, common law spouse, father-in-law, mother-in-law, etc.) of an employee, up to 3 days' bereavement leave is allowed.

ARBITRATOR'S
RULING
Where "immediate family" is not defined, or the definition "includes" certain persons, but is not an exhaustive list, the family of a common law spouse might be covered. However, where "immediate family" is defined, the father or other family of a common law spouse is not covered unless specifically mentioned.

Alberta Wheat Pool (1986), 23 L.A.C. (3d) 316 (Kelleher).

▼

CONTRACT
TERM
When death occurs to a member of a regular full-time employee's *immediate family*, the employee will be granted an appropriate leave of absence; immediate family is defined as the employee's spouse, grandparents, etc.

ARBITRATOR'S
RULING
Bereavement leave clauses should be read broadly
to advance their purpose, which is to accommodate
grief, and "immediate family" includes the grandparents of an employee's spouse.

North Cariboo Labour Relations Association (1985),
19 L.A.C. (3d) 115 (Hope).

INFORMATION

CONTRACT
TERM
The employer shall provide a bulletin board for the
purpose of posting *information* related to the union's
activities.

ARBITRATOR'S
RULING
Information must be factual, not mere propaganda.

Foothills Hospital Board (1985), 23 L.A.C. (3d) 42
(Malone).

INTERMITTENT EMPLOYMENT

CONTRACT
TERM
An employee will be considered on probation until
he has completed 3 months' continuous service or
90 days of *intermittent employment* within any 12
month period.

ARBITRATOR'S
RULING
Absence due to strike, layoff, illness, etc., interrupts
an employee's continuous service for the purpose
of calculating his probationary period, with the result that such an "intermittent employee" must meet
the test of working 90 calendar days in a 12-month
period to achieve seniority status.

Ferro Industrial Products Ltd. (1988), 35 L.A.C. (3d)
324 (Stanley).

J

JOB, *see also* PROMOTION, VACANCY

CONTRACT
TERM

In making promotions to vacant *jobs* coming within the jurisdiction of the union, the required knowledge and skills contained in the job posting shall be the primary considerations and where two or more applicants are equally qualified to fulfill the duties of the *job*, seniority shall be the determining factor. Notices of vacancy required to be filled shall be immediately posted for a period of seven days.

ARBITRATOR'S
RULING

A reclassification of an existing position triggers the posting and seniority provisions of the collective agreement. At the instant a new job (i.e. a specific set of duties assigned to one person) is created or an existing job is changed by the employer, it is vacant for the purposes of the agreement; otherwise, the employer could avoid the posting and seniority provisions by reclassifying current employees, even for new jobs.

City of Edmonton (1987), 30 L.A.C. (3d) 353 (Jones).

▼

CONTRACT
TERM

A vacancy or new *job* shall be posted.

ARBITRATOR'S
RULING

A vacancy or new job is not created merely by alteration of shift hours, work area or days off, and such alteration does not constitute a layoff so as to require re-posting.

Royal Columbian Hospital (1986), 24 L.A.C. (3d) 359 (Kelleher).

▼

CONTRACT
TERM

An employee returning from maternity leave is entitled to resume the normal duties of her *job*.

101

ARBITRATOR'S RULING Since an employer can transfer an employee within a job classification, the term "job" does not relate to specific duties, but to general duties within job classifications; thus, the employer is entitled to assign the returning employee to a different job in the same classification.

DeHavilland Aircraft (1982), 5 L.A.C. (3d) 147 (Palmer).

▼

CONTRACT TERM Notice of a *job vacancy* will be posted; on layoff least senior employees shall be laid off first and called back last.

ARBITRATOR'S RULING A layoff does not create a vacancy because the employer no longer requires the job to be done, but a vacancy does arise where the number of workers to be laid off is reduced because an additional worker is required in a classification. The vacancy exists, and must be posted, even though an employee on layoff may be entitled to fill it under the recall provisions of the collective agreement.

Gray Forging (1981), 30 L.A.C. (2d) 354 (Weatherill).

JOB AVAILABLE

CONTRACT TERM In the event of layoff or recall, seniority shall prevail, provided the senior employee has sufficient ability to do the *job available*.

ARBITRATOR'S RULING "Job available" is any occupied position into which an employee could bump, where the work is performed by any person junior to the more senior person and which the bumper has sufficient ability to do. More senior employees are not restricted to bumping into the job occupied by the most junior employee.

Western Grocers (1989), 6 L.A.C. (4th) 1 (Freedman).

▼

CONTRACT TERM A laid off employee is entitled to recall if he has the greatest seniority and is capable of performing satisfactorily the *job available*.

ARBITRATOR'S RULING The term "job available" refers to work which the employer requires to have done, not the job classification, and it is not sufficient that an employee has done some work within the classification if he cannot perform the tasks for which employees have been recalled.

AEL Microtel (1984), 14 L.A.C. (3d) 113 (Weatherill).

JUST CAUSE

CONTRACT TERM No employee shall be dismissed, suspended or demoted without *just cause*.

ARBITRATOR'S RULING "Just cause" means well-grounded, fair, equitable and proper, and it is the antithesis of the concept to permit an employer to dismiss an employee for medical disability or innocent absenteeism when the effect is to prevent him or her from taking advantage of negotiated benefits, as where continued employment is a condition of entitlement to disability benefits.

Government of Province of Alberta (1987), 29 L.A.C. (3d) 218 (Tadman).

JUSTIFIABLE CAUSE

CONTRACT TERM To be eligible for holiday pay, an employee, unless absent due to *justifiable cause*, must have been present on the work day immediately preceding and following such a holiday.

ARBITRATOR'S RULING Employees who leave work on illegal strike before completing at least half the required shift on the day before a statutory holiday are not in substantial compliance with the agreement and are therefore not entitled to holiday pay. However, employees who work two-thirds of the shift, on the day the illegal strike ends, are in substantial compliance, and are entitled to holiday pay.

Rothesay Paper Ltd. (1989), 5 L.A.C. (4th) 103 (MacLean).

K

KNOWLEDGE, see also SKILL AND ABILITY

CONTRACT
TERM

In making promotions, transfers, and demotions the skill, *knowledge* and work record of the employee shall be the primary considerations. Where two or more applicants are capable of fulfilling the duties of the position and the aforesaid qualifications are otherwise comparable, seniority or years of experience shall be determining factors.

ARBITRATOR'S
RULING

Comparability is defined as "able to be compared, capable of comparison, worthy of comparison", while "equal" denotes possessing a like degree of a quality, on the same level of ability. Relative equality is therefore a higher test than comparability between candidates. A junior employee must be superior to a senior one by a "clear and demonstrable margin".

Board of School Trustees, School District No. 39 (1987), 30 L.A.C. (3d) 257 (Thompson).

▼

CONTRACT
TERM

In making promotions, transfers or filling vacancies, the skill, *knowledge* and efficiency of the employees concerned shall be the primary consideration and where such qualifications are relatively equal, seniority shall be the determining factor.

ARBITRATOR'S
RULING

Previous experience in the same or a similar job shows demonstrated ability, and may be taken into account in assessing competing employees. Relative equality exists unless the difference is substantial and demonstrable — a discernible, material difference, not just a minor one.

Board of School Trustees, District 68 (1985), 19 L.A.C. (3d) 176 (Germaine).

L

LAID OFF EMPLOYEES

CONTRACT
TERM
Laid-off employees shall be recalled in order of seniority provided that they have the required qualifications and ability to do the work available. Seniority shall be a major factor in determining layoffs and recalls, etc.

ARBITRATOR'S
RULING
Laid-off employees who bump into lower-rated jobs are considered to have been laid off, and are entitled to be recalled to their former jobs in advance of more junior employees.

City of Kanata (1987), 31 L.A.C. (3d) 224 (H.D. Brown).

LAWFUL UNION ACTIVITY, *see* UNION ACTIVITY

LAYOFF

CONTRACT
TERM
When the employer decides to *lay off* employees, the following displacement provisions apply: where an employee has the competence, skill and experience to fulfill the requirements of the full-time position concerned, seniority shall apply.

ARBITRATOR'S
RULING
"Position" is defined as the core pattern of duties and responsibilities performed by the incumbent prior to layoff; this basic pattern can be identified by examining the actual work assignments given to the incumbent over an extended period of time.

St. Clair College (1989), 6 L.A.C. (4th) 442.

▼

CONTRACT
TERM
In the event of *layoff* or recall, seniority shall prevail, provided the senior employee has sufficient ability to do the job available.

ARBITRATOR'S RULING "Job available" is any occupied position into which an employee could bump, where the work is performed by any person junior to the more senior person and which the bumper has sufficient ability to do. More senior employees are not restricted to bumping into the job occupied by the most junior employee.

Western Grocers (1989), 6 L.A.C. (4th) 1 (Freedman).

▼

CONTRACT TERM The normal daily hours of work shall be 8 per day. *Layoffs* shall be determined on the basis of the seniority of the employees concerned.

ARBITRATOR'S RULING Specification of normal daily hours of work in an agreement does not constitute a guarantee of such hours, nor does it prevent the employer from reducing the hours of work of all or part of its staff as part of its management rights. However, a 4-hour per day reduction in only one employee's normal daily hours amounts to a layoff and triggers the layoff provisions of the agreement.

Cove Guest Home (1988), 1 L.A.C. (4th) 42 (Scaravelli).

▼

CONTRACT TERM Employees on *layoff* will not be paid for the time the employees are on *layoff*.

ARBITRATOR'S RULING Employees absent on workers' compensation benefits prior to a layoff are not considered to be laid off, since it is the fundamental reason for the employee's absence from work which characterizes the period of absence, which in this case was disability. A layoff entails the necessity of reduction of the workforce due to a shortage of available work, and such a reduction cannot be achieved by laying off an employee already off work on WCB.

City of London (1988), 34 L.A.C. (3d) 92 (Rayner).

▼

CONTRACT TERM Laid-off employees shall be recalled in order of seniority provided that they have the required qualifications and ability to do the work available. Seniority shall be a major factor in determining *layoffs* and recalls, etc.

ARBITRATOR'S RULING Laid-off employees who bump into lower-rated jobs are considered to have been laid off, and are entitled to be recalled to their former jobs in advance of more junior employees.

City of Kanata (1987), 31 L.A.C. (3d) 224 (H.D. Brown).

▼

CONTRACT TERM A *layoff* is a reduction in the workforce or a reduction in the regular hours of work.

ARBITRATOR'S RULING The sending home of casual employees due to inclement weather is a layoff, since it reduces their hours of work; in such circumstances regard must be had to considerations of seniority, even where the layoff is for less than a shift, to the extent that it is practicable to do so.

City of Lethbridge (1987), 30 L.A.C. (3d) 32 (Rigg).

▼

CONTRACT TERM Vacation pay shall be paid to *laid off* employees at the time of *layoff*.

ARBITRATOR'S RULING While vacation pay entitlement may depend on maintaining status as an employee rather than on actually working throughout the year, an employee who is laid off during the year is not entitled to full vacation pay for the balance of the year, but only to a percentage.

Domglas (1986), 26 L.A.C. (3d) 29 (Kelleher).

▼

CONTRACT TERM Seniority governs on *layoff* and recall; on *layoff* the employee must be able to fulfill the normal requirements of the job.

ARBITRATOR'S RULING Unless the collective agreement provides otherwise, upward bumping is not permissible on a layoff since employees should not be allowed to obtain a promotion through a layoff; on the other hand, employees are not required to bump the most junior employee, but can choose the position to bump into. The clause requires present ability, without training, not just potential ability. In the absence of a trial period, the employer is not required to grant the employee an opportunity to demonstrate his or her skills before making an assessment of the employee's ability; however, a short familiarization period is permitted to become familiar with the routine and details of the job.

Denison Mines (1986), 25 L.A.C. (3d) 230 (Springate).

▼

CONTRACT TERM

Layoffs shall proceed in inverse order of seniority provided that no employee is to be displaced by a person with more seniority unless the latter possesses the occupational qualifications of the job.

ARBITRATOR'S RULING

Although management who have previous service in the bargaining unit may retain it and apply it if and when they return, they cannot use their seniority under this collective agreement to bump employees during a layoff. While the word "person" has a more general meaning, it refers here to employees, not management; this is made clear by the French version of the collective agreement, and the provisions of the collective agreement which establish the job security of bargaining unit employees.

CBC (1986), 23 L.A.C. (3d) 394 (M.G. Picher).

▼

CONTRACT TERM

Notice of *layoff* is required in the event of a layoff due to lack of work. If work is not available, an employee shall be paid for 4 hours of work.

ARBITRATOR'S RULING

Where a reporting pay provision exists, a short-term plant closure due to unforeseen circumstances, such as a snowstorm, does not constitute a layoff; in such circumstances, when employees are sent home prior to the completion of their shift, because of the travel difficulties caused by a severe blizzard, the minimum reporting pay provision is applicable.

Peelle Co. (1986), 23 L.A.C. (3d) 1 (Burkett).

▼

CONTRACT TERM

In cases of *layoff* or recall seniority will be the governing factor provided ability to perform the job is demonstrated; in cases of promotion seniority will be the governing factor provided all other factors are relatively equal.

ARBITRATOR'S RULING

Where tests for layoff and promotion are different, an employee is not entitled to bump up when faced with a layoff.

Macotta Co. (1985), 22 L.A.C. (2d) 265 (Burkett).

▼

CONTRACT TERM
Regular employees will be *laid off* according to inverse plant-wide seniority provided that the employees remaining are willing and qualified to do the jobs available.

ARBITRATOR'S RULING
The clause contemplates the right of a laid off employee to bump into a junior job of his choice, which he can perform, even if chain bumping results; the company cannot require him to bump into the most junior job in the plant.

Moloney Electric (1985), 22 L.A.C. (3d) 170 (M.G. Picher).

▼

CONTRACT TERM
Layoffs shall be in accordance with seniority.

ARBITRATOR'S RULING
Sending employees home for less than one shift does not constitute a layoff, particularly where the time required to make the consequential moves would be extensive, and a reporting pay provision exists.

St. Lawrence Cement (1985), 21 L.A.C. (3d) 158 (Palmer). Compare *Brendan Construction*, below.

▼

CONTRACT TERM
Employees shall have certain options (including bumping, severance pay, early retirement, etc.) in the event of *layoff*, defined in the collective agreement as a cessation of employment or elimination of job resulting from reduction of work, re-organization, program termination, closure or other material change in organization.

ARBITRATOR'S RULING
A sale of business does not constitute a layoff where employment under the collective agreement is continued by virtue of successor rights provisions of labour legislation.

Government of B.C. (1985), 21 L.A.C. (3d) 136 (Bird).

▼

CONTRACT TERM
Where employees are to be laid off, such *layoffs* shall proceed in inverse order of Corporation seniority.

ARBITRATOR'S RULING
Under this clause, employees on medical leave of absence may not be laid off or required to bump until termination of leave.

CBC (1985), 18 L.A.C. (3d) 317 (M.G. Picher).

▼

CONTRACT
TERM

Where employees are to be laid off, such *layoffs* shall proceed in inverse order of Corporation seniority, provided the senior employee possesses the occupational qualifications of the job filled by the employee with less seniority. The employee with the most unit or functional group seniority shall be promoted, if he meets the qualifications set for the position.

ARBITRATOR'S
RULING

The collective agreement does not permit upward bumping on layoff since seniority requirements on layoff and promotion are inconsistent; otherwise, an employee could obtain a promotion on layoff for which he could not qualify in a job posting competition.

CBC (1985), 17 L.A.C. (3d) 353 (M.G. Picher).

▼

CONTRACT
TERM

The employer shall give notice of *layoff* or pay in lieu thereof.

ARBITRATOR'S
RULING

"Layoff" includes a reduction in the workforce brought about by a temporary shutdown.

Wilshire Lodge (1984), 17 L.A.C. (3d) 82 (Hope).

▼

CONTRACT
TERM

Layoffs shall be in accordance with seniority, i.e. the employees last appointed, who belong to the staff to be reduced, shall be the first discharged.

ARBITRATOR'S
RULING

A requirement to take a statutory holiday off due to reduced demand for service constitutes a layoff, where the hours of work of all affected employees are not equally reduced and employees with less seniority are scheduled to work.

City of Edmonton (1984), 15 L.A.C. (3d) 137 (Taylor).

▼

CONTRACT
TERM

Layoff shall be in accordance with seniority when an anticipated general plant shortage of work occurs.

ARBITRATOR'S RULING — Layoff involves a planned decrease in production, and seniority provisions apply when management is in a position to plan the reduction of the workforce. Seniority provisions applicable on layoff do not apply in the event of an unexpected breakdown of mechanical equipment, but after a reasonable time (here, a day) an unexpected interruption can become an anticipated shortage of work, and trigger the layoff provisions.

MacMillan Bathurst Inc. (1984), 15 L.A.C. (3d) 114 (Davis).

▼

CONTRACT TERM — *Layoffs* shall be by department by seniority.

ARBITRATOR'S RULING — An unequal reduction in work hours (here, employees on day and afternoon shifts, but not on the night shift) constitutes a layoff so as to trigger seniority provisions.

Ballycliffe Lodge (1984), 14 L.A.C. (3d) 37 (Adams).

▼

CONTRACT TERM — The union acknowledges that it is the exclusive function of the hospital to *lay off*, etc.

ARBITRATOR'S RULING — A layoff is a reduction in working forces, either temporary or permanent, brought about as a result of a consideration of prevailing economic or business conditions; and management's right to lay off is subject to an implied term that the decision will be taken honestly in furtherance of legitimate business interests.

Toronto East General Hospital (1984), 13 L.A.C. (3d) 400 (Burkett).

▼

CONTRACT TERM — Seniority shall govern in the event of a *layoff*.

ARBITRATOR'S RULING — The existence of a layoff does not depend on the length of time off work; thus, a layoff includes interruption of work due to a snowstorm, and the seniority provisions are thereby triggered.

London Transit Commission (1983), 10 L.A.C. (3d) 348 (Rayner).

▼

CONTRACT TERM
Severance pay is not applicable to *layoffs* due to shortage of work.

ARBITRATOR'S RULING
The term "layoff" connotes a severance of the employment relationship brought about by a lack of work, which may be either temporary or permanent, depending on the circumstances.

B.C. Hydro (1983), 10 L.A.C. (3d) 76 (Hope).

▼

CONTRACT TERM
Employees with the greatest plant seniority at the time of layoffs, if they possess the qualifications necessary to perform the available work, shall be the last to be *laid off* and the first to be recalled. Promotions will be made on the basis of plant seniority, provided the employee possesses the requisite ability, skill and job efficiency to perform the duties of the job.

ARBITRATOR'S RULING
Upward bumping is not permitted by the collective agreement, where the tests on layoff and promotion are inconsistent; an employee may possess the necessary qualifications, but not the ability, skill and job efficiency to do the job.

Canadian Mist Distillers (1983), 9 L.A.C. (3d) 385 (Saltman).

▼

CONTRACT TERM
In cases of *layoff* and resulting recalls, provided the employee is able to do the work required, plant seniority shall govern.

ARBITRATOR'S RULING
Where an unequal worksharing or reduction of work results in junior employees working more hours than senior employees, a layoff results, and seniority provisions apply.

Dahmer Steel (1983), 9 L.A.C. (3d) 234 (Hinnegan).

▼

CONTRACT TERM
An employee already on *layoff* will not be required to take vacation during layoff.

ARBITRATOR'S RULING
The clause does not prevent employees from taking a vacation at their discretion during a layoff if the vacation was pre-arranged; since the fundamental reason for the absence is the pre-arrangement of vacations, the employer cannot treat the employees as if they were on layoff.

Nestle Enterprises (1982), 7 L.A.C. (3d) 422 (O'Shea).

▼

CONTRACT
TERM

In the matter of re-hiring following a *layoff*, the last person laid off shall be the first rehired.

ARBITRATOR'S
RULING

Because the word "re-hiring" is used, as opposed to "recall", the clause applies to layoffs "on to the street", not to a bump without loss of employment; as a result, an employee who bumped, when his job was abolished, is not entitled to recall to a newly established job, even though it is identical to the one he held, and the job must be posted.

Board of School Trustees (Surrey) (1982), 7 L.A.C. (3d) 259 (Bird).

▼

CONTRACT
TERM

Seniority shall apply in the event of *layoff* and re-call.

ARBITRATOR'S
RULING

Employees should not be allowed to obtain a promotion through a layoff. Therefore, upward bumping is not required even where, as here, no inconsistency between layoff and promotion provisions would arise, since in both cases seniority governs subject only to ability to perform the job.

Dominion Stores (1982), 7 L.A.C. (3d) 163 (Yeoman). Contrast *Macotta*, above.

▼

CONTRACT
TERM

Contracting out of work is prohibited where it would result in the *layoff* of bargaining unit employees.

ARBITRATOR'S
RULING

The term "layoff" in this clause means initial layoff, not continuing layoff; the clause does not apply to the contracting out of work normally performed by an employee already on layoff, since the layoff precedes and is not caused by the contracting out.

Rockwell International of Canada (1982), 6 L.A.C. (3d) 304 (Rayner).

▼

CONTRACT
TERM

Where a *layoff* may occur by reason of shortage of work or funds or the abolition of a position or other material change in organization, the layoff shall be in accordance with seniority.

ARBITRATOR'S RULING
Relocation of provincial government medicare offices from one city to another constitutes a layoff, and not just a transfer, where the positions are geographically limited, even though employees willing to relocate are guaranteed a position at the new location.

Ministry of Health (1982), 3 L.A.C. (3d) 385 (Kennedy).

▼

CONTRACT TERM
On *layoff* and recall seniority shall be given preference where abilities, etc. are relatively equal.

ARBITRATOR'S RULING
Qualifications of employees are relatively equal unless one employee is better qualified by a substantial and demonstrable margin. Management's decision must not have been made in bad faith or arbitrarily, and it must be reasonable. The less skill and judgment a job requires, the more difficult it is to demonstrate the reasonableness of a decision that there are substantial differences in ability to perform a job as between applicants.

British Leaf Tobacco (1981), 3 L.A.C. (3d) 235 (Kennedy).

▼

CONTRACT TERM
Employees will be *laid off* in accordance with seniority, subject to skill and ability to perform the work; in the case of promotion seniority shall govern where skill, ability and performance are relatively equal between two or more employees.

ARBITRATOR'S RULING
Where tests are different on layoff and promotion, employees who are laid off are not entitled to bump upward, in the absence of specific language in the collective agreement, since employees should not be allowed to obtain a promotion through a layoff.

Electrohome (1981), 30 L.A.C. (2d) 106 (Black).

▼

CONTRACT TERM
In cases of *layoff*, etc., employees shall be entitled to preference based on seniority and ability.

ARBITRATOR'S RULING
A layoff involves sending employees home from work. Normally, it applies to more extensive periods than a part of a shift, but it can include a part day where it is easy to transfer the employees to the work of junior employees.

Brendan Construction (1980), 28 L.A.C. (2d) 375 (Palmer). Compare *St. Lawrence Cement*, above.

▼

CONTRACT TERM — In the event of *reduction of staff*, the principle of seniority will apply subject to qualifications. The company shall have the exclusive right to make appointments to dispatcher-grade 1 vacancies.

ARBITRATOR'S RULING — Upward bumping is not permitted, since it would involve placing the employee in a position to which the company has the exclusive right to appoint (here, dispatcher-grade 1).

Pacific Coach Line (1980), 26 L.A.C. (2d) 270 (Thompson).

▼

CONTRACT TERM — In all cases of *layoff* and recall, preference shall be given to employees based on seniority, provided they are able to fill the requirements of the work available.

ARBITRATOR'S RULING — In cases of promotion, it is generally sufficient, depending on the language of the collective agreement, that an employee have the potential to do the job, but on layoff employees must be able to do the work in question without a training period, because otherwise the operation would be severely impaired by the checkerboard move of employees. Indeed, the word "available" is used to indicate that there is a temporal qualification to the work, and that employees must have the present ability to perform it.

Reynolds Aluminum Company of Canada Ltd. (1980), 26 L.A.C. (2d) 266 (Shime).

▼

CONTRACT TERM — Any employee *laid off* through the application of departmental seniority may exercise his plant-wide seniority and may replace any employee in any department who has less plant-wide seniority, if he is able and willing to do the work.

ARBITRATOR'S RULING — In the absence of a limitation on classifications into which employees may bump, the explicit reference to "any employee" compels the finding that senior employees may bump upwards into higher-rated classifications.

Pioneer Chainsaw Corp. (1980), 26 L.A.C. (2d) 195 (Hinnegan).

▼

CONTRACT
TERM

For the purposes of *layoff* and recall from layoff, the employer shall give preference to employees with the greatest departmental seniority provided such employees have the qualifications to perform the work available.

ARBITRATOR'S
RULING

The reduction in hours of work for a single employee constitutes a layoff, triggering the departmental seniority provisions. Since the clause does not make any distinction between full-time and part-time employees, the employer is not permitted to reduce the hours of a full-time employee while the hours of junior part-time employees are not reduced.

Charlotte Eleanor Englehart Hospital (1980), 25 L.A.C. (2d) 25 (Palmer).

▼

CONTRACT
TERM

In the event of a *layoff*, employees shall be laid off in the reverse order of their seniority, and shall be recalled in order of their seniority, provided they are qualified to do the work.

ARBITRATOR'S
RULING

Employees who bump down are entitled to be recalled to their former jobs; otherwise, they could retain recall rights only by going without work altogether.

Board of School Trustees (Greater Victoria) (1979), 25 L.A.C. (2d) 430 (R.M. Brown).

LEAVE OF ABSENCE

CONTRACT
TERM

Plant holidays shall be recognized with pay provided the employee is not *absent without leave* on the working days immediately preceding and following the holiday.

ARBITRATOR'S
RULING

Absence on disciplinary suspension is not an absence with leave, since "leave" involves an application to be absent for which permission is granted, which does not occur where an employee is suspended for misconduct.

Canadian Timken Ltd. (1989), 8 L.A.C. (4th) 193 (Little).

▼

CONTRACT
TERM

When operational requirements permit, the employer will grant *leave* without pay to union representatives *to undertake training* related to the duties of a representative.

ARBITRATOR'S
RULING

Training includes the receipt of new information, not just the acquisition of practical skills; thus, a one-day union-sponsored seminar on the impact of free-trade qualifies as training.

Treasury Board (Health and Welfare Canada) and Babcock (1989) 5 L.A.C. (4th) 15 (R. Young).

▼

CONTRACT
TERM

Applications for *leaves of absence* without pay will be adjudicated on the basis of merit, compassion, length of service and the operational needs of the store. Leaves of absence shall not be unreasonably withheld.

ARBITRATOR'S
RULING

The employer's policy of refusal to grant extended leaves of absence due to incarceration violates the collective agreement, since it is based on an automatic, rigid policy, and the agreement requires each application to be considered on its own merits. The grievor's application for leave had "merit" since he was attempting to protect his employment status following incarceration, and he had been regarded as a worthy employee. Also, "compassion" can be interpreted to extend beyond family or marital circumstances, and is not precluded by criminal conduct.

Canada Safeway Ltd. (1988), 1 L.A.C. (4th) 435 (McColl).

▼

CONTRACT
TERM

To be eligible for holiday pay, an employee must work the full scheduled work day immediately preceding and following such holiday, unless absent on authorized *leave of absence*, layoff or proven illness or injury.

117

ARBITRATOR'S
RULING
An employee who misses the first hour of work the day following a holiday, and telephones his employer to advise that he will be late, is entitled to a full day's pay for the holiday, where the absence would ordinarily have been authorized by the company after the fact, or where the company would have been obliged to grant a leave of absence for the time involved. Here, the employee's absence would have been considered authorized since he was obliged to deal with his child's recurrent medical problems.

Union Felt Products (Ont.) Ltd. (1988), 1 L.A.C. (4th) 148 (Kennedy).

▼

CONTRACT
TERM
Leave of absence for personal reasons, *religious leave* and special leave in extenuating circumstances, may be granted at the discretion of the employer, without loss of pay; such requests shall not be unreasonably denied.

ARBITRATOR'S
RULING
"Religion" should be interpreted broadly and liberally, and is not restricted to the well-established religious denominations. An adherent of the Wiccan faith is entitled to paid leave of absence for two religious holidays per year, since Wicca qualifies as a religion for the purposes of the agreement.

Humber College (1987), 31 L.A.C. (3d) 266 (Swan).

▼

CONTRACT
TERM
The company will grant *leaves of absence* without pay to employees, retroactively when necessary, *for legitimate personal reasons,* including illness and accident.

ARBITRATOR'S
RULING
Term includes unforeseen situations beyond the employee's control or events that seldom occur but are pressing or important, e.g. marriage followed by honeymoon.

Morton-Parker (1987), 27 L.A.C. (3d) 93 (Willes).

▼

CONTRACT
TERM
Employees are entitled to holiday pay despite absence from work on the day before or after the holiday if the absence is due to *specific authorized absence.*

ARBITRATOR'S
RULING

While employees on layoff remain employees, a layoff is not a specific authorized absence so as to entitle employees laid off for 3 months to 5 holidays occurring during that period.

Baie Verte Mines (1986), 27 L.A.C. (3d) 135 (Easton).

▼

CONTRACT
TERM

The employer may at its discretion grant *leave of absence* without pay *for legitimate personal reasons.*

ARBITRATOR'S
RULING

The clause does not cover non-discretionary absences, such as sick leave, and therefore does not permit the employer to avoid payment of sick leave benefits simply by purporting to grant a personal leave of absence without pay to an employee on sick leave.

Hamilton-Wentworth C.A.S. (1985), 17 L.A.C. (3d) 370 (Foisy).

▼

CONTRACT
TERM

The company may grant a *leave of absence* without pay to an employee *for personal reasons.*

ARBITRATOR'S
RULING

While the employer has a discretion, it must be exercised reasonably and not in an arbitrary fashion. Employers are expected to balance their interest in maintaining sufficient staff to meet production needs against the interests of their employees. Emotional health is a legitimate reason for requesting leave.

Twin Pines Dairy (1981), 30 L.A.C. (2d) 361 (Brent).

▼

CONTRACT
TERM

An employee who assumes a full-time position with the union or a labour organization with which the union is affiliated shall be granted up to one year's *leave of absence.*

ARBITRATOR'S
RULING

Clause is broadly drafted, and includes leave of absence to engage in a Canadian Labour Congress' campaign to support the NDP in a federal election, since that is a union activity within the union's constitution; and a three-week campaign may be considered as full-time since that was the length of the federal campaign.

Borough of Etobicoke (1981), 30 L.A.C. (2d) 289 (McLaren).

▼

CONTRACT TERM

In order to qualify for holiday pay, an employee shall work the full shift on each of the working days immediately preceding and following the plant holidays unless the employee is absent due to a *leave of absence*, etc.

ARBITRATOR'S RULING

A disciplinary suspension is not a leave of absence.

Thomas Built Buses (1980), 27 L.A.C. (2d) 409 (Weatherill).

▼

CONTRACT TERM

The employer may grant an employee *leave of absence* with pay for not more than three days in a year upon special or compassionate grounds.

ARBITRATOR'S RULING

Compassionate leave is granted in situations deserving of sympathetic treatment, including emergencies beyond the control of the employee, and should not be confined to planned events, such as a spouse's major surgery or a child's court date. Compassionate leave is therefore warranted for an employee who wishes to visit another city where her son's wife has been seriously injured in a car accident.

Crown in Right of Ontario (Ministry of Health) (1980), 27 L.A.C. (2d) 283 (Swinton).

▼

CONTRACT TERM

The company may grant a *leave of absence* to an employee *for personal reasons*. In granting such a leave, the company will consider the nature of the personal reasons, seniority, and efficient operation of the plant.

ARBITRATOR'S RULING

To "consider" requires a company to "reckon with" or "make allowances for" an employee's request, i.e. to fairly and reasonably consider the nature of the personal reasons for a request and the effects on other circumstances of the request. A flat denial of a request by the company's most senior employee to add a week's leave of absence to the annual vacation shutdown to visit a sick parent overseas therefore violates the collective agreement.

Whitby Boat Works (1980), 27 L.A.C. (2d) 269 (O'Shea).

LEGITIMATE PERSONAL REASONS, *see* PERSONAL REASONS

LEGITIMATE REASONS

CONTRACT
TERM

The union recognizes that the employer has the exclusive right to manage the business including the right to transfer employees because of lack of work or for other *legitimate reasons.*

ARBITRATOR'S
RULING

The loss of a major customer by the company is a legitimate reason for reducing production, and therefore for reducing the number of shifts, redistributing the workforce over the remaining shifts, and transferring employees to lower-rated job classifications in accordance with their seniority. Where there is no lack of work, there is no requirement to lay off.

Roxul Co. (1988), 2 L.A.C. (4th) 58 (O'Shea).

LOSS OF EMPLOYMENT

CONTRACT
TERM

No regular employees who attain 2 years of regular service will lose their *employment* as a result of technological change.

ARBITRATOR'S
RULING

Relocation to another geographical area, made necessary by declining demand, constitutes a loss of employment, triggering the employment guarantee, but the relocation must be due to a technological change, and here it was not, since closure of the employer's office was due to economic reasons, i.e. failure to achieve growth.

British Columbia Telephone Co. (1989), 7 L.A.C. (4th) 75 (Kelleher).

LOSS OF SENIORITY, *see also* SENIORITY

CONTRACT
TERM

The continuous service and *seniority status of an employee shall be terminated* when an employee has not performed any work for the company for 18 consecutive months as a result of non-Workers' Compensation illness or injury.

ARBITRATOR'S
RULING

Loss of seniority status cannot be equated with loss of employment, since seniority is not a classification of employment, but a factor expressed in terms of time from which specific consequences flow under an agreement. An employee who is disabled more than 18 months remains an employee for the purposes of entitlement to benefits, including long-term disability. This is consistent with the principle that the right of an employer to discharge an employee on long-term disability may be limited where entitlement depends on continued employment.

Harris Rebar Inc. (1988), 35 L.A.C. (3d) 348 (Dunn).

▼

CONTRACT
TERM

Seniority rights shall be terminated if an employee is absent for reasons of sickness or disability for a minimum period of 52 weeks.

ARBITRATOR'S
RULING

An employee absent for more than 52 weeks loses seniority, but does not become a probationer; consequently, he cannot be discharged without just cause and, though he cannot displace other employees, he is entitled to the first vacancy for which he is qualified.

Mack Canada (1986), 23 L.A.C. (3d) 97 (P.C. Picher).

▼

CONTRACT
TERM

Seniority will be lost if an employee after a layoff fails to report for 5 working days after being recalled.

ARBITRATOR'S
RULING

There is an implied exception for *bona fide* circumstances beyond the employee's control, such as sickness or injury. Sick leave should be granted as a matter of course where there is a *bona fide* reason.

Hudson's Bay Co. (1985), 21 L.A.C. (3d) 407 (Bird).

▼

CONTRACT
TERM

An employee shall *lose seniority status* if he is absent from work for 5 consecutive working days without leave or notice unless in the opinion of the company there was reasonable justification.

ARBITRATOR'S
RULING

Unauthorized absence does not reduce an employee to probationary status, but rather renders him an employee with zero seniority who is nonetheless entitled to the full protection of the "just cause" clause of the collective agreement.

Arrowhead Metals (1984), 19 L.A.C. (3d) 59 (Hinnegan).

▼

CONTRACT TERM
An employee shall *lose seniority standing* if he is laid off and fails to return to work within 5 days after he has been notified to do so.

ARBITRATOR'S RULING
Where the employee does not fall within the definition of a probationary employee, he loses his seniority, but retains his right to protection against discharge without just cause.

J.C. Hallman Mfg. (1982), 8 L.A.C. (3d) 164 (Brent).

▼

CONTRACT TERM
An employee's *service shall be considered broken* if absent from work for 3 consecutive days without permission unless he furnishes a satisfactory reason upon his return.

ARBITRATOR'S RULING
Loss of seniority does not result in reversion to probationary status. The employee is not a new hire, and is protected against discharge without just cause.

Collingwood Shipyards (1982), 4 L.A.C. (3d) 132 (Carter).

▼

CONTRACT TERM
An employee will *lose his seniority* for absence for 3 days without notifying the company unless a good reason is given.

ARBITRATOR'S RULING
Loss of seniority does not mean loss of employment, but it does reduce an employee to the status of a probationer, who can be dealt with as such.

Gates Rubber (1981), 29 L.A.C. (2d) 182 (Brandt).

▼

CONTRACT TERM
Failure to notify the company when absent from work for 7 consecutive days shall *terminate all seniority rights*.

ARBITRATOR'S RULING
Under this clause, while the employee loses seniority rights, he does not revert to probationary status, and cannot be discharged without just cause.

Firestone Canada (1980), 28 L.A.C. (2d) 119 (Brunner).

▼

CONTRACT TERM   *Seniority rights shall cease* after one year in the event of inability to work because of illness or injury.

ARBITRATOR'S RULING   Under this clause, while an employee loses seniority, she is not reduced to probationary status, and is therefore entitled to protection against discharge without just cause.

Salvation Army Grace Hospital (1980), 25 L.A.C. (2d) 407 (Brunner).

▼

CONTRACT TERM   An employee shall *lose his seniority* if he fails to report for work for 3 consecutive working days without notifying his immediate supervisor during such period, unless the employee provides an acceptable reason to the company.

ARBITRATOR'S RULING   Under this clause, the employee loses all seniority, but is not reduced to the status of a probationary employee.

Indalloy (1979), 27 L.A.C. (2d) 35 (Kennedy).

LOST TIME

CONTRACT TERM   An employee absent because of sickness or accident will be paid for *lost time* to a maximum of 26 weeks.

ARBITRATOR'S RULING   Absence, even though due to illness, is not lost time where the employee is not scheduled to work, pursuant to a work-sharing program, since this language indicates that sick pay is an indemnity for earnings lost because of time not worked.

B.A. Banknote (1986), 25 L.A.C. (3d) 16 (Emrich).

M

MAKE-UP PAY

CONTRACT TERM — The company will provide *make-up pay* to apprentices while attending vocational school.

ARBITRATOR'S RULING — Term refers to pay the apprentice would otherwise have received, and therefore does not include pay for period when apprentice was on layoff.

Brinco Mining Ltd. (1984), 16 L.A.C. (3d) 236 (Hope).

MATERNITY LEAVE

EDITORS' NOTE — Leave for pregnancy and parental care is provided for and protected by labour standards legislation. See, for example, Ontario's *Employment Standards Act*, R.S.O. 1990, c.E-14.]

CONTRACT TERM — An employee who is frequently absent on account of pregnancy-related illness may be required by the employer to commence her *maternity leave*.

ARBITRATOR'S RULING — "Pregnancy-related illness" does not include pre-existing medical condition of high blood pressure, even though the employee was advised by her doctor to rest at home because medication was restricted by the pregnancy. Alternatively, the clause contravenes the provisions of Ontario's *Employment Standards Act*.

Metropolitan Separate School Board (1984), 16 L.A.C. (3d) 353 (Adams).

▼

CONTRACT TERM — *Maternity leave* up to 6 months will be granted upon request. Seniority is based on continuous service.

ARBITRATOR'S RULING — Since "service" means "employment", temporary absences such as maternity leave do not cause a break in service, and seniority continues to accumulate.

Toronto Star (1981), 30 L.A.C. (2d) 267 (Weatherill).

▼

CONTRACT
TERM
Any employee who becomes pregnant shall be entitled to a *maternity leave* up to five months in duration. It is understood and agreed that such employees shall retain and accumulate full seniority rights and benefits while on such leave.

ARBITRATOR'S
RULING
"Retain and accumulate" means that employees on maternity leave are entitled to have benefits remain intact and inviolate, in the same way and to the same extent as if they were at work during the period in question. The cost of any benefit premiums is to be borne by the employer.
Corporation of County of Essex (1980), 25 L.A.C. (2d) 283 (Brunner).

MERIT, *see also* **SKILL AND ABILITY**

CONTRACT
TERM
Applications for leaves of absence without pay will be adjudicated on the basis of *merit*, compassion, length of service and the operational needs of the store. Leaves of absence shall not be unreasonably withheld.

ARBITRATOR'S
RULING
The employer's policy of refusal to grant extended leaves of absence due to incarceration violates the collective agreement, since it is based on an automatic, rigid policy, and the agreement requires each application to be considered on its own merits. The grievor's application for leave had "merit" since he was attempting to protect his employment status following incarceration, and he had been regarded as a worthy employee. Also, "compassion" can be interpreted to extend beyond family or marital circumstances, and is not precluded by criminal conduct.
Canada Safeway Ltd. (1988), 1 L.A.C. (4th) 435 (McColl).

METHODS, *see* **TECHNOLOGICAL CHANGE**

MODIFICATION

CONTRACT
TERM
Exceptional circumstances may arise which, although not covered by the schedule, may, in the judgment of management, warrant a *modification* of the schedules. Such cases will be dealt with as they occur.

ARBITRATOR'S
RULING

A modification involves a slight or partial change or moderation; changing employees' schedules from 8-hour to 12-hour shifts is a major change, not a modification. The right to modify the schedule cannot be used as a Trojan horse to take away overtime and other benefits based on the schedule.

Miramichi Pulp and Paper Inc. (1987), 29 L.A.C. (3d) 48 (Stanley).

MONTH

CONTRACT
TERM

After a period of 6 *months* with no recorded offences, all previous offences of the type set forth above shall be cancelled and the employee's record considered clear.

ARBITRATOR'S
RULING

In the absence of any qualification, "months" means calendar months; therefore, absence from work due to layoff does not extend the six-month period.

Robertson Building Systems (1985), 19 L.A.C. (3d) 427 (H.D. Brown).

▼

CONTRACT
TERM

When an employee is promoted permanently into a higher paid position, the designated rate for the position will begin immediately after a *month*'s probationary period.

ARBITRATOR'S
RULING

In the context of a probationary period the term month is to be construed as a working month, not a calendar month, since the employer must be able to observe and assess the employee on probation, and this is possible only when he is working.

Dartmouth General Hospital (1982), 3 L.A.C. (3d) 420 (Langille).

MONTHLY DUES

CONTRACT
TERM

The employer shall deduct such *monthly dues*, or the equivalent, as are set forth in the constitution and by-laws of the union.

ARBITRATOR'S
RULING

Nothing prevents a union from assessing higher dues in the first month of employment, and the phrase "monthly dues" includes such higher amount.

Metro Toronto (1979), 23 L.A.C. (2d) 381 (Teplitsky).

MOTHER-IN-LAW, *see also* BEREAVEMENT LEAVE

CONTRACT TERM
When the current spouse, *mother-in-law*, etc. dies, the employee will be excused for a period not exceeding 3 days.

ARBITRATOR'S RULING
"Mother-in-law" includes the mother of an employee's common law spouse.

Lakeview Development (1987), 31 L.A.C. (3d) 85 (Haefling).

▼

CONTRACT TERM
In the event of the death of an employee's immediate relative, an employee will be granted leave of absence with pay; immediate relative shall mean: wife, *mother-in-law*, etc.

ARBITRATOR'S RULING
"Mother-in-law" includes the mother of an employee's common law wife.

Genaire Ltd. (1987), 27 L.A.C. (3d) 188 (Weatherill).

▼

CONTRACT TERM
In the event of the death of an employee's spouse, *mother-in-law*, etc., 3 working days' leave of absence shall be granted with pay.

ARBITRATOR'S RULING
"Mother-in-law" does not include the mother of an employee's common law spouse.

Peel Board of Health (1983), 9 L.A.C. (3d) 94 (Shime). Contrast *Lakeview Development* and *Genaire Ltd.*, above.

MUTUAL AGREEMENT

CONTRACT TERM
A schedule of work shall be established upon *mutual agreement*.

ARBITRATOR'S RULING
This clause imposes an obligation to meet and bargain in good faith, and a schedule cannot be instituted or changed unilaterally by the employer.

Algoma Steel (1986), 27 L.A.C. (3d) 113 (Brunner).

▼

CONTRACT TERM
There shall be no unilateral change in hours of work, etc. until *mutually agreed* to by both parties.

ARBITRATOR'S
RULING

Mutual agreement does not mean simply an attempt to try to reach an agreement, or merely a requirement to consult or negotiate; without agreement in advance, a unilateral change cannot be made by the employer.

Alberni Board of School Trustees (1981), 29 L.A.C. (2d) 129 (Christie).

N

NECESSARY MEDICAL TREATMENT

CONTRACT TERM — Sick leave with full salary will be granted for the purpose of obtaining *necessary medical treatment.*

ARBITRATOR'S RULING — Necessary medical treatment means treatment that is necessary for the health of the employee, and does not include voluntary treatment to induce ovulation for fertility purposes.

Fritze (1985), 19 L.A.C. (3d) 353 (Elliott).

NEW EMPLOYEES/NEWLY HIRED EMPLOYEES

CONTRACT TERM — *Newly hired employees* shall be on a probationary basis for a period of six months.

ARBITRATOR'S RULING — Part-time employees transferred to a full-time unit are not newly hired employees, and so are not required to serve a probationary period, where the collective agreement provides that seniority is portable.

Sudbury and District Association for Mentally Retarded (1984), 13 L.A.C. (3d) 385 (Egan).

▼

CONTRACT TERM — *New employees* shall be considered as probationary employees.

ARBITRATOR'S RULING — Laid off employees recalled to work are not new employees even though their seniority may have been lost due to the length of the layoff; they do not have to repeat the probationary period.

Northern Telecom (1983), 9 L.A.C. (3d) 253 (Burkett).

▼

CONTRACT TERM The first 44 days worked in the bargaining unit by all *new employees* shall be a probationary period.

ARBITRATOR'S RULING A part-time employee hired on the full-time staff is a new employee for purposes of the probation period, where the collective agreement elsewhere speaks of the "hiring" of part-time employees for the full-time staff, and makes it clear that they are to serve a probationary period.

Dominion Stores (1981), 30 L.A.C. (2d) 194 (Brunner).

NEW JOB CLASSIFICATION

CONTRACT TERM The company will notify the union upon the creation of any *new job classification* and will discuss with the union matters related to newly created positions such as wages and hours of work.

ARBITRATOR'S RULING An addition to the job content of an existing classification does not result in a new job classification; there must be a substantial, qualitative change in the employee's actual functions.

Sperry Inc. (1985), 20 L.A.C. (3d) 385 (Hinnegan).

NEW METHODS, see TECHNOLOGICAL CHANGE

NON-OCCUPATIONAL SICKNESS

CONTRACT TERM For the purposes of sickness benefits, an employee will be considered disabled if he is unable to perform the duties of his employment as a result of *non-occupational sickness or accident* and is under the care of a licensed physician.

ARBITRATOR'S RULING Alcoholism, with its related mental and physical symptoms, is a non-occupational sickness or accident, and an employee is therefore entitled to sick pay while undergoing treatment for alcoholism.

American Can (1981), 3 L.A.C. (3d) 283 (Somjen).

NORMAL HOURS OF WORK

CONTRACT TERM The *normal daily hours of work* shall be 8 per day. Layoffs shall be determined on the basis of the seniority of the employees concerned.

131

ARBITRATOR'S RULING   Specification of normal daily hours of work in an agreement does not constitute a guarantee of such hours, nor does it prevent the employer from reducing the hours of work of all or part of its staff as part of its management rights. However, a 4-hour per day reduction in only one employee's normal daily hours amounts to a layoff and triggers the layoff provisions of the agreement.
Cove Guest Home (1988), 1 L.A.C. (4th) 42 (Scaravelli).

▼

CONTRACT TERM   Time and a half shall be paid for all authorized work performed in excess of the employee's *normal scheduled daily working hours*.

ARBITRATOR'S RULING   Overtime provisions fall into two categories: those in which overtime becomes payable after an employee has worked a specified number of hours in a day or week, and those in which an employee is entitled to overtime pay whenever he works outside of the periods of time when he has been scheduled to work. Where the collective agreement refers to both an 8-hour day and posting of schedules, this clause requires overtime pay outside the scheduled hours, whether or not a full 8-hour day is worked.
Domglas (1985), 19 L.A.C. (3d) 156 (Kennedy).

▼

CONTRACT TERM   The *normal hours of work per day* are as follows: (a) nursing department 7-1/2 hours; (b) other departments 8 hours.

ARBITRATOR'S RULING   This provision does not guarantee hours of work, and there can be a deviation from the normal hours, but a new norm cannot be established by unilateral management initiative. A reduction of hours, even if uniform, may breach a "normal hours of work" provision, if the reduction constitutes a new norm by unilateral action.
Ballycliffe Lodge (1984), 14 L.A.C. (3d) 37 (Adams).

▼

CONTRACT TERM   Employees required to work on a recognized holiday shall be paid at the rate of two and a half times the base rate for all hours worked. If hours actually worked are outside of the employee's *normal shift hours*, he shall also be entitled to the 8 hours recognized holiday pay at his base rate.

ARBITRATOR'S RULING Any work outside the normal workweek, and not just the normal workday, is "outside normal shift hours". Employees required to work on a recognized holiday on a scheduled day off are therefore entitled to two and a half times the base rate plus the 8 hours' base pay, whether or not the employees are required to work the same hours they would have worked had they been scheduled to work on the recognized holiday.

Fiberglas Canada Ltd. (1980), 26 L.A.C. (2d) 145 (Sychuk).

NORMAL WORKING WEEK

CONTRACT TERM A *normal working week* shall consist of 5 normal working days Monday through Friday.

ARBITRATOR'S RULING This clause does not constitute a minimum guarantee of work, and a reduction of hours (in this case, one day a month for four successive months) is not a breach. However, although abnormal hours can be scheduled (as here, to deal with an emergency for a limited period of time), the employer cannot institute a new schedule of normal hours.

City of Nanaimo (1982), 7 L.A.C. (3d) 245 (Getz).

NORMALLY PERFORM THE WORK, *see also* WORK, WORK NORMALLY PERFORMED

CONTRACT TERM Scheduled overtime shall be offered by seniority amongst the employees who *normally perform the work* by department.

ARBITRATOR'S RULING "Work" refers to a separate and identifiable task or set of tasks which constitutes a type of job. A classification, on the other hand, is a grouping of the same or similar types of jobs under a single title. Work "normally performed by employees" does not embrace all job functions ever performed by employees in a particular classification, but only work for which an employee is qualified and which he or she has performed on a regular basis.

Strudex Fibres (1989), 6 L.A.C. (4th) 226 (Roberts).

▼

CONTRACT
TERM
The company will attempt to distribute overtime work equitably among the employees who *normally perform the work.*

ARBITRATOR'S
RULING
"Equitably" does not mean "equally", but rather "fairly", e.g. if two or more employees normally perform similar work, the overtime assigned should be roughly the same.

Worthington Pump (1989), 3 L.A.C. (4th) 399 (Samuels).

NOTIFY

CONTRACT
TERM
Where a reduction of forces is caused by emergency conditions the application of plant seniority may be postponed for up to 5 working days; if the company decides to exercise its right under this provision it shall *notify* the shop committee as soon as possible.

ARBITRATOR'S
RULING
An emergency is "a sudden juncture demanding immediate action" and therefore includes burnout of a motor, since although this was anticipated there was no way of anticipating when it would happen. However, although no special words are required, notice must be given to a representative of the shop committee as soon as possible that the company intends to invoke the emergency clause; it cannot be given after the layoff is over.

Gregory Manufacturing (1981), 30 L.A.C. (2d) 427 (Bird).

O

ON CALL, *see* STAND-BY PAY

ON-THE-JOB EXPERIENCE

CONTRACT
TERM

Annual increments are based upon experience, at the rate of one step for each completed year of *on-the-job experience.*

ARBITRATOR'S
RULING

Term refers to actual performance of the job, not simply a period of employment; thus, it does not include extended leaves of absence, although short absences do not interrupt progression.

Fanshawe College (1982), 4 L.A.C. (3d) 10 (Swinton).

ONE

CONTRACT
TERM

In order to qualify for a paid holiday, an employee must work the full scheduled shift preceding and immediately following the statutory holiday, unless the employee is absent on *one* of the aforementioned days due to illness, injury, or an approved leave of absence.

ARBITRATOR'S
RULING

"One" does not mean only one, but any of the qualifying days; an employee absent on *both* days due to compensable illness is entitled to holiday pay. Moreover, the employee is entitled under this clause, not just to the first holiday, but to whatever number of holidays occur during the absence, so long as the employer-employee relationship continues.

Chelsey Park Oxford (1989), 8 L.A.C. (4th) 1 (Mitchnick).

OPERATING NEEDS

CONTRACT
TERM

Subject to the *operating needs* of the business, management will consider senior employees with respect to assignment of shifts and hours.

ARBITRATOR'S
RULING

"Operating needs" means *bona fide* business reasons, whether or not wise, and "consider" means only to take into consideration, or be aware of; once the employer satisfies this requirement, it can institute rotating shifts.

Arbutus Club (1986), 23 L.A.C. (3d) 241 (MacIntyre).

OPERATIONAL PRACTICES, *see* PRACTICES

OPINION OF THE EMPLOYER

CONTRACT
TERM

Where it is the *opinion of the employer* that two or more applicants for a vacant position are qualified and of equal merit, preference shall be given to the senior applicant.

ARBITRATOR'S
RULING

The employer is obliged to assess qualifications and abilities fairly and, while the employer has considerable discretion, the decision must not be unreasonable.

N.S. Civil Service Commission (1986), 25 L.A.C. (3d) 404 (Outhouse).

OR

CONTRACT
TERM

Notice or pay in lieu of notice is required of layoffs, depending on an employee's length of service, e.g. if an employee has more than 10 years' service, he shall receive eight weeks' notice of layoff *or* eight weeks' pay in lieu of eight weeks' notice.

ARBITRATOR'S
RULING

"Or" is to be interpreted disjunctively, i.e. employees are to be given *either* eight weeks' notice *or* eight weeks' pay in lieu, for example. The employer cannot give employees a *combination* of notice and pay in lieu, to total the specified number of weeks.

Domgroup Ltd. (1988), 33 L.A.C. (3d) 269 (T.A.B. Jolliffe).

▼

CONTRACT TERM
In order to qualify for payment of statutory holidays, an employee must have worked the whole of his regularly scheduled shift prior to and immediately following the holiday; an employee who is absent from his regularly scheduled duties before *or* after the holiday due to an authorized leave of absence shall be entitled to the holiday.

ARBITRATOR'S RULING
Since the language is personalized, the clause refers to the shift regularly scheduled for the individual claimant, rather than to shifts worked by employees of the plant as a group. Thus, an employee is entitled to pay for a holiday occurring during pregnancy leave, where she works her regularly scheduled shifts before the leave and upon her return, but she is not entitled to pay for a holiday occurring during an extended unpaid pregnancy leave. The word "or", which may be either conjunctive or disjunctive, is here both conjunctive and disjunctive, i.e. it means before, after or before, and after the holiday.

FBI Foods (1986), 22 L.A.C. (3d) 157 (Emrich).

▼

CONTRACT TERM
Supervisors will not do bargaining unit work except for emergency work when employees are absent *or* not available when required, etc.

ARBITRATOR'S RULING
There is a presumption that "and" is conjunctive and "or" is disjunctive; thus, a supervisor may perform emergency work in circumstances where the employee who would otherwise be assigned the work is absent or where that employee is present in the plant but otherwise not available. If the employee is absent, the supervisor may perform emergency work, and there is no obligation on the employer to attempt to find out if the employee is available.

Burlington Steel (1983), 11 L.A.C. (3d) 97 (Swan).

OVERTIME

CONTRACT TERM
Scheduled *overtime* shall be offered by seniority amongst the employees who normally perform the work by department.

ARBITRATOR'S RULING "Work" refers to a separate and identifiable task or set of tasks which constitutes a type of job. A classification, on the other hand, is a grouping of the same or similar types of jobs under a single title. Work "normally performed by employees" does not embrace all job functions ever performed by employees in a particular classification, but only work for which an employee is qualified and which he or she has performed on a regular basis.

Strudex Fibres (1989), 6 L.A.C. (4th) 226 (Roberts).

▼

CONTRACT TERM The company will attempt to distribute *overtime* work equitably among the employees who normally perform the work.

ARBITRATOR'S RULING "Equitably" does not mean "equally", but rather "fairly", e.g. if two or more employees normally perform similar work, the overtime assigned should be roughly the same.

Worthington Pump (1989), 3 L.A.C. (4th) 399 (Samuels).

▼

CONTRACT TERM *Overtime* will be paid for all time worked in excess of a normal 8-hour working period. "Time worked" may include a period in which no work is actually performed, but in which the employee remains under the employer's direction and control and/or in which the employee's responsibilities to the employer continue.

ARBITRATOR'S RULING Employees who are required to remain in company vehicles during their lunch breaks, except in certain circumstances, are entitled to be paid overtime for their lunch breaks, since they remain under the employer's direction and control and are not free to use the lunch break as they wish.

Town of Midland (1987), 31 L.A.C. (3d) 251 (Saltman).

▼

CONTRACT TERM Employees working *overtime* on Sundays shall receive double time; workweek is Monday to Friday starting at 7 a.m. Monday.

ARBITRATOR'S RULING If an employee's regular shift commences late on a particular day and overlaps into a second day, as for example a Friday evening into a Saturday morning, the shift worked is viewed as a "day" corresponding to the day on which the shift commenced. Where a 3-shift operation is in effect, and the collective agreement provides that the workweek begins at 7 a.m. Monday, work between 5 a.m. and 7 a.m. on Monday is to be treated as work on a Sunday, and double time is payable.

Canron Inc. (1987), 27 L.A.C. (3d) 379 (M.G. Picher).

▼

CONTRACT TERM *Overtime* at time and a half is payable after 40 hours in a workweek; time and a half is payable for work on a holiday.

ARBITRATOR'S RULING A workweek consists of days and hours spent working within a given time frame, and for purposes of calculating overtime it includes a holiday on which the employee works. No question of pyramiding arises because the purpose of overtime is to compensate for the effort and inconvenience of having to work beyond the normal work schedule, whereas the purpose of holiday pay, an earned benefit, is to ensure enjoyment of a holiday without loss of pay.

J. Xavier Enterprises (1987), 26 L.A.C. (3d) 289 (T.A.B. Jolliffe).

▼

CONTRACT TERM Employee required to work *overtime* on his first scheduled day of rest shall be paid overtime pay.

ARBITRATOR'S RULING Where attendance at a driver education course is voluntary and unrelated to employment in the bargaining unit, it is not "required", and does not constitute "work", even though some benefit may accrue to the employer.

N.S. Civil Service Commission (1986), 25 L.A.C. (3d) 5 (Outhouse).

▼

CONTRACT TERM [*Overtime*] at time and a half is payable for time worked in excess of 8 hours per day or in excess of 8 continuous hours.

ARBITRATOR'S RULING "Days" means calendar days, not a 24-hour period commencing at the start of an employee's shift.

139

Chrysler Canada (1985), 22 L.A.C. (3d) 342 (O'Shea).

▼

CONTRACT
TERM

If the employer is unable to find employees within the department to perform the *overtime*, then the *overtime* will be assigned to the least senior employee within the department who has the ability to perform the work required; each employee is expected to co-operate with the employer in the performance of such work.

ARBITRATOR'S
RULING

Words "will be assigned" plus expectation of co-operation make overtime compulsory, and amount to consent to overtime as required by Ontario's *Employment Standards Act*.

Seven-Up/Pure Spring (1985), 22 L.A.C. (3d) 83 (H.D. Brown).

▼

CONTRACT
TERM

Employees will be paid [*overtime*] at time and a half for time worked outside their daily scheduled hours.

ARBITRATOR'S
RULING

"Time worked" may include activities other than those included in an employee's job description and those which he usually performs every day. Authorized, albeit voluntary, attendance at a training session organized by management constitutes work, but attendance at a wine and cheese party thereafter does not.

Steinberg Inc. (1985), 20 L.A.C. (3d) 289 (Foisy).

▼

CONTRACT
TERM

Overtime shall be on a voluntary basis; however, it is also agreed that the least senior employee shall be required to work if no one shall volunteer.

ARBITRATOR'S
RULING

Where it is impractical to run an assembly line with only one employee, this phrase must be intended to refer to the least senior employees, and the company is not restricted to compelling only one employee, the most junior employee, to work overtime.

Sealy (1985), 20 L.A.C. (3d) 45 (Wakeling).

▼

CONTRACT
TERM

[*Overtime*] at time and a half shall be paid for all authorized work performed in excess of the employee's normal scheduled daily working hours.

ARBITRATOR'S RULING
Overtime provisions fall into two categories: those in which overtime becomes payable after an employee has worked a specified number of hours in a day or week, and those in which an employee is entitled to overtime pay whenever he works outside of the periods of time when he has been scheduled to work. Where the collective agreement refers to both an 8-hour day and posting of schedules, this clause requires overtime pay outside the scheduled hours, whether or not a full 8-hour day is worked.

Domglas (1985), 19 L.A.C. (3d) 156 (Kennedy).

▼

CONTRACT TERM
Overtime work shall be compensated at time and a half for every hour worked over 40 hours.

ARBITRATOR'S RULING
Whether travel time is work depends on the circumstances. Authorized travel to and from a professional development conference is work, entitling an employee to overtime pay, even though attendance may not be mandatory.

London Ass'n for Mentally Retarded (1984), 16 L.A.C. (3d) 165 (Saltman).

▼

CONTRACT TERM
Overtime is payable for time worked in excess of the regular working day.

ARBITRATOR'S RULING
"Time worked" includes time during which employees are under the direction and control of the employer and during which the employees' responsibilities continue even though services are not performed for the employer; hence, lunch period is time worked where employees are required to remain at the workplace in order to be available in case of an emergency.

Religious Hospitallers (1983), 11 L.A.C. (3d) 151 (Saltman).

▼

CONTRACT TERM
Any time worked by an employee, in addition to working 7-1/2 hours in any one day, shall be [*overtime*] paid for at time and one-half.

141

ARBITRATOR'S
RULING

Under this language, it does not matter that the employee has gone home after his regular shift; for overtime purposes, there is no requirement of continuity with a regular shift, as long as the additional hours are worked on the same day. If call-back pay is also payable, the employee may select the most favourable option.

Humber Memorial Hospital (1982), 5 L.A.C. (3d) 324 (Kennedy).

▼

CONTRACT
TERM

An employee will be paid *overtime* at straight-time rates for travel outside regular hours provided it is essential. Employees will be paid overtime at time and one-half for the first 2 hours of authorized overtime worked in excess of the regular hours, and double time thereafter.

ARBITRATOR'S
RULING

Travel time outside regular hours is authorized overtime worked, even though paid at straight-time rates, and should be included in calculating the overtime payable for other overtime work.

Alberta Housing Corp. (1982), 4 L.A.C. (3d) 228 (Taylor).

▼

CONTRACT
TERM

An employee who is requested by the company to work on his regular days off will be paid at the rate of time and one-half for all time so worked.

ARBITRATOR'S
RULING

"Work" does not require employees to be actually performing their duties. Employees were entitled to be paid for sleeping over at a remote location where they were obliged to remain to finish the job, since they were subject to the direction of management and thus were not free to engage in personal activities of their choice.

Hamilton Street Railway (1981), 1 L.A.C. (3d) 355 (Shime).

▼

CONTRACT
TERM

Seniority shall be followed when scheduling *overtime.*

ARBITRATOR'S
RULING

The term "scheduling" signifies a written time-table posted in advance, and is not synonymous with "assigned" or "requested" or "ordered". An obligation to follow seniority where overtime is scheduled cannot apply to unanticipated or emergency overtime, which is usually due to the absence of one or more employees. Scheduled overtime refers to anticipated overtime, and not to overtime which is assigned or distributed on very short notice.

Reid Dominion Packaging (1981), 1 L.A.C. (3d) 314 (Jolliffe).

▼

CONTRACT
TERM

The company shall pay [*overtime*] at time and a half for all hours an employee is required to work over 8 a day, and double time for all work performed on each shift on a Saturday.

ARBITRATOR'S
RULING

A "shift" is a pre-determined period of time that would ordinarily constitute a day's work. Employees who work an extra three hours overtime at the end of a shift from midnight Friday are not entitled to the Saturday premium, since the three hours are an extension of the Friday shift, and are not a separate shift.

Dominion Bridge Co. Ltd. (1980), 27 L.A.C. (2d) 399 (Adams).

▼

CONTRACT
TERM

An employee shall be paid [*overtime*] at the rate of time and one-half for all work performed in excess of the normal weekly hours of work. An employee who is called in and reports for work outside his regularly scheduled hours of work will be paid a minimum of 4 hours pay.

ARBITRATOR'S
RULING

Employees required to wear paging devices off-duty are not performing work entitling them to overtime by doing so. However, when an employee responds to such a call, he or she is entitled to overtime pay for the period of time spent dealing with the call, if it is in excess of the normal weekly hours of work, since no other reasonable meaning can be attached to the term "work performed". However, the call-in provision applies only to an employee who is called in and then reports for work at the company's premises.

143

Leco Industries Ltd. (1980), 26 L.A.C. (2d) 80 (Brunner).

▼

CONTRACT TERM

There shall be no pyramiding of premiums. *Overtime* will be paid at time and a half for all time worked in excess of 8 hours per day or 40 hours per week. In any split shift which extends beyond 12 hours, overtime at the rate of time and one-half shall be paid for the excess over 12 hours.

ARBITRATOR'S RULING

Employees (transit crews) working 8 hours per day spread over a period of 13 hours (6:15 a.m. to 9:45 a.m.; 2:15 p.m. to 7:15 p.m.) are entitled to both a daily overtime premium for work in excess of 8 hours per day, and a split shift premium since the schedule is spread over more than 12 hours. "Pyramiding" occurs only when overtime is calculated on a base to which a shift premium has already been added, or when overtime is paid more than once for the same hours worked. Here, payment of overtime for part of the total span of a split shift is a special form of shift premium, not payment for overtime work in the usual sense; the one premium is not incorporated in the base rate on which the other is calculated. The two payments, overtime and split shift, are independently payable under separate provisions.

City of Brampton (1980), 25 L.A.C. (2d) 165 (Weatherill).

▼

CONTRACT TERM

All [*overtime*] work in excess of 12 hours shall be paid at the rate of double time. Employees required to work on a Sunday shall be paid at the rate of double time for all hours worked, and double time and a half after an employee has worked 40 hours in that week. In no case will overtime and premium compensation be duplicated or pyramided.

ARBITRATOR'S RULING

Overtime or premium hours are those which fall outside an employee's regularly scheduled hours. There is a presumption that double premiums will not be paid for the same work, and this presumption is confirmed by the collective agreement language. Thus, an employee cannot claim both Sunday and daily overtime premiums for the same hours, since the purpose is the same. A different result will flow where separate and distinct reasons exist for two different types of premiums, e.g. overtime and shift premium, weekend premium and statutory holiday premium.

Labatt's Ltd. (1980), 24 L.A.C. (2d) 312 (Burkett).

P

PAY

CONTRACT TERM   Employees are entitled to vacation with *pay*.

ARBITRATOR'S RULING   A distinction is to be made between clauses which use such language as "total earnings" or "gross earnings" and clauses which base vacation pay on wages or earnings received for "time worked", "total hours worked", or "all work done". In the absence of a definition in the collective agreement, it is reasonable to look to labour standards legislation, which uses "total wages earned by the employee for the hours worked". Based on this language, vacation pay does not include holiday pay and sick leave pay.

Frelco Limited (1980), 27 L.A.C. (2d) 123 (Thistle).

PAYROLL

CONTRACT TERM   An employee shall not be eligible for holiday pay if he is absent on the scheduled workday immediately preceding or next following the holiday; employees on the *payroll* as of November 1st in each year are entitled to and shall be granted an additional holiday.

ARBITRATOR'S RULING   An extended layoff during plant renovations does not disentitle employees to holiday pay where they were not scheduled to work during layoff. Use of the word "the" does not mean that grievors become disentitled when some employees are recalled early and plant is again in operation, because the objective/subjective distinction between "his" and "the" is a sterile distinction, and anyway the use of the phrase "absent on the scheduled workday" requires that employees themselves be scheduled to work. Workers remain "employees" as long as they retain seniority for purposes of recall, but qualification "on the payroll" requires active employment around the date specified and continuing beyond it.

Canada Packers (1985), 21 L.A.C. (3d) 289 (Swan).

▼

CONTRACT TERM
Employees who are on the *payroll* as of July 1 shall be entitled to vacation pay.

ARBITRATOR'S RULING
Employees are not entitled to vacation pay where they are not on the payroll for the entire year.

S.K.D. Manufacturing (1982), 7 L.A.C. (3d) 443 (Weatherill).

▼

CONTRACT TERM
A cost of living bonus is payable to employees on the active *payroll* of the employer.

ARBITRATOR'S RULING
Phrase includes employees on unpaid sick leave even though they are not in receipt of wages from the employer.

Metro Toronto (1977), 14 L.A.C. (2d) 395 (Brent).

PERMANENT

CONTRACT TERM
New employees shall be on a probationary period normally not exceeding 6 consecutive calendar months. All vacancies and new positions of a *permanent* nature shall be posted. Any general conditions of employment not specifically mentioned in this agreement and not contrary to its intent shall continue in force and effect.

ARBITRATOR'S RULING
Temporary employment on fixed term contracts does not prevent the accumulation of seniority where there is no provision for temporary employees in the collective agreement. Allowing non-permanent vacancies to be filled without posting does not give an employer the right to employ people on temporary contracts. A practice of hiring employees on temporary contracts does not make it a general condition where there is no evidence the union acquiesced in the practice and it has applied only to a transitory 5% of the bargaining unit; such a practice is contrary to the intent of the agreement, since it denies rights set out in the agreement; and it is immaterial that individual employees accepted the contracts.

Ottawa-Carleton (1981), 4 L.A.C. (3d) 77 (Swan).

PERMANENT REDUCTION

CONTRACT
TERM

Employees with more than one year's service who are displaced and for whom no job is available due to *permanent reduction* in the number of employees will be entitled to severance pay.

ARBITRATOR'S
RULING

Displacement embraces a layoff. Permanent reduction means a reduction of the employee complement due to lack of work, with no fixed date for recall, that is not part of the usual cyclical pattern of layoffs, and lasts for the period during which recall rights may be exercised.

Council of Marine Canners (1983), 10 L.A.C. (3d) 375 (Munroe).

PERMISSION TO BE ABSENT

CONTRACT
TERM

In order to be entitled to payment for a plant holiday an employee must have worked the full working day immediately preceding and following the holiday except where management has given *permission to be absent* on either of these days.

ARBITRATOR'S
RULING

Because "the" is used, rather than "his", the qualifying days are to be determined objectively for all employees, and not subjectively for individual employees. Where employees are on layoff on the day preceding a holiday, they are not scheduled to work, and are not entitled to holiday pay. A layoff is not synonymous with permission to be absent.

Caravelle Foods (1980), 26 L.A.C. (2d) 1 (O'Shea).

PERSONS, *see also* EMPLOYEES, *compare* CONTRACTING OUT

CONTRACT
TERM

Persons not covered by this collective agreement shall not do work normally performed by clerical employees except in emergencies and for training.

ARBITRATOR'S RULING The test is not whether the work is done only by employees in the bargaining unit, but whether the work would have been done by employees in the bargaining unit had the contracting out not occurred. Here, that test is satisfied. However, "persons" refers only to other non-bargaining-unit employees of the employer, so that the employer does not violate the collective agreement by having bargaining unit work performed by outside agents if it is contracted out for valid business reasons.

Maritime Telegraph and Telephone Co. Ltd. (1989), 8 L.A.C. (4th) 22 (Archibald).

▼

CONTRACT TERM No *person outside the bargaining unit* shall perform work normally done by employees in the bargaining unit except for the purpose of instruction, experimentation, making process adjustments or in an emergency.

ARBITRATOR'S RULING This phrase is to be interpreted to mean only those employees expressly excluded from the bargaining unit. The employer does not violate the agreement by transferring certain job duties to non-union employees at another location of the employer.

Indusmin (1988), 2 L.A.C. (4th) 321 (Weatherill).

▼

CONTRACT TERM Layoffs shall proceed in inverse order of seniority provided that no employee is to be displaced by a *person* with more seniority unless the latter possesses the occupational qualifications of the job.

ARBITRATOR'S RULING Although management who have previous service in the bargaining unit may retain it and apply it if and when they return, they cannot use their seniority under this collective agreement to bump employees during a layoff. While the word "person" has a more general meaning, it refers here to employees, not management; this is made clear by the French version of the collective agreement, and the provisions of the collective agreement which establish the job security of bargaining unit employees.

CBC (1986), 23 L.A.C. (3d) 394 (M.G. Picher).

▼

CONTRACT TERM
Persons employed outside the bargaining unit shall not perform work of union members except in an emergency.

ARBITRATOR'S RULING
This clause prevents non-bargaining unit personnel of the company from doing bargaining unit work except in emergencies. It does not prevent contracting out.

Nabob Foods (1982), 5 L.A.C. (3d) 256 (Munroe).

▼

CONTRACT TERM
No bargaining unit employee shall be laid off as a direct result of a *non-bargaining unit person* performing the work of the said bargaining unit employee.

ARBITRATOR'S RULING
In the absence of a provision limiting "persons" to employees, the term "person" includes supervisors, others employed outside the bargaining unit, and employees of independent contractors.

Country Place Nursing Home (1981), 1 L.A.C. (3d) 341 (Prichard).

▼

CONTRACT TERM
Persons whose regular jobs are not in the bargaining unit shall not work on any jobs which are included in the bargaining unit, except for the purpose of instruction, experimenting or when regular employees are not available.

ARBITRATOR'S RULING
This is a "working foreman" clause, designed to prevent the assignment of bargaining unit work to supervisory employees; persons in this context means employees, and does not include independent contractors.

Ivaco Rolling Mills (1981), 1 L.A.C. (3d) 186 (Adell).

▼

CONTRACT TERM
All work within the bargaining unit shall be performed only by those *persons coming within the bargaining unit* who are members of the union or who are eligible to become members, except in cases of *bona fide* emergency or for instructional purposes.

ARBITRATOR'S RULING
The word "persons" means non-bargaining unit employees of the employer, and the clause does not prohibit contracting out to persons other than employees.

150

Robin Hood Multifoods Ltd. (1980), 26 L.A.C. (2d) 371 (Ladner).

PERSONAL REASONS

CONTRACT TERM — The company will grant leaves of absence without pay to employees, retroactively when necessary, for legitimate *personal reasons*, including illness and accident.

ARBITRATOR'S RULING — Term includes unforeseen situations beyond the employee's control or events that seldom occur but are pressing or important, e.g. marriage followed by honeymoon.

Morton-Parker (1987), 27 L.A.C. (3d) 93 (Willes).

▼

CONTRACT TERM — The employer may at its discretion grant leave of absence without pay for legitimate *personal reasons*.

ARBITRATOR'S RULING — The clause does not cover non-discretionary absences, such as sick leave, and therefore does not permit the employer to avoid payment of sick leave benefits simply by purporting to grant a personal leave of absence without pay to an employee on sick leave.

Hamilton-Wentworth C.A.S. (1985), 17 L.A.C. (3d) 370 (Foisy).

▼

CONTRACT TERM — The company may grant a leave of absence without pay to an employee for *personal reasons*.

ARBITRATOR'S RULING — While the employer has a discretion, it must be exercised reasonably and not in an arbitrary fashion. Employers are expected to balance their interest in maintaining sufficient staff to meet production needs against the interests of their employees. Emotional health is a legitimate reason for requesting leave.

Twin Pines Dairy (1981), 30 L.A.C. (2d) 361 (Brent).

▼

CONTRACT TERM — The company may grant a leave of absence to an employee for *personal reasons*. In granting such a leave, the company will consider the nature of the personal reasons, seniority, and efficient operation of the plant.

151

ARBITRATOR'S RULING To "consider" requires a company to "reckon with" or "make allowances for" an employee's request, i.e. to fairly and reasonably consider the nature of the personal reasons for a request and the effects on other circumstances of the request. A flat denial of a request by the company's most senior employee to add a week's leave of absence to the annual vacation shutdown to visit a sick parent overseas therefore violates the collective agreement.
Whitby Boat Works (1980), 27 L.A.C. (2d) 269 (O'Shea).

POLICY

CONTRACT TERM It is the exclusive right of the employer to determine its *policy* and direct its operations.

ARBITRATOR'S RULING This clause gives the employer the right to establish a mandatory retirement policy, subject to restrictions in the collective agreement, in this case an express obligation not to discriminate, and an implied duty to implement its policy in a manner that is not unreasonable, discriminatory, arbitrary or in bad faith.
Queensway General Hospital (1981), 30 L.A.C. (2d) 177 (P.C. Picher).

POLITICAL MATTER, see also UNION ACTIVITY

CONTRACT TERM The employer agrees to provide bulletin boards for posting notices of union activities; there shall be no posting of *political matter* on the employer's property.

ARBITRATOR'S RULING Notice of a Labour Day rally featuring a prominent politician on the day before a federal election is not political matter since it does not support a political party or candidate or espouse a political point of view.
Salvation Army Grace Hospital (1985), 19 L.A.C. (3d) 441 (Burkett).

POSITION

CONTRACT TERM When the employer decides to lay off employees, the following displacement provisions apply: where an employee has the competence, skill and experience to fulfill the requirements of the full-time *position* concerned, seniority shall apply.

ARBITRATOR'S
RULING

"Position" is defined as the core pattern of duties and responsibilities performed by the incumbent prior to layoff; this basic pattern can be identified by examining the actual work assignments given to the incumbent over an extended period of time.

St. Clair College (1989), 6 L.A.C. (4th) 442.

▼

CONTRACT
TERM

If any employee's *position* is reclassified downward, his wages shall not be reduced.

ARBITRATOR'S
RULING

"Position" means a collection of job duties; it does not mean the same as a "classification".

City of Lethbridge (1982), 4 L.A.C. (3d) 289 (England).

POSSIBLE

CONTRACT
TERM

The employer shall eliminate, *as far as possible*, all part-time employees.

ARBITRATOR'S
RULING

During a layoff for economic reasons, the employer is required by this clause to eliminate part-time positions, to the extent that it is feasible or practical to do so, without incurring undue financial obligations or liabilities.

Shaughnessy Hospital Society (1988), 33 L.A.C. (3d) 385 (McPhillips).

PRACTICABLE

CONTRACT
TERM

The company shall continue to use outside contractors but shall, *wherever practicable*, have such work performed by employees within the bargaining unit, provided they have the necessary skills.

ARBITRATOR'S
RULING

The word "practicable" means "possible or feasible", whereas the word "practical" means "efficient and workable"; thus, "wherever practicable" does not mean "unless it is more efficient to do otherwise". As a result, where bargaining unit members are capable of doing the work, during regular hours or on overtime, the mere fact that outside contractors are better or faster does not make it impracticable to use bargaining unit employees.

Ivaco Rolling Mills (1981), 1 L.A.C. (3d) 186 (Adell).

PRACTICAL

CONTRACT TERM The company agrees to carry out in practice *wherever practical* the principle of promotion of staff members within the bargaining unit. Promotions shall be based on merit and ability; where in the opinion of the company two or more applicants are equal, the position shall be given to the senior applicant.

ARBITRATOR'S RULING "Wherever practical" means what is practical for the company in the business sense, and not what is practical from the union's perspective; it means that the company is allowed reasonable scope in making decisions based on economic factors or considerations.

The Tribune (1989), 4 L.A.C. (4th) 390 (Chertkow).

PRACTICES

CONTRACT TERM Area or operational *practices* will be maintained unless otherwise mutually agreed.

ARBITRATOR'S RULING The introduction of a demerit point system for preventable accidents by company drivers does not violate the agreement by infringing an area or operational practice; it is rather an exercise of management's right to make rules concerning the safe operation of the enterprise.

Canadian Motorways Ltd. (1988), 34 L.A.C. (3d) 76 (McLaren).

▼

CONTRACT TERM Area or operational *practices* will be maintained unless otherwise mutually agreed.

ARBITRATOR'S RULING The installation of electronic surveillance cameras violates the guarantee that operational practices will be maintained. Practices are the accepted way of doing things, the uniform and constant response to a recurring set of circumstances. Where the action of management involves a core management activity, and there is a change in circumstances, the test is whether the company was obligating itself to act in the same manner regardless of the circumstances. Here, the employer had not demonstrated a change in the circumstances, such as a pilferage problem of substantial proportions, that would warrant any change in operational practices.

Thibodeau-Finch Express Inc. (1988), 32 L.A.C. (3d) 271 (Burkett).

▼

CONTRACT TERM
Area or operational *practices* will be maintained unless otherwise mutually agreed.

ARBITRATOR'S RULING
The party asserting a practice must show that the employer was obligating itself to act in the same manner for the foreseeable future, regardless of circumstances. The more critical the activity to efficient management, the more evidence is required, in addition to mere consistent action. At best, smoking on the job is an unintentional benefit enjoyed by reason of the employer's failure to exercise its power to make a rule concerning that particular aspect of safe operation.

Thibodeau-Finch Express Inc. (1987), 31 L.A.C. (3d) 191 (Brent).

▼

CONTRACT TERM
Area or operational *practices* will be maintained unless otherwise mutually agreed to.

ARBITRATOR'S RULING
The practice by highway drivers of stopping for lunch en route when they please is an operational practice, and the employer cannot impose lunch period rules, to satisfy customers' demands created by a "just-in-time inventory system" without the agreement of the union.

McKinlay Transport (1986), 24 L.A.C. (3d) 396 (O'Shea).

▼

CONTRACT TERM
Area or operational *practices* enjoyed by any local union and/or company will be maintained (despite the existence of a master collective agreement).

ARBITRATOR'S RULING
A "practice" refers to an accepted way of doing things, a uniform and constant response to a recurring set of circumstances; it must occur with sufficient regularity, and continue long enough to be accepted by both parties as the normal way of operating presently and in the future; it can benefit either employees or employers, and arise by verbal agreement or by a course of conduct, even without words. While a practice may involve the exercise of management rights, the test is whether the union could reasonably believe that the company was ob-

ligating itself to act in the same manner for the foreseeable future regardless of the circumstances. The more critical the activity to efficient management, the more unlikely the question can be answered affirmatively without evidence additional to mere consistent action. A practice can include, as here, more favourable bumping rights than the master agreement provides. However, certain employee benefits initiated by management may always be withdrawn at management's discretion, such as gratuities or bonuses, and unintentional benefits, e.g. parking privileges flowing from nearby unutilized land.

Dominion Consolidated Truck Lines (1980), 28 L.A.C. (2d) 45 (Adams).

PREFERENCE

CONTRACT TERM
Before the company seeks candidates for vacancies from outside the bargaining unit, *preference* shall be given to senior qualified applicants.

ARBITRATOR'S RULING
The word "preference" does not give an employee an unrestricted right to be transferred to a lower paying position in another department, but rather leaves a discretion to management which must be fairly and reasonably exercised. Management may decide to refuse a transfer for good and sufficient reason, as where the efficient operation of the employee's department would be disrupted.

Suncor (1983), 13 L.A.C. (3d) 432 (Mason).

PREGNANCY-RELATED ILLNESS, *see also* ILLNESS

CONTRACT TERM
An employee who is frequently absent on account of *pregnancy-related illness* may be required by the employer to commence her maternity leave.

ARBITRATOR'S RULING
Term does not include pre-existing medical condition of high blood pressure, even though the employee was advised by her doctor to rest at home because medication was restricted by the pregnancy. Alternatively, the clause contravenes the provisions of Ontario's *Employment Standards Act*.

Metropolitan Separate School Board (1984), 16 L.A.C. (3d) 353 (Adams).

PRESCRIBED DRUG

CONTRACT TERM   The company agrees to administer a major medical plan covering the cost of *prescribed drugs* and medicines.

ARBITRATOR'S RULING   A "prescribed drug" includes a drug available over the counter where it is prescribed by a physician; the term is broader than a "prescription drug", which is a drug which by law requires a prescription to dispense.

Domglas Inc. (1985), 22 L.A.C. (3d) 355 (Beattie).

PRESENT

CONTRACT TERM   The company shall ensure that a union steward from the employee's division is *present* when an employee with seniority is being discharged or suspended for a period of 5 days or more.

ARBITRATOR'S RULING   The presence of a union steward beside a representative of the employer who is discharging an employee over the telephone does not satisfy the requirement that a steward be present, since the employee would have no opportunity to consult with and be represented by the steward. As well, the steward would hear only half the conversation, and the fact that the union official was willing to listen did not amount to a waiver of the grievor's rights. A three-way telephone call, through the use of an extension phone or other device, would have satisfied the requirement.

Denison Mines Ltd. (1988), 1 L.A.C. (4th) 391 (Freedman).

PRESENT EMPLOYEES, see also EMPLOYEES

CONTRACT TERM   In job postings, the employer shall first consider all applications received from *present employees*.

ARBITRATOR'S RULING   "Employees" refers only to employees in the same bargaining unit, not all employees of the company. The word "present" may have a temporal limitation, but it does not expand the meaning to include non-bargaining unit employees. Thus, persons excluded from the bargaining unit, such as part-time employees, may not be considered on the same footing in a job posting competition as bargaining unit employees, in the absence of express language.

157

Religious Hospitallers of Hotel Dieu (1989), 9 L.A.C. (4th) 296 (Palmer).

PRESENT PRACTICES

CONTRACT
TERM

All work performed in the skilled trades shall be done by employees who are covered by the classification and rate as outlined in this agreement within the framework of *present practices.*

ARBITRATOR'S
RULING

"Present practices" contemplates practices in existence prior to the signing of the collective agreement. The words refer to practices in existence immediately prior to the signing of the collective agreement and which continue during the collective agreement.

Rockwell International (1982), 6 L.A.C. (3d) 304 (Rayner).

PRESENT PRIVILEGES

CONTRACT
TERM

Nothing contained in this agreement shall be deemed to take away any *present privilege* enjoyed by employees within the bargaining unit.

ARBITRATOR'S
RULING

The word "present" is intended to refer to something which precedes the collective agreement, so that the privilege claimed must have been in existence prior to the effective date of the collective agreement.

Religious Hospitallers (1982), 7 L.A.C. (3d) 131 (Saltman).

PRIVILEGE

CONTRACT
TERM

It is agreed that no right, benefit or *privilege* enjoyed or possessed but not set down in this agreement shall be altered or revoked without the consent of the union.

ARBITRATOR'S
RULING

A privilege is a right or advantage enjoyed beyond the common advantage of other persons; a private or personal favour enjoyed; a peculiar advantage. Smoking is such a privilege, and the employer violates the collective agreement if it removes a designated smoking room without the union's consent.

Regional Municipality of Ottawa-Carleton (1989), 7 L.A.C. (4th) 178 (Simmons).

▼

CONTRACT
TERM

All rights, benefits, *privileges* and working conditions which employees now enjoy, receive or possess, which the employer has knowledge of, shall continue to be enjoyed and possessed insofar as they are consistent with this agreement, but may be modified by mutual agreement between the employer and the union.

ARBITRATOR'S
RULING

The introduction of a requirement that employees punch in and out for paid coffee breaks is not an alteration of a right, benefit or privilege, because these relate to something positive which flows from one person to another, and the employer never by any positive act conferred on employees a right, benefit or privilege of not punching in and out at breaks. However, the change does constitute an alteration of a working condition. The existence of a working condition does not necessarily imply a positive act on the part of the employer; it is simply a circumstance under which work is to be performed, or a condition under which employees work.

Glades Lodge Ltd. (1988), 1 L.A.C. (4th) 257 (Veniot).

▼

CONTRACT
TERM

All rights, benefits, *privileges* and working conditions which employees enjoy shall be continued, but may be modified by agreement of the parties.

ARBITRATOR'S
RULING

A "right" implies an unfettered claim to something, while a privilege or benefit is an advantage enjoyed by one beyond others. An allowance to smoke is not a privilege, and institution of a no-smoking policy does not violate the collective agreement, where there was always a potential, if not actual, control placed on it. The ability to smoke is also not a working condition, where the practice varies from one location to another within the bargaining unit, and it has simply been licensed to a limited degree.

Board of Education for City of Toronto (1988), 33 L.A.C. (3d) 149 (Knopf).

▼

CONTRACT
TERM

Nothing contained in this agreement shall be deemed to take away any present *privilege* enjoyed by employees within the bargaining unit.

ARBITRATOR'S
RULING

The term "privilege" is extremely broad and extends to all those benefits which an employee is accustomed to receiving but to which he is not legally entitled and which cannot therefore be considered a "right"; in this case, the employees enjoyed the privilege of working past age 65, and that privilege must be continued.

Religious Hospitallers (1982), 7 L.A.C. (3d) 131 (Saltman).

PROBATION/PROBATIONARY EMPLOYEE

CONTRACT
TERM

An employee will be on *probation* until s(he) has completed 50 scheduled days of employment on plant work within a consecutive nine-month period.

ARBITRATOR'S
RULING

"Scheduled" means time worked which was planned in advance and assigned compulsorily to particular employees. An employee who is required to work Saturday and Sunday during his probationary period, even if it is not regularly scheduled, is entitled to count such time as "scheduled". This is in accord with the function of a probation period, which is to allow assessment and evaluation.

Burns Meats (1989), 7 L.A.C. (4th) 374 (Bowman).

▼

CONTRACT
TERM

Newly hired employees shall be considered on *probation* for a period of 6 months.

ARBITRATOR'S
RULING

A probationary period runs from the date of hire, excluding that date itself. Thus, the 6-month probationary period of an employee hired June 13 elapses at the end of the day on December 13.

Ontario Public Service Employees' Union (1989), 7 L.A.C. (4th) 53 (T.A.B. Jolliffe).

▼

CONTRACT
TERM

An employee will be considered on *probation* until he has completed 3 months' continuous service or 90 days of intermittent employment within any 12 month period.

ARBITRATOR'S
RULING
Absence due to strike, layoff, illness, etc. interrupts an employee's continuous service for the purpose of calculating his probationary period, with the result that such an "intermittent employee" must meet the test of working 90 calendar days in a 12-month period to achieve seniority status.

Ferro Industrial Products Ltd. (1988), 35 L.A.C. (3d) 324 (Stanley).

▼

CONTRACT
TERM
New employees will be considered *probationary employees* for the first 45 workdays on the active payroll of the employer. Upon completion of 30 days worked, probationary employees shall be entitled to payment for the paid holidays specified.

ARBITRATOR'S
RULING
Because management needs a reasonable opportunity to assess an employee, paid holidays to which a probationer becomes entitled are not counted in calculating the probationary period; "workdays" and "days worked" are synonymous.

General Coach (1988), 35 L.A.C. (3d) 235 (Roberts).

▼

CONTRACT
TERM
There shall be a 30-day period of *probation*.

ARBITRATOR'S
RULING
An employee is probationary where he was previously laid off and re-hired after his recall rights expired. The question, on termination of a probationary employee, is whether he has been properly measured in a manner which is not arbitrary, discriminatory or in bad faith.

Westar Timber (1985), 22 L.A.C. (3d) 406 (Vickers).

▼

CONTRACT
TERM
An employee shall acquire seniority rights when he has worked 90 days; a *probationary employee* may be separated without reference to seniority, but if he is continued in employment, his seniority shall be accumulated from the original date of his employment.

ARBITRATOR'S
RULING
For purposes of probation, which involves assessment of the employee's performance, a "day" means a "working day", but interruption of the probationary period by a brief layoff due to lack of work does not result in termination so as to require a new probation period.

Gainers Inc. (1985), 22 L.A.C. (3d) 214 (Owen).

▼

CONTRACT TERM
: The company has full rights to discharge *probationary employees* if in the opinion of the company they do not meet the standards required of them by the company.

ARBITRATOR'S RULING
: This clause entitles the company to consider, not only work performance, but "suitability" for permanent employment, a term which is broader than just cause, and which includes character, compatibility with fellow employees, potential for advancement, etc. However, the decision to discharge may not be arbitrary or capricious, discriminatory or in bad faith.

Nordair (1985), 22 L.A.C. (3d) 177 (Frumkin).

▼

CONTRACT TERM
: A *probationary employee* may be rejected for just cause. The test of just cause for rejection shall be suitability for continued employment.

ARBITRATOR'S RULING
: An employer must justify termination of a probationary employee albeit according to a lesser standard of cause. Where termination is for "unsuitability", the employer must show (1) legitimate standards of work performance; (2) communication of standards to the employee, and proper and ample direction; (3) adequate opportunity for the employee to meet the standards; (4) proper evaluation by employer; (5) failure to meet standards for no apparent reason; and (6) absence of unreasonable or discriminatory acts.

Government Employee Relations Bureau (1984), 15 L.A.C. (3d) 177 (Larson).

▼

CONTRACT TERM
: Newly hired employees shall be on a *probationary* basis for a period of six months.

ARBITRATOR'S RULING
: Part-time employees transferred to a full-time unit are not newly hired employees, and so are not required to serve a probationary period, where the collective agreement provides that seniority is portable.

Sudbury and District Association for Mentally Retarded (1984), 13 L.A.C. (3d) 385 (Egan).

▼

CONTRACT TERM
New employees shall be on a *probationary* period normally not exceeding 6 consecutive months. Seniority shall mean length of continuous service.

ARBITRATOR'S RULING
Successive 3-month terms of employment interrupted by one working day off without pay do not prevent the completion of a continuous probation period.

City of Ottawa (1984), 13 L.A.C. (3d) 293 (Little).

▼

CONTRACT TERM
New employees shall be considered as *probationary* employees.

ARBITRATOR'S RULING
Laid off employees recalled to work are not new employees even though their seniority may have been lost due to the length of the layoff; they do not have to repeat the probationary period.

Northern Telecom (1983), 9 L.A.C. (3d) 253 (Burkett).

▼

CONTRACT TERM
An employee shall be on *probation* until he has been actively at work for a total of 65 working days.

ARBITRATOR'S RULING
The probation period is not shortened simply because the employee on probation works 11-hour days while most employees work 7 hour days. Sick days and paid statutory holidays not worked do not count, given the purpose of the probationary period.

Metro Toronto Ass'n for the Mentally Retarded (1983), 9 L.A.C. (3d) 58 (Langille).

▼

CONTRACT TERM
An employee on being hired will be considered temporary and placed on *probation* until he or she has worked continuously for a period of 60 calendar days.

ARBITRATOR'S RULING
Requiring students hired on a temporary basis, for vacation relief, to resign, and them immediately rehiring them, in order to avoid the accrual of seniority rights, is not permitted by the collective agreement, although the union's acquiescence in such a practice may bar relief.

Consolidated Bathurst (1982), 6 L.A.C. (3d) 30 (MacDowell).

▼

163

CONTRACT TERM — When an employee is promoted permanently into a higher paid position, the designated rate for the position will begin immediately after a month's *probationary* period.

ARBITRATOR'S RULING — In the context of a probationary period the term month is to be construed as a working month, not a calendar month, since the employer must be able to observe and assess the employee on probation, and this is possible only when he is working. *Dartmouth General Hospital* (1982), 3 L.A.C. (3d) 420 (Langille).

▼

CONTRACT TERM — New employees shall be on a *probationary* period normally not exceeding 6 consecutive calendar months. All vacancies and new positions of a permanent nature shall be posted. Any general conditions of employment not specifically mentioned in this agreement and not contrary to its intent shall continue in force and effect.

ARBITRATOR'S RULING — Temporary employment on fixed term contracts does not prevent the accumulation of seniority where there is no provision for temporary employees in the collective agreement. Allowing non-permanent vacancies to be filled without posting does not give an employer the right to employ people on temporary contracts. A practice of hiring employees on temporary contracts does not make it a general condition where there is no evidence the union acquiesced in the practice and it has applied only to a transitory 5% of the bargaining unit; such a practice is contrary to the intent of the agreement, since it denies rights set out in the agreement; and it is immaterial that individual employees accepted the contracts. *Ottawa-Carleton* (1981), 4 L.A.C. (3d) 77 (Swan).

▼

CONTRACT TERM — Seniority shall be established after a *probationary* period of 45 working days during a six-month period.

ARBITRATOR'S RULING — Since the purpose of a probationary period is to give the employer an opportunity to assess an employee, Saturdays and Sundays are included in working days, where they are worked, even though they may be overtime, and not part of the normal workweek.

Edwards, Owen Sound Operations (1981), 2 L.A.C. (3d) 348 (Linden).

▼

CONTRACT TERM

The first 44 days worked in the bargaining unit by all new employees shall be a *probationary* period.

ARBITRATOR'S RULING

A part-time employee hired on the full-time staff is a new employee for purposes of the probation period, where the collective agreement elsewhere speaks of the "hiring" of part-time employees for the full-time staff, and makes it clear that they are to serve a probationary period.

Dominion Stores (1981), 30 L.A.C. (2d) 194 (Brunner).

▼

CONTRACT TERM

The company has the right to make any decision regarding the retention of a *probationary employee.*

ARBITRATOR'S RULING

This clause entitles the employer to discharge a probationary employee, provided that the employer's decision is not arbitrary, discriminatory or in bad faith. The onus is on the employer to establish a *prima facie* case that there were grounds to terminate the probationary employee and that the decision was made in good faith. If the employer does so, the onus shifts to the employee to prove that the decision was arbitrary, discriminatory and in bad faith. In establishing good faith, the employer must verify that the employee has been given a fair opportunity to demonstrate the qualifications and suitability appropriate for permanent employment and that it has made a fair assessment, e.g. has not set unreasonable standards.

Pacific Western Airlines (1981), 30 L.A.C. (2d) 68 (Sychuk).

PROMOTION, *see also* SKILL AND ABILITY, *compare* TRANSFER

CONTRACT TERM

The company agrees to carry out in practice wherever practical the principle of *promotion* of staff members within the bargaining unit. Promotions shall be based on merit and ability; where in the opinion of the company two or more applicants are equal, the position shall be given to the senior applicant.

ARBITRATOR'S RULING "Wherever practical" means what is practical for the company in the business sense, and not what is practical from the union's perspective; it means that the company is allowed reasonable scope in making decisions based on economic factors or considerations.

The Tribune (1989), 4 L.A.C. (4th) 390 (Chertkow).

▼

CONTRACT TERM In making staff changes, transfers, or *promotions*, appointment shall be made of applicants having the required qualifications and where qualifications are equal, seniority shall be the governing factor. Management rights shall not be exercised in an arbitrary or discriminatory manner.

ARBITRATOR'S RULING Under this agreement, transfer involves a move outside the bargaining unit, or to another classification, while promotion constitutes either an advancement within a classification or a move to a higher classification. "Staff change" is a broad concept, and includes a reassignment of employees within the same classification to different locations. The employer's decision to make a staff change by reassigning two workers away from their usual stations is arbitrary where it is done without explanation or advance consultation.

Metropolitan Toronto Zoo (1989), 4 L.A.C. (4th) 46 (Swan).

▼

CONTRACT TERM Selection of employees for *promotion* shall be based upon seniority, ability, skill.

ARBITRATOR'S RULING Promotion involves a move up, and does not include a lateral move, from one clerical position to another, with the same pay rate, within the same classification.

N.S. Liquor Comm'n. (1983), 13 L.A.C. (3d) 438 (MacDougall).

▼

CONTRACT TERM Seniority shall be the governing factor regarding *promotion*, where ability and qualifications are relatively equal among employees.

ARBITRATOR'S
RULING

A promotion occurs when an employee advances to a position with higher pay and/or greater responsibility or promotional opportunities. Depending on the language of the agreement, it may refer to permanent promotions only, and exclude the assignment of relief work. Again, transfers may be permanent or temporary, based on the collective agreement language. A transfer may, depending on the context, mean a move within a classification, or only a move between classifications, or even just a shift change. Ability refers to an employee's inherent capacities whereas qualifications refer to some form of training or experience.

Dominion Stores (1983), 9 L.A.C. (3d) 47 (Saltman).

▼

CONTRACT
TERM

Seniority shall govern *promotion*.

ARBITRATOR'S
RULING

Promotion includes movement to a higher paying position even though it is within the same classification, provided the higher pay is not simply a nominal amount.

Town of Dieppe (1982), 9 L.A.C. (3d) 76 (Stanley).

▼

CONTRACT
TERM

The company will post a notice of a job vacancy on the bulletin board for 2 consecutive days, providing an opportunity to those for whom the posted job represents a *promotion* to apply.

ARBITRATOR'S
RULING

A promotion means advancement to a higher position, grade or rank, usually though not necessarily at a higher rate of pay. A job with more desirable characteristics from a subjective point of view for an employee at the same wage rate is therefore not a promotion, but a lateral transfer.

Ascolectric Ltd. (1980), 26 L.A.C. (2d) 390 (Weatherill).

PROPERLY SECURED AREA

CONTRACT
TERM

The company agrees to provide a *properly secured area* in which employees may keep their personal effects while on duty.

167

ARBITRATOR'S
RULING

A properly secured area for employees' personal effects is an area sufficient to secure the safety of the personal effects which employees may reasonably be expected to wear or bring to work with them, such as coats, jackets, hats, shoes and overshoes, purses, wallets, handbags and lunches. A lunch room coat rack is not a properly secured area where it is open and unsupervised, and small open lockers are not properly secured areas; moreover, without locks, lockers are not secured areas.

Dominion Stores (1981), 29 L.A.C. (2d) 239 (O'Shea).

PROTECTIVE DEVICES

CONTRACT
TERM

The employer agrees to provide safe working conditions, proper and adequate tools, equipment and *protective devices.*

ARBITRATOR'S
RULING

"Protective devices" includes safety shoes and boots. The company can only be required, however, to pay a reasonable price for safety shoes or boots and to replace them when reasonably required.

Island Telephone Co. Ltd. (1984), 17 L.A.C. (3d) 47 (Christie).

PYRAMIDING

CONTRACT
TERM

Overtime premium will not be duplicated for the same hours worked, nor shall there be any *pyramiding* with respect to any other premiums.

ARBITRATOR'S
RULING

There is an implied presumption against pyramiding, i.e. paying double premiums for the same hours, but it does not apply where the premiums are intended for different purposes. However, the above language prevents pyramiding regardless of the purpose for which the premiums are designed.

St. Thomas-Elgin General Hospital (1984), 17 L.A.C. (3d) 202 (Burkett).

▼

CONTRACT
TERM

There shall be no *pyramiding* of premiums. Overtime will be paid at time and a half for all time worked in excess of 8 hours per day or 40 hours per week. In any split shift which extends beyond 12 hours, overtime at the rate of time and one-half shall be paid for the excess over 12 hours.

ARBITRATOR'S
RULING

Employees (transit crews) working 8 hours per day spread over a period of 13 hours (6:15 a.m. to 9:45 a.m.; 2:15 p.m. to 7:15 p.m.) are entitled to both a daily overtime premium for work in excess of 8 hours per day, and a split shift premium since the schedule is spread over more than 12 hours. "Pyramiding" occurs only when overtime is calculated on a base to which a shift premium has already been added, or when overtime is paid more than once for the same hours worked. Here, payment of overtime for part of the total span of a split shift is a special form of shift premium, not payment for overtime work in the usual sense; the one premium is not incorporated in the base rate on which the other is calculated. The two payments, overtime and split shift, are independently payable under separate provisions.

City of Brampton (1980), 25 L.A.C. (2d) 165 (Weatherill).

▼

CONTRACT
TERM

All work in excess of 12 hours shall be paid at the rate of double time. Employees required to work on a Sunday shall be paid at the rate of double time for all hours worked, and double time and a half after an employee has worked 40 hours in that week. In no case will overtime and premium compensation be duplicated or *pyramided*.

ARBITRATOR'S
RULING

Overtime or premium hours are those which fall outside an employee's regularly scheduled hours. There is a presumption that double premiums will not be paid for the same work, and this presumption is confirmed by the collective agreement language. Thus, an employee cannot claim both Sunday and daily overtime premiums for the same hours, since the purpose is the same. A different result will flow where separate and distinct reasons exist for two different types of premiums, e.g. overtime and shift premium, weekend premium and statutory holiday premium.

Labatt's Ltd. (1980), 24 L.A.C. (2d) 312 (Burkett).

Q

QUALIFICATIONS

CONTRACT
TERM

Employees shall be selected for positions on the basis of their skill, ability, experience and *qualifications*. Where these factors are relatively equal, seniority shall govern provided the successful applicant is qualified to perform the available work within an appropriate familiarization period.

ARBITRATOR'S
RULING

While they are not distinct, and there is considerable overlap, "skill" is competence in particular tasks; "qualifications" refers to possession of necessary education, training and certification; "abilities" relates to overall qualities of an employee with respect to the work to be done; and "experience" refers to the breadth and length of actual experience. Relative equality involves a determination of whether one employee is more qualified than another by a substantial and demonstrable margin in relation to the relevant circumstances. The employer cannot seize on minor differences between candidates to defeat the application of seniority.

Wellesley Hospital (1989), 5 L.A.C. (4th) 55 (Weatherill)

▼

CONTRACT
TERM

Employees shall be selected for positions on the basis of their skill, ability, experience and *qualifications*. Where these factors are relatively equal, seniority shall govern.

ARBITRATOR'S
RULING

"Qualifications" means accomplishments by way of education, training, familiarity or other means which make the applicant a fit and proper person to perform the tasks of the position.

Greater Niagara General Hospital (1988), 2 L.A.C. (4th) 416 (Brunner).

▼

CONTRACT TERM
Where skill, ability, experience and *qualifications* are relatively equal, seniority shall govern.

ARBITRATOR'S RULING
Qualifications established by the employer must be reasonably related to the work to be done. Depending on the job, bilingualism may be a reasonable requirement justified by a legitimate business need.

Cornwall General Hospital (1986), 22 L.A.C. (3d) 141 (Burkett).

▼

CONTRACT TERM
In making promotions, transfers or filling vacancies, the skill, knowledge and efficiency of the employees concerned shall be the primary consideration and where such *qualifications* are relatively equal, seniority shall be the determining factor.

ARBITRATOR'S RULING
Previous experience in the same or a similar job shows demonstrated ability, and may be taken into account in assessing competing employees. Relative equality exists unless the difference is substantial and demonstrable; there must be a discernible, material difference, not just a minor one.

Board of School Trustees, District 68 (1985), 19 L.A.C. (3d) 176 (Germaine).

▼

CONTRACT TERM
In all cases of promotion, where ability and *qualifications* are relatively equal, departmental seniority shall prevail.

ARBITRATOR'S RULING
An employer can demand formal qualifications, provided they are consistent with the collective agreement, and are reasonable in relation to the work to be done. Equivalent academic qualifications may be acceptable, since otherwise the legitimate expectations of employees would be defeated without advancing any legitimate interest of the employer.

Sunbeam Home (1983), 13 L.A.C. (3d) 183 (Rayner).

▼

171

CONTRACT TERM

Where *qualifications* and ability to perform the work are relatively equal, seniority shall govern in filling vacancies and new positions.

ARBITRATOR'S RULING

Qualifications may be established by management, but they must be reasonably relevant to the position. Education and training may be required, but they must be relevant to the job classification to be filled.

London P.U.C. (1983), 12 L.A.C. (3d) 378 (Palmer).

▼

CONTRACT TERM

Seniority shall be the governing factor regarding promotion, transfer, etc. where ability and *qualifications* are relatively equal among employees.

ARBITRATOR'S RULING

Ability refers to an employee's inherent capacities whereas qualifications refer to some form of training or experience.

Dominion Stores (1983), 9 L.A.C. (3d) 47 (Saltman).

▼

CONTRACT TERM

When selecting employees to fill vacancies the company will recognize seniority, ability and *qualifications*. Where these factors are relatively equal, the senior employee will be selected.

ARBITRATOR'S RULING

Unless expressly limited by the collective agreement, management has power to determine qualifications, provided it acts in good faith, and the qualifications bear a reasonable relationship to the work to be done.

Island Telephone (1983), 8 L.A.C. (3d) 132 (Christie).

▼

CONTRACT TERM

Vacancies will be filled in order of seniority after due consideration is given to the employee's *qualifications* and the requirements of the operation.

ARBITRATOR'S RULING

Depending on the job, qualifications may include the ability to maintain composure under pressure, to handle peaks in workload, and to maintain regular attendance.

Air Canada (1981), 2 L.A.C. (3d) 314 (Burkett).

QUALIFIED

CONTRACT TERM

Management shall award a posted position, as between two equally *qualified* applicants, to the senior employee.

ARBITRATOR'S RULING   Unless management is entitled under the collective agreement to establish special qualifications, a qualified applicant is one who is competent to perform the work required by the classification, whether or not the applicant has achieved a stipulated level of education.

St. Catharines General Hospital (1984), 13 L.A.C. (3d) 378 (Teplitsky).

▼

CONTRACT TERM   No new teacher will be hired for a position for which a teacher with a right of recall is *qualified*.

ARBITRATOR'S RULING   An employer can establish qualifications, but they must bear a reasonable relationship to the work to be done, and must be established in good faith, and applied consistently or uniformly to all applicants.

Essex Co. School Board (1983), 8 L.A.C. (3d) 322 (Hinnegan).

R

REASON SATISFACTORY TO THE EMPLOYER, *see also* SATISFACTORY REASON

CONTRACT TERM — An employee shall lose seniority and be deemed to have terminated her employment if she is absent from work without permission, unless she furnishes a reason *satisfactory to the employer.*

ARBITRATOR'S RULING — Under this language, the issue is not whether the employee's explanation would be accepted by an arbitrator; the question is whether the employer's decision is arbitrary, discriminatory or in bad faith. *Guelph General Hospital* (1982), 5 L.A.C. (3d) 289 (Saltman).

▼

CONTRACT TERM — An employee shall lose seniority and be deemed to have quit if he is absent for 3 consecutive working days without notifying the Personnel Office unless a *reason satisfactory to the company* is given.

ARBITRATOR'S RULING — While the clause gives the company the initial right to assess the validity of the reasons given, the company must do so reasonably, and cannot act in an arbitrary or capricious manner; the company cannot refuse to accept a valid reason. *Welmet Industries* (1980), 28 L.A.C. (2d) 84 (Rayner).

REASONABLE CAUSE, *see also* UNSAFE WORK

CONTRACT TERM — If an employee has *reasonable cause* to believe that a machine, device or thing is unsafe to use or operate, or that a work situation is unsafe, because such operation is likely to endanger himself or another, the employee may refuse to use or operate the machine, device or thing, or continue to work in that situation.

ARBITRATOR'S RULING — While employees must act in good faith, "reasonable cause" must also be assessed on an objective basis from the perspective of the average employee. In any event, it does not include dangers inherent in an employee's work, or fear of minor injuries, such as cuts, nicks or bruises. In this case, employees' reluctance to operate a special type of loom was based on fears of danger inherent in the employees' work (cuts, nicks and bruises of the same nature as with any other type of loom).

Crossley Carpet Mills Ltd. (1989), 3 L.A.C. (4th) 199 (Darby).

REASONABLE EXCUSE

CONTRACT TERM — In order to qualify for holiday pay, an employee must work his last full scheduled shift immediately preceding and his first full scheduled shift immediately following the holiday, unless he is excused because of illness or for other *reasonable excuse.*

ARBITRATOR'S RULING — Employees on workers' compensation on the qualifying days are entitled to holiday pay for all holidays occurring during the absence. Absence for such a reason, which is beyond the employee's control, is a reasonable excuse. Holiday pay is an earned benefit, not to be taken away without clear language. Moreover, the receipt of holiday pay and workers' compensation is not double payment, since workers' compensation is not provided by the employer, nor does it flow from the collective agreement.

Caressant Care (1987), 29 L.A.C. (3d) 347 (Walters).

REASONABLE RATIO

CONTRACT TERM — The employer is required to use a *reasonable ratio* of 1st, 2nd, 3rd and 4th year apprentices.

ARBITRATOR'S RULING — Clause means that a numerically proportionate ratio of apprentices by category should, where possible, be maintained and any departure should not be immoderate or excessive.

Easco Electric Ltd. (1984), 17 L.A.C. (3d) 415 (MacDougall).

REASONS FOR DISCIPLINE

CONTRACT
TERM
If an employee is disciplined, he shall be advised of the *reasons for the discipline* in writing.

ARBITRATOR'S
RULING
The requirement to give reasons for discipline requires that sufficient information be given to permit an employee to know the basis on which discipline is being imposed, and whether he or she should grieve the discipline.

City of Calgary (1989), 9 L.A.C. (4th) 1 (Rooke).

REGULAR/REGULARLY

CONTRACT
TERM
The employer agrees to pay 100% of the rates charged for welfare benefit plans for each employee *regularly* working 30 hours per week or longer.

ARBITRATOR'S
RULING
The meaning of the words "regular" and "regularly" may vary with the circumstances and the context. While it can mean steadiness or uniformity, it can also be defined against the background of generally accepted labour relations practice, and thus in accordance with the practice of the Ontario Labour Relations Board. Thus, even though it is an exception rather than the norm for the employee to work over 30 hours per week, the appropriate test is that of the OLRB which requires that the employee work in excess of the specified hours for the majority of weeks in the seven-week period immediately preceding the claim.

Welland District Association (1982), 5 L.A.C. (3d) 315 (Devlin).

REGULAR EMPLOYEE

CONTRACT
TERM
Persons employed on a temporary basis are not covered by the terms of this agreement and shall not accumulate seniority, unless later employed as *regular employees.*

ARBITRATOR'S
RULING
Continuing the employment of a temporary employee beyond the end of the agreed temporary employment period does not confer employment status. Mere passage of time on the job does not make a temporary employee a regular employee; this requires some action by the company evidencing a change in status.

Maple Leaf Monarch (1984), 13 L.A.C. (3d) 307 (Gorsky).

REGULAR HOURS OF WORK

CONTRACT TERM
The *regular hours of work* shall be 5 consecutive days of 8 hours per day to a maximum of 40 per week.

ARBITRATOR'S RULING
"Regular hours of work" is not synonymous with "day shift", and the employer is therefore not prohibited from introducing an evening shift.

Lewisporte Wholesalers Ltd. (1988), 3 L.A.C. (4th) 338 (Harris).

REGULAR INCOME

CONTRACT TERM
Pay for sick leave is for the sole and only purpose of protecting the employee against loss of *regular income* when she is legitimately ill and unable to work. An employee required to work on a designated holiday shall be paid at time and a half her regular straight time rate of pay for all hours worked on such holiday, and will receive in addition a lieu day off at her regular straight time rate of pay.

ARBITRATOR'S RULING
An employee who is scheduled to work on a statutory holiday but is unable to do so because of *bona fide* illness is entitled to both holiday and sick pay, since both are earned benefits. Had she worked on the holiday, the employee would have been entitled to both payments, which are for separate purposes, and are not duplications. Once scheduled to work a statutory holiday, entitlement to holiday pay becomes part of an employee's regular income since the employee is expected to attend work at that time.

North York General Hospital (1980), 27 L.A.C. (2d) 64 (Shime).

REGULAR RATE

CONTRACT TERM
An employee who is required to work on a designated holiday shall be entitled to time and a half, and in addition shall either be paid for a full day at his *regular rate* of pay or take a lieu day off with pay.

ARBITRATOR'S
RULING
"Regular rate of pay" encompasses straight time rate or overtime rate depending on the rate the employee would have received if he had worked the day as a non-holiday.

Metro Toronto (1984), 13 L.A.C. (3d) 356 (P.C. Picher).

REGULAR SALARY

CONTRACT
TERM
An injured worker shall receive from the employer the difference between the amount payable by the Workers' Compensation Board and his *regular salary*.

ARBITRATOR'S
RULING
Regular salary is the amount of compensation an employee is entitled to be paid by the employer for a specified period. It is not the amount of his paycheque, since deductions must be taken from the regular salary. The employer must therefore make up the "regular gross salary" without deductions for injured employees in receipt of WCB benefits.

Newfoundland Hospital Association (1987), 32 L.A.C. (3d) 55 (Thistle).

REGULAR SCHEDULE

CONTRACT
TERM
An employee will be compensated for time lost by him from his *regular schedule* due to bereavement.

ARBITRATOR'S
RULING
Term does not include vacation, so that bereavement leave pay is not due where bereavement occurs during vacation, since time is not lost from regular schedule.

City of Toronto (1981), 2 L.A.C. (3d) 61 (Beatty).

REGULAR TAKE-HOME PAY

CONTRACT
TERM
The employer agrees to pay any employee on workers' compensation the difference between compensation payments and *regular take-home pay* for up to a maximum of one year.

ARBITRATOR'S
RULING

"Regular take-home pay" refers to what the employee would have earned had he worked during the compensable period. It does not mean the amount determined by the Workers' Compensation Board, nor does it mean the take-home pay of a regular employee working full-time. Allowance must therefore be made where the employee would have been subject to layoffs.

Canvin Products (1981), 30 L.A.C. (2d) 300 (Ladner).

REGULARLY EMPLOYED

CONTRACT
TERM

The union is sole bargaining agent for laboratory technologists except persons *regularly employed* for not more than 15 hours per week.

ARBITRATOR'S
RULING

"Regularly employed" is not necessarily the same as "regularly scheduled". An employee hired on a casual basis who works a minimum of 11 hours per week, but on average more than 15 hours per week, as a result of frequently replacing absent employees, is regularly employed, despite the fact that the additional hours are not "scheduled" work and she has the option to refuse to do it. "Regular" is to be interpreted as meaning "recurring uniformly according to a predictable time and manner" or as "constant". It involves a pattern to the employment history which indicates some order and predictability. Uninterrupted or continuous employment is not required.

Salvation Army Grace Hospital (1987), 31 L.A.C. (3d) 1 (Brandt).

RELATIVE EFFICIENCY AND SUITABILITY

CONTRACT
TERM

The employer undertakes to observe seniority with regard to transfers, so far as it is practicable to do so, as well as *relative efficiency and suitability*.

ARBITRATOR'S
RULING

Under this hybrid clause, the employer can take into account the relative absenteeism and work experience of applicants. The burden is on the employer to show why ability is given greater weight than seniority, especially where the job is not a complex one.

Wellesley Hospital (1981), 2 L.A.C. (3d) 193 (Kennedy).

RELATIVELY EQUAL

CONTRACT TERM
Employees shall be selected for positions on the basis of their skill, ability, experience and qualifications. When these factors are *relatively equal* amongst the employees considered, seniority shall govern.

ARBITRATOR'S RULING
Relative equality is to be determined having regard to the nature of the job to be done. The kind of difference between candidates which can defeat seniority rights must not be a slight one, but rather be composed of a substantial and demonstrable margin, in areas relevant to the performance of the job in question.

Ottawa Civic Hospital (1989), 9 L.A.C. (4th) 348 (Mitchnick).

▼

CONTRACT TERM
Employees shall be selected for positions on the basis of their skill, ability, experience and qualifications. Where these factors are *relatively equal*, seniority shall govern provided the successful applicant is qualified to perform the available work within an appropriate familiarization period.

ARBITRATOR'S RULING
While they are not distinct, and there is considerable overlap, "skill" is competence in particular tasks; "qualifications" refers to possession of necessary education, training and certification; "abilities" relates to overall qualities of an employee with respect to the work to be done; and "experience" refers to the breadth and length of actual experience. Relative equality involves a determination of whether one employee is more qualified than another by a substantial and demonstrable margin in relation to the relevant circumstances. The employer cannot seize on minor differences between candidates to defeat the application of seniority.

Wellesley Hospital (1989), 5 L.A.C. (4th) 55 (Weatherill)

▼

CONTRACT TERM
In making promotions, transfers or filling vacancies, the skill, knowledge and efficiency of the employees concerned shall be the primary consideration, and where such qualifications are *relatively equal* seniority shall be the determining factor.

ARBITRATOR'S RULING
Previous experience in the same or a similar job shows demonstrated ability, and may be taken into account in assessing competing employees. Relative equality exists unless the difference is substantial and demonstrable; there must be a discernible, material difference, not just a minor one.

Board of School Trustees, District 68 (1985), 19 L.A.C. (3d) 176 (Germaine).

▼

CONTRACT TERM
Where skills, competence, efficiency and qualifications are *relatively equal*, seniority shall be the directing factor.

ARBITRATOR'S RULING
"Relative equality" means approximate equality; thus, minor differences cannot defeat the application of seniority.

Elisabeth Bruyere Health Centre (1982), 6 L.A.C. (3d) 119 (Saltman).

▼

CONTRACT TERM
On layoff and recall seniority shall be given preference where abilities, etc. are *relatively equal* in the opinion of management.

ARBITRATOR'S RULING
A "relatively equal" clause involves a competition among employees; in these circumstances, employees will be considered relatively equal unless one employee is better qualified by a substantial or demonstrable margin. Management's decision must be *bona fide*, and not be arbitrary, discriminatory or unreasonable. The less skill and judgment a job requires, the more difficult it is to demonstrate the reasonableness of a decision that there are substantial differences in ability to perform a job as between applicants. Where the clause does not refer to the "opinion of management", the decision must not only be reasonable; it must be correct.

British Leaf Tobacco (1981), 3 L.A.C. (3d) 235 (Kennedy).

▼

CONTRACT TERM
On promotion or transfer, where the employer determines that the qualifications for the position are *relatively equal* between the applicants, seniority shall be the governing factor.

ARBITRATOR'S RULING
Under this clause, the arbitrator is not bound by the employer's assessment, and need pay no special deference to the employer's views.

University of Toronto (1981), 30 L.A.C. (2d) 187 (Palmer).

▼

CONTRACT TERM
Vacancies will be filled on the basis of ability, skill and experience. When these factors are *relatively equal*, the employee with the greatest seniority will be given preference.

ARBITRATOR'S RULING
The successful candidate must have substantially superior ability. The employer must determine whether there is a substantial and demonstrable margin of difference in ability, skill and experience before awarding the job to a less senior candidate. The decision must be reasonable, and the procedures must be fair and unbiased.

Northern Telecom Ltd. (1980), 25 L.A.C. (2d) 379 (Fraser).

RELIGIOUS LEAVE

CONTRACT TERM
Religious leave may be granted at the discretion of the employer without loss of pay; such requests shall not be unreasonably denied.

ARBITRATOR'S RULING
"Religion" should be interpreted broadly and liberally, and is not restricted to the well-established religious denominations. An adherent of the Wiccan faith is entitled to paid leave of absence for two religious holidays per year, since Wicca qualifies as a religion for the purposes of the agreement.

Humber College (1987), 31 L.A.C. (3d) 266 (Swan).

REPORT FOR WORK/REPORTING PAY

CONTRACT TERM
When an employee, because of failure of the company to inform him that no work will be available, *reports for work* on schedule and is advised that there is no work available, he shall suffer no loss of salary for that day.

ARBITRATOR'S
RULING

Employees who do not cross a picketline due to fear of assault and damage to vehicles cannot be said to report for work and are not entitled to a reporting allowance. The work is available, though inaccessible, because of the picketline.

Denison Mines Ltd. (1988), 3 L.A.C. (4th) 1 (M.G. Picher).

▼

CONTRACT
TERM

An employee *reporting for work* on the call of the company shall be paid a minimum of 2 hours pay.

ARBITRATOR'S
RULING

Employees who report for work but cannot do so because the shift has been cancelled, due to an illegal work stoppage by other employees, are entitled to reporting pay, since the clause does not make an exception for causes beyond the control of the employer.

Crestbrook Forest Industries (1987), 10 L.A.C. (3d) 91 (Ladner).

▼

CONTRACT
TERM

An employee *reporting for work* on the call of the company shall be paid a minimum of 4 hours' pay.

ARBITRATOR'S
RULING

The phrase "report for work" applies where management exercises authority over employees; it does not apply where employees attend at a pick-up point for transportation to a remote mine site, and buses are cancelled due to weather conditions.

Westmin Resources (1985), 21 L.A.C. (3d) 27 (McColl).

▼

CONTRACT
TERM

An employee upon *reporting for work* at the commencement of his regular shift, unless notified in advance not to do so, shall receive a minimum of 4 hours' work or pay.

ARBITRATOR'S
RULING

This clause does not apply where an employee is sent home because of a possible illness or is disciplined at the beginning of his regularly scheduled shift.

Thomas Built Buses (1980), 27 L.A.C. (3d) 409 (Weatherill).

▼

CONTRACT TERM
An employee shall be paid at the rate of time and one-half for all work performed in excess of the normal weekly hours of work. An employee who is called in and *reports for work* outside his regularly scheduled hours of work will be paid a minimum of 4 hours pay.

ARBITRATOR'S RULING
Employees required to wear paging devices off-duty are not performing work entitling them to overtime by doing so. However, when an employee responds to such a call, he or she is entitled to overtime pay for the period of time spent dealing with the call, if it is in excess of the normal weekly hours of work, since no other reasonable meaning can be attached to the term "work performed". However, the call-in provision applies only to an employee who is called in and then reports for work at the company's premises.

Leco Industries Ltd. (1980), 26 L.A.C. (2d) 80 (Brunner).

REQUIRED TO WORK

CONTRACT TERM
Should an employee be *required to work* on his scheduled day off, he may be given another day off in lieu if mutually agreed. Otherwise, he shall be paid in accordance with overtime rates.

ARBITRATOR'S RULING
An employee who agrees to work an extra day on the weekend when asked by the employer is required to work where the employer alters the posted schedule to make the additional hours part of the employee's schedule.

Halifax Infirmary Hospital (1989), 5 L.A.C. (4th) 138 (Veniot).

▼

CONTRACT TERM
An employee *required to work* overtime on his first scheduled day of rest shall be paid overtime pay.

ARBITRATOR'S RULING
Where attendance at a driver education course is voluntary and unrelated to employment in the bargaining unit, it is not "required", and does not constitute "work", even though some benefit may accrue to the employer.

N.S. Civil Service Commission (1986), 25 L.A.C. (3d) 5 (Outhouse).

184

RESIGNATION

CONTRACT
TERM
Severance pay on termination of employment is not payable when an employee *resigns* or is discharged for just cause.

ARBITRATOR'S
RULING
The term "resignation" includes voluntary retirement, including voluntary retirement at age 65.

Mainland Engine Rebuilders (1982), 5 L.A.C. (3d) 90 (MacIntyre).

RETAIN AND ACCUMULATE

CONTRACT
TERM
Any employee who becomes pregnant shall be entitled to a maternity leave up to five months in duration. It is understood and agreed that such employees shall *retain and accumulate* full seniority rights and benefits while on such leave.

ARBITRATOR'S
RULING
"Retain and accumulate" means that employees on maternity leave are entitled to have benefits remain intact and inviolate, in the same way and to the same extent as if they were at work during the period in question. The cost of any benefit premiums is to be borne by the employer.

Corporation of County of Essex (1980), 25 L.A.C. (2d) 283 (Brunner).

RETURN TO UNIT, *see also* SENIORITY

CONTRACT
TERM
In the event an employee is transferred to a non-bargaining unit position, seniority shall be considered unbroken if he *returns* to the status of an employee within one year; if he returns after one year, his seniority upon returning shall be that which he had on the date of transfer.

ARBITRATOR'S
RULING
The right to use seniority to return to the bargaining unit depends on the contractual language. Here, in light of the elaborate job security provisions for bargaining unit employees, the clause does not allow management personnel to use seniority to bump bargaining unit employees in the event of a layoff, but only to retain bargaining unit seniority in the event of a return to the unit.

CBC (1986), 23 L.A.C. (3d) 394 (M.G. Picher).

▼

CONTRACT
TERM
An employee accepting a transfer to a position not covered by the collective agreement shall retain rights and continue to accumulate seniority for a period of 6 months from date of transfer. Thereafter, his rights and accumulated seniority shall be temporarily suspended until such time as he *returns to the bargaining unit*; in such event, only the seniority accumulated while in the bargaining unit shall be taken into consideration when exercising seniority.

ARBITRATOR'S
RULING
Although the collective agreement does not expressly provide for a return to the bargaining unit after 6 months, that right arises by clear implication; since the language provides for retention of seniority rights, without restriction as to their use, a returning supervisor can use retained seniority to bump into the bargaining unit.

B.C. Rail (1985), 20 L.A.C. (3d) 163 (Hope).

▼

CONTRACT
TERM
Where an employee previously in the bargaining unit *re-enters* the bargaining unit, full credit will be given for all seniority to his credit at the time of his departure from the bargaining unit.

ARBITRATOR'S
RULING
Though the employee does not accumulate seniority while outside the unit, he can use the seniority he retains to bump back into the unit.

Atomic Energy (1983), 12 L.A.C. (3d) 252 (Saltman).

▼

CONTRACT
TERM
An hourly employee who transfers to the salaried bargaining unit and is subsequently declared surplus within 3 years shall *return* to the hourly unit and bump the most junior employee whose job he is qualified to perform based on total seniority acquired in both units.

ARBITRATOR'S
RULING
In the absence of clear language to the contrary, an employee may exercise seniority rights within a bargaining unit for employment service outside the unit. Here, the employee is entitled to return, and if there are no junior employees to bump, to recall rights.

Northern Telecom (1983), 9 L.A.C. (3d) 224 (M.G. Picher).

RIGHT

CONTRACT
TERM

All *rights*, benefits, privileges and working conditions which employees now enjoy, receive or possess, which the employer has knowledge of, shall continue to be enjoyed and possessed insofar as they are consistent with this agreement, but may be modified by mutual agreement between the employer and the union.

ARBITRATOR'S
RULING

The introduction of a requirement that employees punch in and out for paid coffee breaks is not an alteration of a right, benefit or privilege, because these relate to something positive which flows from one person to another, and the employer never by any positive act conferred on employees a right, benefit or privilege of not punching in and out at breaks. However, the change does constitute alteration of a working condition. The existence of a working condition does not necessarily imply a positive act on the part of the employer; it is simply a circumstance under which work is to be performed, or a condition under which employees work.

Glades Lodge Ltd. (1988), 1 L.A.C. (4th) 257 (Veniot).

▼

CONTRACT
TERM

All *rights*, benefits, privileges and working conditions which employees enjoy shall be continued, but may be modified by agreement of the parties.

ARBITRATOR'S
RULING

A "right" implies an unfettered claim to something, while a privilege or benefit is an advantage enjoyed by one beyond others. An allowance to smoke is not a privilege, and institution of a no-smoking policy does not violate the collective agreement, where there was always a potential, if not actual, control placed on it. The ability to smoke is also not a working condition, where the practice varies from one location to another within the bargaining unit, and it has simply been licensed to a limited degree.

Board of Education for City of Toronto (1988), 33 L.A.C. (3d) 149 (Knopf).

187

RULES AND REGULATIONS

CONTRACT TERM

The parties having taken notice of the working conditions, plant rules and regulations now in existence, declare them to be acceptable. Any new or amended *rules or regulations* shall be discussed and agreed to between the company and the union before they become effective.

ARBITRATOR'S RULING

"Rules" and "regulations" mean a set of written directives posted to the attention of employees which must be observed in their day-to-day conduct. Unwritten conventions may also be encompassed where, by the usage of a trade or long practice within the workplace, they have become so widely accepted by both management and employees that they have gained the force of a rule or regulation. While the term "working condition" refers to privileges, and not merely rights, which employees have enjoyed on an established basis, a distinction must be drawn between working conditions or rules which arise by a conscious decision and outcomes which have been dictated by circumstances. The fact that the company has had a practice, which was not required by the collective agreement, of filling temporary vacancies, to satisfy production requirements, does not mean that it has become a rule or regulation or a working condition so as to prevent the company from altering it in order to respond to declining production needs.

Rothmans (1983), 12 L.A.C. (3d) 329 (M.G. Picher).

S

SATISFACTORY REASON

CONTRACT
TERM

Seniority rights shall be terminated if the employee is absent from work for 3 consecutive days without a *satisfactory reason.*

ARBITRATOR'S
RULING

Management must exercise its discretion by balancing its interests against those of the employee, and each application for leave of absence must be given fair and proper consideration. Here, the company based its decision on the application of a fixed policy of limiting the number of employees absent within each zone as opposed to the required balancing of interests. In the contemporary industrial context, an employee is assumed to have a life outside and opportunities can occur which constitute a satisfactory reason, especially where the employer is not taken by surprise and has an opportunity to deal with the grievor's absence in advance.

Mack Canada Inc. (1988), 33 L.A.C. (3d) 320 (Kennedy).

SATISFACTORY IN HIS SUPERVISOR'S OPINION

CONTRACT
TERM

To be eligible for sick leave, an employee is required to have a *satisfactory record of attendance in his supervisor's opinion.*

ARBITRATOR'S
RULING

In coming to a conclusion on whether or not an employee's record of attendance is satisfactory, the supervisor does not have to be correct, but he must consider factors relevant to the issue, and act for business reasons. In addition, the supervisor must not discriminate against the employee or single the employee out for special treatment.

Air Canada (1981), 30 L.A.C. (2d) 28 (Burkett).

SCHEDULE

CONTRACT TERM
Exceptional circumstances may arise which, although not covered by the schedule, may, in the judgment of management, warrant a modification of the *schedules*. Such cases will be dealt with as they occur.

ARBITRATOR'S RULING
A modification involves a slight or partial change or moderation; changing employees' schedules from 8-hour to 12-hour shifts is a major change, not a modification. The right to modify the schedule cannot be used as a Trojan horse to take away overtime and other benefits based on the schedule.

Miramichi Pulp and Paper Inc. (1987), 29 L.A.C. (3d) 48 (Stanley).

SCHEDULED

CONTRACT TERM
An employee will be on probation until s(he) has completed 50 *scheduled* days of employment on plant work within a consecutive nine-month period.

ARBITRATOR'S RULING
"Scheduled" means time worked which was planned in advance and assigned compulsorily to particular employees. An employee who is required to work Saturday and Sunday during his probationary period, even if it is not regularly scheduled, is entitled to count such time as "scheduled". This is in accord with the function of a probation period, which is to allow assessment and evaluation.

Burns Meats (1989), 7 L.A.C. (4th) 374 (Bowman).

SCHEDULED TO WORK

CONTRACT TERM
A union official will be paid by the company for time he takes for administration of this agreement for a period of 40 hours per week if he would otherwise have been *scheduled to work* for the company.

ARBITRATOR'S RULING
Term "scheduled to work" applies during plant shutdown, when no other employees are working, since the work the union official is scheduled to do is the administration of the collective agreement, which is not dependent on the presence of employees in the plant.

Massey-Ferguson (1983), 9 L.A.C. (3d) 413 (Brent).

SCHEDULED WORKING DAY

CONTRACT TERM
Where bereavement leave falls on a *scheduled working day* for the employee, he shall be paid a bereavement allowance.

ARBITRATOR'S RULING
Where entitlement to bereavement leave is unrestricted, it is payable regardless whether the individual is on vacation; but where it is restricted to attendance at the funeral on scheduled working days, it is not payable when the employee is on vacation at the time of death.

Rio Algom (1986), 24 L.A.C. (3d) 194 (Tacon).

SCHEDULING

CONTRACT TERM
Seniority shall be followed when *scheduling* overtime.

ARBITRATOR'S RULING
The term "scheduling" signifies a written time-table posted in advance, and is not synonymous with "assigned" or "requested" or "ordered". An obligation to follow seniority where overtime is scheduled cannot apply to unanticipated or emergency overtime, which is usually due to the absence of one or more employees. Scheduled overtime refers to anticipated overtime, and not to overtime which is assigned or distributed on very short notice.

Reid Dominion Packaging (1981), 1 L.A.C. (3d) 314 (Jolliffe).

SCOPE OF HIS EMPLOYMENT

CONTRACT TERM
Where an employee is made party to criminal, civil or quasi-judicial proceedings, by reason of conduct within the *scope of his employment*, the employer agrees to retain and pay counsel the legal fees incurred in defending the employee.

ARBITRATOR'S RULING
Term refers to conduct occurring in the course of employment, or arising out of the employer's enterprise, whether or not it involves an excess of actual authority, or actions which the employer could reasonably be expected to approve.

191

Ottawa-Carleton Treatment Centre (1985), 18 L.A.C. (3d) 350 (Weatherill).

SENIORITY, *see also* LOSS OF SENIORITY

CONTRACT TERM *Seniority* is defined as the length of service (excluding overtime) with the employer in a bargaining unit position. An employee with 9 or more years of continuous service in the employ of the employer is entitled to severance pay based on the number of years of continuous employment.

ARBITRATOR'S RULING "Service" is not synonymous with bargaining unit seniority, but is length of continuous employment with the employer.

Victoria Order of Nurses (1989), 6 L.A.C. (4th) 50 (Easton).

▼

CONTRACT TERM The *seniority* of each employee shall count from the date of employment with the company. An employee's *seniority date* shall be his last hiring date except that, on return to work following a layoff or illness of more than 24 months, his *seniority date* shall be adjusted.

ARBITRATOR'S RULING The seniority of an employee is not broken by a legal strike, where it is not one of the listed events interrupting the accumulation of seniority.

Camco Inc. (1988), 33 L.A.C. (3d) 144 (Foisy).

▼

CONTRACT TERM *Seniority* shall be determined by an employee's length of continuous service in the company. Promotions, demotions and transfers will be made on the basis of seniority provided the senior employee has the necessary ability, etc. to perform the job.

ARBITRATOR'S RULING Seniority is a collective bargaining concept, and its application is therefore restricted to members of the bargaining unit. For the purposes of competition for a job posting, seniority does not accumulate while an employee is outside the bargaining unit unless the collective agreement so provides, but in the absence of language to the contrary, seniority accumulated while in the bargaining unit will not be lost if the employee leaves and later returns.

Domtar Inc. (1987), 30 L.A.C. (3d) 115 (Haefling).

▼

CONTRACT
TERM

Employees whenever mentioned in the agreement shall not be deemed to include foremen; *seniority* shall be broken by resignation, discharge, or long-term sickness or disability.

ARBITRATOR'S
RULING

Clause entitles returning supervisor to retain bargaining unit seniority but not to accumulate seniority while a foreman.

Pacific Truck (1986), 24 L.A.C. (3d) 299 (Munroe).

▼

CONTRACT
TERM

In the event an employee is transferred to a non-bargaining unit position, *seniority* shall be considered unbroken if he *returns* to the status of an employee within one year; if he returns after one year, his seniority upon returning shall be that which he had on the date of transfer.

ARBITRATOR'S
RULING

The right to use seniority to return to the bargaining unit depends on the contractual language. Here, in light of the elaborate job security provisions for bargaining unit employees, the clause does not allow management personnel to use seniority to bump bargaining unit employees in the event of a layoff, but only to retain bargaining unit seniority in the event of a return to the unit.

CBC (1986), 23 L.A.C. (3d) 394 (M.G. Picher).

▼

CONTRACT
TERM

An employee accepting a transfer to a position not covered by the collective agreement shall retain rights and continue to accumulate *seniority* for a period of 6 months from date of transfer. Thereafter, his rights and accumulated seniority shall be temporarily suspended until such time as he *returns to the bargaining unit*; in such event, only the seniority accumulated while in the bargaining unit shall be taken into consideration when exercising seniority.

ARBITRATOR'S
RULING

Although the collective agreement does not expressly provide for a return to the bargaining unit after 6 months, that right arises by clear implication; since the language provides for retention of seniority rights, without restriction as to their use, a returning supervisor can use retained seniority to bump into the bargaining unit.

B.C. Rail (1985), 20 L.A.C. (3d) 163 (Hope).

▼

CONTRACT
TERM

Where an employee previously in the bargaining unit *re-enters* the bargaining unit, full credit will be given for all *seniority* to his credit at the time of his departure from the bargaining unit.

ARBITRATOR'S
RULING

Though the employee does not accumulate seniority while outside the unit, he can use the seniority he retains to bump back into the unit.

Atomic Energy (1983), 12 L.A.C. (3d) 252 (Saltman).

▼

CONTRACT
TERM

An hourly employee who transfers to the salaried bargaining unit and is subsequently declared surplus within 3 years shall *return* to the hourly unit and bump the most junior employee whose job he is qualified to perform based on total *seniority* acquired in both units.

ARBITRATOR'S
RULING

In the absence of clear language to the contrary, an employee may exercise seniority rights within a bargaining unit for employment service outside the unit. Here, the employee is entitled to return, and if there are no junior employees to bump, to recall rights.

Northern Telecom (1983), 9 L.A.C. (3d) 224 (M.G. Picher).

▼

CONTRACT
TERM

Employees who leave the bargaining unit to work in a staff position will maintain but not accumulate their *seniority* (length of service with the company).

ARBITRATOR'S
RULING

Given the definition of "seniority" in the collective agreement, management who return to the bargaining unit can use their seniority to bump into the unit, and are not restricted to using their seniority only after they have been transferred into the unit.

Windsor Machine Co. (1982), 4 L.A.C. (3d) 331 (Munroe).

▼

CONTRACT
TERM

Maternity leave up to 6 months will be granted upon request. *Seniority* is based on continuous *service*.

ARBITRATOR'S Since "service" means "employment", temporary
RULING absences such as maternity leave do not cause a
break in service, and seniority continues to accumulate.

Toronto Star (1981), 30 L.A.C. (2d) 267 (Weatherill).

SENIORITY LIST

CONTRACT A *seniority list* shall be completed based on the date
TERM each employee last commenced continuous employment with the company.

ARBITRATOR'S Where employees commence employment on the
RULING same date, the seniority ranking cannot be established by alphabetical order or drawing of lots, but
must be done on a rational basis (e.g. by taking into
account previous part-time employment with the
company).

Ellenzweig Bakery (1985), 20 L.A.C. (3d) 407
(Weatherill).

SENIORITY WITH ABILITY, *see* SKILL AND ABILITY

SERVICE, *see also* CONTINUOUS SERVICE

CONTRACT Seniority is defined as the length of service (ex-
TERM cluding overtime) with the employer in a bargaining unit position. An employee with 9 or more years
of continuous *service* in the employ of the employer
is entitled to severance pay based on the number
of years of continuous employment.

ARBITRATOR'S "Service" is not synonymous with bargaining unit
RULING seniority, but is length of continuous employment
with the employer.

Victoria Order of Nurses (1989), 6 L.A.C. (4th) 50
(Easton).

▼

CONTRACT Employees who have completed 6 months' *service*
TERM shall be entitled to one week's vacation, to 2 weeks'
vacation after 1 year's *service*, etc.

ARBITRATOR'S "Service" includes time spent on disability leave,
RULING since vacation entitlement based on length of service should not be affected by involuntary absences, unless there is clear language to the contrary
in the collective agreement.

195

Rahey's Supermarket (1989), 3 L.A.C. (4th) 311 (MacDonald).

▼

CONTRACT
TERM

Payment for cumulative sick leave credits shall be subject to the following conditions: upon death or termination of employment after 5 years of *service*, an employee or her representative shall be entitled to an amount equal to 50% of her accumulated sick leave credits.

ARBITRATOR'S
RULING

Part-time or casual employment is to be counted as "service" for the purposes of payout of unused sick leave, since there is no indication that service is to be calculated only on the basis of full-time service.

Regional Municipality of Niagara (1988), 2 L.A.C. (4th) 314 (Thorne).

▼

CONTRACT
TERM

Employees with less than one year's *service* at date of vacation shall be paid 6% of gross earnings; employees with one year's *service* or more shall have 3 weeks' paid vacation.

ARBITRATOR'S
RULING

Service continues to accrue during layoff since periods of layoff do not sever employment so long as recall rights are retained. There is no indication in the language that vacation entitlement is linked to actual performance of work, active employment, or working a specific number of hours or days.

Ron May Pontiac GMC Ltd. (1988), 33 L.A.C. (3d) 129 (MacDougall).

▼

CONTRACT
TERM

Vacation entitlement is based on years of *service*.

ARBITRATOR'S
RULING

Term includes service with previous employer where the business is sold or transferred; otherwise, vacation entitlement would be less than that provided under employment standards legislation, which counts service with the previous employer in calculating minimum vacation entitlement on sale of a business.

Middlesex-London District Health Unit (1984), 16 L.A.C. (3d) 98 (Saltman).

▼

CONTRACT TERM Sabbatical leave follows six years' *service* from commencement of employment.

ARBITRATOR'S RULING In the case of a bargaining unit employee who has spent some time outside the unit, and then transferred back, the term "service" includes all service with the employer, including service outside the unit.

Ryerson Polytechnical Institute (1980), 27 L.A.C. (2d) 378 (MacDowell).

▼

CONTRACT TERM Vacations shall be based on years of *service*.

ARBITRATOR'S RULING Service is not interrupted by period on layoff.

Sola Basic (1976), 11 L.A.C. (2d) 328 (Beck).

SEVERANCE PAY

CONTRACT TERM In the event the company ceases operations and lays off employees, the employees so displaced shall receive a *severance allowance* of one week's pay for each year of service to a maximum of 10 weeks. Seniority shall terminate and an employee shall cease to be employed by the company when he is off work for a continuous period of 24 months or the length of employee's seniority, whichever is shorter.

ARBITRATOR'S RULING Severance denotes a complete separation of the employment relationship. Employees laid off but retaining recall rights are not entitled to a severance allowance.

Max Factor Canada Ltd. (1988), 33 L.A.C. (3d) 274 (Simmons).

SEXUAL HARASSMENT

CONTRACT TERM There shall be no harassment by reason of sex.

ARBITRATOR'S RULING Sexual harassment runs the gamut from overt gender-based activity, such as coerced intercourse, to unsolicited physical contact, to persistent propositions, to more subtle conduct such as gender-based insults and taunting which may reasonably be perceived to create a negative psychological and emotional work environment.

Canada Post (1983), 11 L.A.C. (3d) 13 (Norman).

SHIFT

CONTRACT TERM The company shall pay time and a half for all hours an employee is required to work over 8 a day, and double time for all work performed on each *shift* on a Saturday.

ARBITRATOR'S RULING A "shift" is a pre-determined period of time that would ordinarily constitute a day's work. Employees who work an extra three hours overtime at the end of a shift from midnight Friday are not entitled to the Saturday premium, since the three hours are an extension of the Friday shift, and are not a separate shift.

Dominion Bridge Co. Ltd. (1980), 27 L.A.C. (2d) 399 (Adams).

SICKNESS/SICK LEAVE/SICK LEAVE BENEFITS

CONTRACT TERM Upon proof that an employee has become totally disabled, the company will pay a weekly indemnity benefit; totally disabled means wholly or continuously disabled by *sickness* or an accidental bodily injury which prevents one from working for remuneration or profit.

ARBITRATOR'S RULING An employee who is unable to work the night shift due to stress reaction, identified and confirmed by physicians, suffers from a permanent disability and is entitled to disability protection in the agreement until he can bump into an available day job.

Hickeson-Lang Supply Co. (1988), 34 L.A.C. (3d) 62 (Mitchnick).

▼

CONTRACT TERM Employees who are totally disabled are entitled to *sick pay benefit* for the purposes of sick pay; totally disabled means a state of bodily injury or disease which prevents the employee from performing the regular duties of the occupation.

ARBITRATOR'S RULING Participation in an *in vitro* fertilization program involving medical and surgical treatment qualifies an employee for sick leave benefits, since the grievor's absence results from an underlying diseased condition.

Hamilton Civic Hospitals (1988), 32 L.A.C. (3d) 284 (Saltman).

▼

CONTRACT TERM
Sick pay benefits shall be paid if an employee is totally disabled; totally disabled means an employee's inability to perform the regular duties pertaining to her occupation due to illness or injury.

ARBITRATOR'S RULING
Participation in an *in vitro* fertilization program, involving medical and surgical procedures to remedy infertility, entitles an employee to short-term sick leave benefits, because it is a recognized medical treatment for a pre-existing abnormal condition, which causes physical incapacity. Infertility itself qualifies as an illness or disease according to worldwide medical standards.

Metropolitan General Hospital (1987), 32 L.A.C. (3d) 10 (H.D. Brown).

▼

CONTRACT TERM
Weekly indemnity insurance benefits include sickness and accident insurance up to 66-2/3% of basic weekly earnings, for a maximum period of 32 weeks on the fourth day of *sickness*, on the first day for hospitalization or accident.

ARBITRATOR'S RULING
An accident is an injury that is the fortuitous and unexpected result of natural causes; an injury to the back while bending over to put on one's socks qualifies as an accident. By contrast, sickness is a disability arising from the operation of natural causes such as old age, congenital or insidious disease, or the natural progression of some constitutional, physical or mental defect.

Long Manufacturing (1987), 30 L.A.C. (3d) 156 (Swan).

▼

CONTRACT TERM
A teacher shall be granted 20 days' [sick] leave per teaching year to a maximum of 75 days.

ARBITRATOR'S RULING
"Sickness" means a condition of ill health preventing an employee from working. While pregnancy itself is not an illness, and a normal pregnancy does not entitle an employee to sick leave, inability to work due to or consequential upon pregnancy does entitle an employee to sick leave, and this includes disability due to pain and discomfort following a caesarean birth.

199

Agassiz School Division No. 13 (1987), 28 L.A.C. (3d) 420 (Freedman).

▼

CONTRACT TERM

Employees are entitled to sick leave pay where they are absent from work by virtue of being *sick* or disabled.

ARBITRATOR'S RULING

An employee may be so affected by the alcoholism of a spouse as to become herself sick or disabled; indeed, the condition of co-alcoholism is recognized as a disease entitling the spouse of an alcoholic to participation in rehabilitation and treatment programs and financial assistance from the employer.

South Sask. Hospital Centre (1986), 25 L.A.C. (3d) 361 (Allbright).

▼

CONTRACT TERM

Disability benefits shall be paid if an employee is unable to work because of accident or *sickness*.

ARBITRATOR'S RULING

Inability to work due to a particular sensitivity to cigarette smoke is a sickness entitling an employee to disability benefits.

De Havilland Aircraft (1986), 25 L.A.C. (3d) 249 (Davis).

▼

CONTRACT TERM

The company shall provide employees with *sick leave benefits*.

ARBITRATOR'S RULING

Clause covers pregnancy-related illness, i.e. a pre-existing back condition aggravated by pregnancy.

Cominco (1986), 24 L.A.C. (3d) 32 (Chertkow).

▼

CONTRACT TERM

Sick leave with full salary will be granted for the purpose of obtaining necessary medical treatment.

ARBITRATOR'S RULING

Necessary medical treatment means treatment that is necessary for the health of the employee, and does not include voluntary treatment to induce ovulation for fertility purposes.

Fritze (1985), 19 L.A.C. (3d) 353 (Elliott).

▼

CONTRACT TERM

The company agrees to provide sick benefits, provided that no *sick leave pay* shall be paid for days paid by the Workers' Compensation Board.

ARBITRATOR'S RULING
Attendance at work is not a condition precedent to receiving benefits under the collective agreement unless the language so provides. Accordingly, this language does not restrict the accumulation of sick pay credits during absence on workers' compensation.
Forsyth (1984), 17 L.A.C. (3d) 257 (Hope).

▼

CONTRACT TERM
Teachers are entitled to 20 days' annual sick pay in case of *sickness*.

ARBITRATOR'S RULING
While sickness includes a pre-existing weakness or genetic defect which, when combined with pregnancy, produces a disability, it does not include a pre-existing condition which creates a risk of illness (in this case, a lack of immunity to rubella causing the teacher to stay away from school during the early stages of pregnancy).
Boards of Education (1983), 12 L.A.C. (3d) 309 (Smith).

▼

CONTRACT TERM
Employees shall receive 11 statutory holidays. Vacation shall be based on years of continuous service. *Sick leave credits* shall accumulate based on months or years worked.

ARBITRATOR'S RULING
Some benefits accrue by virtue of employment, others depend on the employee's presence at the workplace and performance of work. It all depends on the agreement. Here, in the absence of restrictions, employees absent from work because of a compensable disability are entitled to holiday pay and vacations, since continuous service is synonymous with seniority, but sick leave credits do not accumulate since they are based on months or years worked.
City of Trail (1983), 10 L.A.C. (3d) 251 (Munroe).

▼

CONTRACT TERM
Employees are entitled to *sick leave*.

ARBITRATOR'S RULING
While pregnancy itself is not an illness, a pregnant employee is entitled to sick leave where she is unable to work due to back pain arising from or exacerbated by pregnancy. The employer's right to require an employee to commence maternity leave, pursuant to employment standards legislation, does not oust the employee's entitlement to sick leave.

Simon Fraser University (1983), 8 L.A.C. (3d) 395 (Hope).

▼

CONTRACT TERM
For the purposes of sickness benefits, an employee will be considered disabled if he is unable to perform the duties of his employment as a result of *non-occupational sickness* or accident and is under the care of a licensed physician.

ARBITRATOR'S RULING
Alcoholism, with its related mental and physical symptoms, is a non-occupational sickness or accident, and an employee is therefore entitled to sick pay while undergoing treatment for alcoholism.
American Can (1981), 3 L.A.C. (3d) 283 (Somjen).

▼

CONTRACT TERM
Pay for *sick leave* is for the sole and only purpose of protecting the employee against loss of regular income when she is legitimately ill and unable to work. An employee required to work on a designated holiday shall be paid at time and a half her regular straight time rate of pay for all hours worked on such holiday, and will receive in addition a lieu day off at her regular straight time rate of pay.

ARBITRATOR'S RULING
An employee who is scheduled to work on a statutory holiday but is unable to do so because of *bona fide* illness is entitled to both holiday and sick pay, since both are earned benefits. Had she worked on the holiday, the employee would have been entitled to both payments, which are for separate purposes, and are not duplications. Once scheduled to work a statutory holiday, entitlement to holiday pay becomes part of an employee's regular income since the employee is expected to attend work at that time.
North York General Hospital (1980), 27 L.A.C. (2d) 64 (Shime).

SKILL AND ABILITY

EDITORS' NOTE
Three types of clauses are to be found: (1) "required ability" clauses, under which seniority governs provided that the employee can perform the job; (2) "relatively equal" clauses, under which seniority prevails only if the senior employee is relatively equal in ability to junior contestants; and (3) "hybrid clauses", which combine seniority with ability without indicating the weight to be given to each factor.]

CONTRACT TERM
Seniority shall govern in all cases of promotions, transfers and demotions when the *qualifications and ability* of the applicants concerned are *equal.*

ARBITRATOR'S RULING
The word "equal" is not an invitation to consider insignificant differences between applicants, but to determine whether one employee is more qualified than another by a "substantial and demonstrable margin", having regard to the particular job in question.

Board of School Trustees, School District #88 (Terrace) (1989), 9 L.A.C. (4th) 432 (Kelleher).

▼

CONTRACT TERM
Employees shall be selected for positions on the basis of their *skill, ability, experience and qualifications.* When these factors are *relatively equal* amongst the employees considered, seniority shall govern.

ARBITRATOR'S RULING
Relative equality is to be determined having regard to the nature of the job to be done. The kind of difference between candidates which can defeat seniority rights must not be a slight one, but rather be composed of a substantial and demonstrable margin, in areas relevant to the performance of the job in question.

Ottawa Civic Hospital (1989), 9 L.A.C. (4th) 348 (Mitchnick).

▼

CONTRACT TERM
In filling vacancies, a current regular full-time or regular part-time employee having the required *qualifications, experience, skill and ability* to do the work will be given *first consideration* over an external applicant.

ARBITRATOR'S RULING
"First consideration" means preference; an employee with the required qualifications, experience, skill and ability goes to the top of the list and is awarded the job in question, even if an external applicant is demonstrably superior.

Capital Regional District (1989), 8 L.A.C. (4th) 307 (Munroe).

▼

CONTRACT TERM
Employees shall be selected for positions on the basis of their *skill, ability, experience and qualifications*. Where these factors are *relatively equal*, seniority shall govern provided the successful applicant is qualified to perform the available work within an appropriate familiarization period.

ARBITRATOR'S RULING
While they are not distinct, and there is considerable overlap, "skill" is competence in particular tasks; "qualifications" refers to possession of necessary education, training and certification; "abilities" relates to overall qualities of an employee with respect to the work to be done; and "experience" refers to the breadth and length of actual experience. Relative equality involves a determination of whether one employee is more qualified than another by a substantial and demonstrable margin in relation to the relevant circumstances. The employer cannot seize on minor differences between candidates to defeat the application of seniority.

Wellesley Hospital (1989), 5 L.A.C. (4th) 55 (Weatherill)

▼

CONTRACT TERM
In making promotions, transfers and appointments, ability and qualifications are the primary considerations; where *ability and qualifications* are adjudged to be *substantially equal*, seniority shall be the determining factor.

ARBITRATOR'S RULING
The term "substantially equal" is synonymous with relative equality, and requires that a junior applicant's abilities and qualifications must exceed those of the senior applicant "by a substantial and demonstrable margin". There must be a discernible, material difference around which a reasonable and objective employer might pivot his decision. Moreover, reliance on an interview to the exclusion of past experience is improper.

Workers' Compensation Board of British Columbia (1989), 4 L.A.C. (4th) 141 (Hope).

▼

CONTRACT TERM
When selecting an applicant for a regular vacancy or newly created position, seniority, *qualifications, ability, service requirements and acceptable performance* will be considered. Seniority shall be the governing factor in the case of *equally rated* applicants.

ARBITRATOR'S RULING

"Equally rated" is a narrower concept than "relatively equal", but still does not require that there be mathematical equality in point scores between competing applicants for a job. However, a 5.5 point difference in scores between two applicants, out of a possible score of 90, is sufficiently significant to reject the assertion that they are equally rated.

Manitoba Telephone System (1988), 2 L.A.C. (4th) 136 (Bowman).

▼

CONTRACT TERM

In the filling of vacancies, new positions, transfers or promotions, appointments shall be made to the employee with the required *qualifications, and level of competency and efficiency,* and where such requirements are *equal,* seniority shall be the determining factor.

ARBITRATOR'S RULING

Under this clause, the junior applicant must be better by a substantial and demonstrable margin; there must be a discernible, material difference. Management must reach a decision fairly, on the basis of relevant factors.

Princeton General Hospital (1987), 32 L.A.C. (3d) 35 (Hope).

▼

CONTRACT TERM

In making promotions, transfers, and demotions the *skill, knowledge and work record* of the employee shall be the primary considerations. Where two or more applicants are capable of fulfilling the duties of the position and the aforesaid qualifications are otherwise *comparable,* seniority or years of experience shall be determining factors.

ARBITRATOR'S RULING

Comparability is defined as "able to be compared, capable of comparison, worthy of comparison", while "equal" denotes possessing a like degree of a quality, on the same level of ability. Relative equality is therefore a higher test than comparability between candidates. A junior employee must be superior to a senior one by a "clear and demonstrable margin".

Board of School Trustees, School District No. 39 (1987), 30 L.A.C. (3d) 257 (Thompson).

▼

CONTRACT TERM	On promotion and transfer, where *skill, capabilities and required qualifications* are *relatively equal*, seniority shall be the determining factor.
ARBITRATOR'S RULING	Term allows employer to rely on disciplinary notations that identify shortcomings related to the criteria for selection.

Prince George Senior Citizens Housing Society (1987), 27 L.A.C. (3d) 410 (Kelleher).

▼

CONTRACT TERM	Appointments to positions shall be filled on the basis of *seniority with ability*.
ARBITRATOR'S RULING	Under this clause, the senior employee is entitled to the job provided only that he has the required ability; it does not refer to "seniority *and* ability", and accordingly is not a "hybrid clause" (which would require that both be taken into account).

C.A.S. Cape Breton (1987), 27 L.A.C. (3d) 289 (Outhouse).

▼

CONTRACT TERM	Where it is the opinion of the employer that two or more applicants for a vacant position are *qualified* and of *equal merit*, preference shall be given to the senior applicant.
ARBITRATOR'S RULING	The employer is obliged to assess qualifications and abilities fairly and, while the employer has considerable discretion, the decision must not be unreasonable.

N.S. Civil Service Commission (1986), 25 L.A.C. (3d) 404 (Outhouse).

▼

CONTRACT TERM	Appointments will be made on the basis of *merit, efficiency and seniority*.
ARBITRATOR'S RULING	This is a "hybrid" clause, which requires that all factors be weighed and considered; while it does not require that seniority govern where the senior employee has "sufficient ability" to do the job, it also does not allow the employer to consider seniority only where an assessment of the "relative ability" of employees is inconclusive.

B.C. Hydro (1985), 21 L.A.C. (3d) 422 (Munroe).

▼

CONTRACT TERM — In making promotions, transfers or filling vacancies, the *skill, knowledge and efficiency* of the employees concerned shall be the primary consideration and where such *qualifications* are *relatively equal*, seniority shall be the determining factor.

ARBITRATOR'S RULING — Previous experience in the same or a similar job shows demonstrated ability, and may be taken into account in assessing competing employees. Relative equality exists unless the difference is substantial and demonstrable; there must be a discernible, material difference, not just a minor one.

Board of School Trustees, District 68 (1985), 19 L.A.C. (3d) 176 (Germaine).

▼

CONTRACT TERM — Appointments will be made on the basis of *merit, efficiency and seniority.*

ARBITRATOR'S RULING — This is a "hybrid" clause; it does not permit the employer to compare competing candidates before applying seniority (i.e. a contest or "relatively equal" clause), nor does it require the employer to award the position to the senior candidate provided he or she has sufficient ability to do the job (i.e. a "sufficient ability" clause); a hybrid clause requires the employer to give reasonable consideration to all factors, and to make a decision that is honest, reasonable and, according to some arbitrators, correct. All relevant considerations must be taken into account and the decision must not be based on improper factors.

B.C. Hydro (1983), 10 L.A.C. (3d) 56 (Germaine).

▼

CONTRACT TERM — Where *skills, competence, efficiency and qualifications* are *relatively equal*, seniority shall be the directing factor.

ARBITRATOR'S RULING — "Relative equality" means approximate equality; thus, minor differences cannot defeat the application of seniority.

Elisabeth Bruyere Health Centre (1982), 6 L.A.C. (3d) 119 (Saltman).

▼

CONTRACT TERM

In making staff changes, transfers or promotions, where *efficiency, work history and qualifications* are judged to be *equal*, seniority shall be the determining factor.

ARBITRATOR'S RULING

Absolute equality is a futile concept. Applicants are equal unless there is a discernible, material difference around which a reasonable and objective employer might pivot his decision.

University of British Columbia (1982), 5 L.A.C. (3d) 69 (Munroe).

▼

CONTRACT TERM

On layoff and recall seniority shall be given preference where *abilities, etc.* are *relatively equal* in the opinion of management.

ARBITRATOR'S RULING

A "relatively equal" clause involves a competition among employees; in these circumstances, employees will be considered relatively equal unless one employee is better qualified by a substantial or demonstrable margin. Management's decision must be *bona fide*, and not be arbitrary, discriminatory or unreasonable. Where the clause does not refer to the "opinion of management", the decision must not only be reasonable; it must be correct.

British Leaf Tobacco (1981), 3 L.A.C. (3d) 235 (Kennedy).

▼

CONTRACT TERM

The employer undertakes to observe *seniority* with regard to transfers, so far as it is practicable to do so, *as well as relative efficiency and suitability.*

ARBITRATOR'S RULING

Under this hybrid clause, the employer can take into account the relative absenteeism and work experience of applicants. The burden is on the employer to show why ability is given greater weight than seniority, especially where the job is not a complex one.

Wellesley Hospital (1981), 2 L.A.C. (3d) 193 (Kennedy).

▼

CONTRACT TERM

On promotion or transfer, where the employer determines that the *qualifications* for the position are *relatively equal* between the applicants, seniority shall be the governing factor.

ARBITRATOR'S RULING
Under this clause, the arbitrator is not bound by the employer's assessment, and need pay no special deference to the employer's views.

University of Toronto (1981), 30 L.A.C. (2d) 187 (Palmer).

▼

CONTRACT TERM
Vacancies will be filled on the basis of *ability, skill and experience*. When these factors are *relatively equal*, the employee with the greatest seniority will be given preference.

ARBITRATOR'S RULING
The successful candidate must have substantially superior ability. The employer must determine whether there is a substantial and demonstrable margin of difference in ability, skill and experience before awarding the job to a less senior candidate. The decision must be reasonable, and the procedures must be fair and unbiased.

Northern Telecom Ltd. (1980), 25 L.A.C. (2d) 379 (Fraser).

▼

CONTRACT TERM
Recommendations for all promotions shall be based on *seniority, efficiency and the ability to perform.*

ARBITRATOR'S RULING
This is a "hybrid" clause requiring that the employer give reasonable consideration to all factors, and weigh them prior to making a decision.

City of Stratford (1980), 25 L.A.C. (2d) 170 (Shime).

SPECIFIED CLOTHING

CONTRACT TERM
A clothing maintenance allowance will be paid if the employer requires an employee to supply and/or maintain *specified clothing* in place of a uniform that would otherwise be supplied and maintained.

ARBITRATOR'S RULING
A dress code does not constitute the establishment of "specified clothing", so as to attract a uniform allowance, where it does not specify what staff can wear, but is designed simply to ensure that employees are neat, clean and tidy. Only when a dress code extends beyond a minimum standard of dress and serves some productive purpose of the employer does it attract a uniform allowance.

Green Memorial Home Society (1982), 4 L.A.C. (3d) 438 (Ladner).

209

SPOUSE, *see also* BEREAVEMENT LEAVE

CONTRACT
TERM
It is agreed that there will be no discrimination by either party on the basis of sexual orientation in relation to salary or fringe benefits. *Spouse* designates a husband or wife in law or in common law.

ARBITRATOR'S
RULING
The restriction of certain fringe benefits (free tuition, bereavement leave) to partners of the opposite sex does not constitute discrimination on the basis of sexual orientation, since even the *Human Rights Code*, which prohibits sexual orientation discrimination, defines spouse to mean, not a same-sex partner, but a person of the opposite sex who is either married or living in a common law relationship.
Carleton University (1988), 35 L.A.C. (3d) 96 (Wright).

▼

CONTRACT
TERM
Bereavement leave with pay shall be available in the event of the critical illness or death of any of the following relatives of the employee or his *spouse*, child, etc.

ARBITRATOR'S
RULING
The clause covers not just blood relationships but relationships through marriage, including a spouse's stepchild, where there has been a real life relationship.
Southern Alberta School Authorities Assn. (1981), 5 L.A.C. (3d) 351 (Mason).

STAFF CHANGE

CONTRACT
TERM
In making *staff changes,* transfers, or promotions, appointment shall be made of applicants having the required qualifications and where qualifications are equal, seniority shall be the governing factor. Management rights shall not be exercised in an arbitrary or discriminatory manner.

ARBITRATOR'S
RULING
Under this agreement, transfer involves a move outside the bargaining unit, or to another classification, while promotion constitutes either an advancement within a classification or a move to a higher classification. "Staff change" is a broad concept, and includes a reassignment of employees within the same classification to different locations. The employer's decision to make a staff change by reassigning two workers away from their usual stations is arbitrary where it is done without explanation or advance consultation.

Metropolitan Toronto Zoo (1989), 4 L.A.C. (4th) 46 (Swan).

STANDARD WORK WEEK

CONTRACT TERM
: The *standard work week* shall consist of 40 hours per week comprised of 5 eight-hour days.

ARBITRATOR'S RULING
: "Week" may mean a calendar week, Sunday to Saturday, or a period of 7 consecutive days; the reference to hours, rather than particular calendar days, indicates a consecutive day week. The employer violates the agreement when it denies overtime to employees working a continental workweek (7 days on, 2 days off), if they do not work more than 5 days in a calendar week.

Sunny Orange Ltd. (1981), 1 L.A.C. (3d) 381 (McLaren).

STAND-BY PAY

CONTRACT TERM
: *Stand-by pay* is payable (1/2 hour's pay for 4 hours on stand-by) when an employee is designated to be immediately available to return to work during a period he is not on regular duty. Call-back pay is payable (at the overtime rate) when an employee is called back to work for a period in excess of 2 hours.

ARBITRATOR'S RULING
: Stand-by pay and call-back pay are both payable, and pyramiding of benefits is not involved, since the purpose of stand-by pay is to compensate an employee for the inconvenience of arranging his life to be able to respond to a call-back, whereas the purpose of call-back pay is to compensate the employee for the actual work done once the employee is called back.

Crown in Right of Alberta (1986), 25 L.A.C. (3d) 276 (Elliott).

START OF OPERATIONS, *see also* HOLIDAY PAY

CONTRACT TERM
: An employee will be entitled to payment for specified holidays only if he or she has completed the probationary period and attends for the declared working day immediately preceding the holiday and reports back at the *start of operations* immediately following the holiday.

211

ARBITRATOR'S RULING   Exact performance is required, subject to the rule that "minute and unimportant deviations" from exact compliance will be ignored. Although the employer was prepared to excuse lateness of up to 5 minutes, as constituting substantial performance, lateness for longer periods disentitles employees to holiday pay.

Patons & Baldwins (Canada) Ltd. (1980), 25 L.A.C. (2d) 332 (Brunner).

STATUTORY HOLIDAY, *see also* HOLIDAY PAY

CONTRACT TERM   Any employee required to work on a day observed by the company as a *statutory holiday* shall be paid at double time in addition to his regular holiday pay.

ARBITRATOR'S RULING   Term includes holidays set out in the collective agreement even though they are in addition to those required by labour standards legislation since they are observed as holidays by the company.

Dunbar Aluminum (1981), 2 L.A.C. (3d) 261 (H.D. Brown).

STRIKE

CONTRACT TERM   It is agreed that there shall be no *strike*, lockout or other similar interruption of work during the period of the agreement.

ARBITRATOR'S RULING   The concerted refusal of employees to work overtime, albeit voluntary, as a result of the banning of overtime by the union during layoffs, constitutes a strike.

MacMillan Bathurst Inc. (1988), 1 L.A.C. (4th) 207 (E.B. Jolliffe).

SUBJECT TO DISCHARGE

CONTRACT TERM   Possession of alcoholic beverages while on duty ... 1st offence, *subject to discharge*.

ARBITRATOR'S RULING   This clause does not contain a specific penalty within the meaning of labour legislation that empowers an arbitrator to modify penalties where the collective agreement does not contain a specific penalty for the infraction.

Concrete Supplies of Windsor Inc. (1984), 14 L.A.C. (3d) 1 (Barton).

EDITORS' NOTE Section 45(9) of the Ontario *Labour Relations Act* has been amended, and no longer precludes an arbitrator from substituting a lesser penalty simply because the collective agreement contains a specific penalty for the infraction.

SUBSTANTIALLY EQUAL, see also RELATIVELY EQUAL

CONTRACT TERM In making promotions, transfers and appointments, ability and qualifications are the primary considerations; where ability and qualifications are adjudged to be *substantially equal*, seniority shall be the determining factor.

ARBITRATOR'S RULING The term "substantially equal" is synonymous with relative equality, and requires that a junior applicant's abilities and qualifications must exceed those of the senior applicant "by a substantial and demonstrable margin". There must be a discernible, material difference around which a reasonable and objective employer might pivot his decision. Moreover, reliance on an interview to the exclusion of past experience is improper.

Workers' Compensation Board of British Columbia (1989), 4 L.A.C. (4th) 141 (Hope).

SUITABILITY, see also PROBATION

CONTRACT TERM A probationary employee may be rejected for just cause. The test of just cause for rejection shall be *suitability* for continued employment.

ARBITRATOR'S RULING An employer must justify termination of a probationary employee albeit according to a lesser standard of cause. Where termination is for "unsuitability", the employer must show (1) legitimate standards of work performance; (2) communication of standards to the employee, and proper and ample direction; (3) adequate opportunity for the employee to meet the standards; (4) proper evaluation by employer; (5) failure to meet standards for no apparent reason; and (6) absence of unreasonable or discriminatory acts.

Government Employee Relations Bureau (1984), 15 L.A.C. (3d) 177 (Larson).

213

SUMMARY DISMISSAL

CONTRACT TERM
The employer shall have the right to *summary dismissal* or discharge of employees for specified serious offences; in such cases, an arbitrator shall not substitute any other penalty for that of discharge.

ARBITRATOR'S RULING
Term means that the employer can dismiss without notice, not that the employer must dismiss without delay.

Becker's Milk (1978), 20 L.A.C. (2d) 1 (Weatherill).

T

T-4 EARNINGS

CONTRACT
TERM

Employees will receive vacation pay equal to the greater of 4% of their *T-4 earnings* in the preceding calendar year or 96 hours' pay.

ARBITRATOR'S
RULING

Term includes vacation pay and holiday pay received in the previous year since these payments are included in the T-4 forms submitted by the company to Revenue Canada.

Canso Seafoods Ltd. (1984), 16 L.A.C. (3d) 253 (Kelly).

TECHNOLOGICAL CHANGE

CONTRACT
TERM

No regular employees who attain 2 years of regular service will lose their employment as a result of *technological change.*

ARBITRATOR'S
RULING

Relocation to another geographical area, made necessary by declining demand, constitutes a loss of employment, triggering the employment guarantee, but the relocation must be due to a technological change, and here it was not, since closure of the employer's office was due to economic reasons, i.e. failure to achieve growth.

British Columbia Telephone Co. (1989), 7 L.A.C. (4th) 75 (Kelleher).

▼

CONTRACT
TERM

Technological change: no employee will be laid off or suffer a reduction in salary because of the introduction of new or modified equipment and/or associated changes in methods of operation.

ARBITRATOR'S
RULING

Although there is no definition in the agreement, the *Canada Labour Code* defines technological change as the introduction of equipment "of a different nature or kind than previously utilized". The new or modified equipment must encompass a change in technology. Otherwise, the introduction of every updated piece of equipment of essentially the same technology would trigger the technological change provisions. Here, the technology of the Betacam is substantially similar to its predecessors. The introduction of electronic portable camera-recorder units by the CBC, to replace the combined use of portable electronic cameras and videotape recorder units, represents the improvement of existing technology and updating of equipment and is therefore not technological change for the purposes of the agreement.

Canadian Broadcasting Corp. (1988), 34 L.A.C. (3d) 140 (P.C. Picher).

▼

CONTRACT
TERM

Six months' notice is required before the introduction of *new methods, new equipment or organization* which will result in regular personnel becoming redundant.

ARBITRATOR'S
RULING

Technological change implies the introduction of a new approach which will achieve continued performance of the work in a more efficient manner resulting in a reduction of the number of employees required to perform the same work. It would not ordinarily include a reduction of the work or the workforce, or a closure of all or part of an operation, in response to reduced market demand and reduced revenues.

B.C. Hydro (1983), 10 L.A.C. (3d) 76 (Hope).

▼

CONTRACT
TERM

Piece rates will be maintained unless there is a *measurable change* because of new *methods*, etc.

ARBITRATOR'S
RULING

A new method includes a change in the order or sequence in which tasks or functions of an assembly operation are performed; a measurable change occurs where less time is required to perform the operation.

Westclox (1982), 3 L.A.C. (3d) 68 (Beatty).

▼

CONTRACT
TERM

The employer guarantees that no employees will lose employment by the introduction of *technological change*, defined to include any change in technology, method or procedure which decreases the number of employees, except for normal layoff.

ARBITRATOR'S
RULING

While technological change need not involve the introduction of new machinery or improved methods, it must involve something more than just a change in the employer's operation; it does not include a simple curtailment of operations or cutback in production arising from reduced demand or, as in this case, a merger of two newspapers.

Canadian Newspapers (1980), 29 L.A.C. (2d) 85 (Ladner).

TEMPORARY EMPLOYEE, *compare* PROBATION

CONTRACT
TERM

Persons employed on a *temporary* basis are not covered by the terms of this agreement and shall not accumulate seniority, unless later employed as regular employees.

ARBITRATOR'S
RULING

Continuing the employment of a temporary employee beyond the end of the agreed temporary employment period does not confer employment status. Mere passage of time on the job does not make a temporary employee a regular employee; this requires some action by the company evidencing a change in status.

Maple Leaf Monarch (1984), 13 L.A.C. (3d) 307 (Gorsky).

▼

CONTRACT
TERM

A *temporary employee* shall not accumulate seniority but shall be entitled to all other benefits. *Temporary employee* means an employee who is employed for a definite period not longer than 6 months.

ARBITRATOR'S
RULING

The essence of temporary employment is that it is for a certain term; both the commencement and termination dates must be fixed at the time of hiring, although the term can be fixed by reference to the duration of a specified project as well as by reference to actual dates. Re-hiring an employee for successive terms of less than 6 months does not establish regular employment status; however, it

217

may be evidence that work is not temporary, but ongoing, and should be posted.

Pacific Northern Gas (1983), 13 L.A.C. (3d) 216 (Larson).

▼

CONTRACT TERM

An employee on being hired will be considered *temporary* and placed on probation until he or she has worked continuously for a period of 60 calendar days.

ARBITRATOR'S RULING

Requiring students hired on a temporary basis, for vacation relief, to resign, and them immediately rehiring them, in order to avoid the accrual of seniority rights, is not permitted by the collective agreement, although the union's acquiescence in such a practice may bar relief.

Consolidated Bathurst (1982), 6 L.A.C. (3d) 30 (MacDowell).

THE REGULARLY SCHEDULED SHIFT/WORKDAY

CONTRACT TERM

Each employee shall receive holiday pay provided he is at work on *the last regular scheduled workday* before and the first regular scheduled workday after the holiday.

ARBITRATOR'S RULING

Some arbitrators consider holiday pay as compensation for work done, while others regard it as a consequence of the fact that an employment relationship exists. Here, since the phrase is not personalized by use of the pronoun "his", it is not sufficient that an employee work his last regular scheduled workday; he must work on the regular scheduled workday before and after the holiday.

Browing Harvey Ltd. (1986), 27 L.A.C. (3d) 239 (Dicks).

▼

CONTRACT TERM

An employee is entitled to holiday pay where he works *the last working day* immediately before and the first scheduled working day immediately after the holiday.

ARBITRATOR'S
RULING

Substantial compliance is sufficient, so that it is not necessary to work the full shift if there is no work to do, but this does not entitle a worker to holiday pay where he simply leaves early without a valid reason.

Magnetic Metals (1986), 25 L.A.C. (3d) 93 (Rayner).

▼

CONTRACT
TERM

To qualify for holiday pay employees are required to work *the normal scheduled day* immediately preceding and immediately following the holiday except in the case of absence due to sickness, injury or other reason satisfactory to the company.

ARBITRATOR'S
RULING

When an employee is laid off indefinitely, so that she does not work the normal scheduled day following the holiday, she is not entitled to holiday pay; layoff is not a reason satisfactory to the company.

C.R. Snelgrove Co. (1986), 24 L.A.C. (3d) 127 (Solomatenko).

▼

CONTRACT
TERM

To qualify for holiday pay an employee must work *the full workday* immediately preceding and the full workday immediately following the holiday unless absent due to illness, etc.

ARBITRATOR'S
RULING

The qualifying days are not the workdays on which employees are personally scheduled to work, but rather the workdays scheduled for employees generally.

Dorr-Oliver Canada (1986), 23 L.A.C. (3d) 92 (Weatherill).

▼

CONTRACT
TERM

An employee shall not be eligible for holiday pay if he is absent on *the scheduled workday* immediately preceding or next following the holiday; employees on the payroll as of November 1st in each year are entitled to and shall be granted an additional holiday.

ARBITRATOR'S
RULING

An extended layoff during plant renovations does not disentitle employees to holiday pay where they were not scheduled to work during layoff. Use of the word "the" does not mean that grievors become disentitled when some employees are recalled early and plant is again in operation, because the objective/subjective distinction between "his" and "the" is a sterile distinction, and anyway the use of the phrase "absent on the scheduled workday" requires that employees themselves be scheduled to work. Workers remain "employees" as long as they retain seniority for purposes of recall, but qualification "on the payroll" requires active employment around the date specified and continuing beyond it.

Canada Packers (1985), 21 L.A.C. (3d) 289 (Swan).

▼

CONTRACT
TERM

Employees must have worked *the complete shift* before and after the holiday to qualify for holiday pay.

ARBITRATOR'S
RULING

As a result of the use of the definite article "the", the clause refers to shifts which employees generally are scheduled to work, even if the grievor personally is not scheduled to work because of layoff; it would be a different matter if the clause referred to "his scheduled shift".

Hamilton Gear Machine (1982), 6 L.A.C. (3d) 311 (Brown).

▼

CONTRACT
TERM

To obtain holiday pay employees must work on *the last regularly scheduled shift* prior to the holiday.

ARBITRATOR'S
RULING

A shift may be scheduled prior to a holiday even though employees are on strike; where it is so scheduled, then the last day before the strike is not the last regularly scheduled shift before the holiday. [This ruling must be reconsidered in light of present Ontario legislation which prohibits bargaining unit employees from working during a legal strike.]

3M Canada (1982), 4 L.A.C. (3d) 420 (M.G. Picher).

▼

CONTRACT TERM
In order to be entitled to payment for a plant holiday an employee must have worked *the full working day* immediately preceding and following the holiday except where management has given permission to be absent on either of these days.

ARBITRATOR'S RULING
Because "the" is used, rather than "his", the qualifying days are to be determined objectively for all employees, and not subjectively for individual employees. Where employees are on layoff on the day preceding a holiday, they are not scheduled to work, and are not entitled to holiday pay. A layoff is not synonymous with permission to be absent.

Caravelle Foods (1980), 26 L.A.C. (2d) 1 (O'Shea).

THEFT

CONTRACT TERM
The specific penalty for the following infractions shall be discharge: ... *theft* or aiding in the commission of *theft*.

ARBITRATOR'S RULING
"Theft" is the dishonest intention to benefit from another's property, as understood in common usage; it should not be defined to include all the legal and technical requirements of the *Criminal Code* definition. An employee who inadvertently gives free drinks to customers does not commit theft because there is no dishonest intention or personal gain involved.

Berto's Restaurant (1989), 8 L.A.C. (4th) 87 (Dissanayake).

▼

CONTRACT TERM
If it is decided that the employee was unjustly dismissed or suspended or, except in the case of *theft*, that the penalty was inappropriate, he should be reinstated to his former position.

ARBITRATOR'S RULING
"Theft" incorporates all the elements of the *Criminal Code* definition of theft, including intent. That is, the taking must be done fraudulently, without any colour of right, i.e. apparent right to the item, and with the intent of depriving the owner of it. While unauthorized taking of the employer's property may warrant discipline, it does not amount to theft, unless there is intent to deprive the employer of it, without any honest belief that he has the right or permission to do so.

Canada Packers Inc. (1989), 6 L.A.C. (4th) 25 (Swan).
Contrast *Ed Mirvish Enterprises*, below.

▼

CONTRACT
TERM

The specific penalty for the following infractions shall be discharge: ... *theft.*

ARBITRATOR'S
RULING

The use of something belonging to the employer, obtained through deception and turned to the use of oneself or another, constitutes theft. It is inappropriate to import the *Criminal Code* definition of theft, which requires fraudulent intent, into a collective agreement where the parties themselves have not done so. A waiter's serving of complimentary drinks to long-standing patrons constitutes theft under the collective agreement, where the waiter knew he required permission from the hotel, and deceived the bartender.

Ed Mirvish Enterprises Ltd. (1988), 34 L.A.C. (3d) 1 (Haefling). Contrast *Canada Packers Inc.*, above.

TIME WORKED, *see also* WORK

CONTRACT
TERM

For the purposes of calculating vacation pay and vacation bonus, where an employee has been absent on WCB benefits, such time will be considered as *time worked*, provided that such employee actually worked for some period during the vacation eligibility period in question.

ARBITRATOR'S
RULING

An employee absent on WCB who shows up to work on only one day during the year, without authorization by the employer, is not entitled to vacation monies for the year in question. He cannot be said to have actually worked, since he was not directed or assigned work by the employer. One cannot establish a claim to vacation and bonus pay simply by volunteering for work or by assigning oneself to perform work.

Rio Algom Ltd. (1988), 2 L.A.C. (4th) 151 (O'Shea).

▼

CONTRACT
TERM

Overtime will be paid for all *time worked* in excess of a normal 8-hour working period. "Time worked" may include a period in which no work is actually performed, but in which the employee remains under the employer's direction and control and/or in which the employee's responsibilities to the employer continue.

ARBITRATOR'S RULING Employees who are required to remain in company vehicles during their lunch breaks, except in certain circumstances, are entitled to be paid overtime for their lunch breaks, since they remain under the employer's direction and control and are not free to use the lunch break as they wish.

Town of Midland (1987), 31 L.A.C. (3d) 251 (Saltman).

▼

CONTRACT TERM Employees will be paid time and a half for *time worked* outside their daily scheduled hours.

ARBITRATOR'S RULING "Time worked" may include activities other than those included in an employee's job description and those which he usually performs every day. Authorized, albeit voluntary, attendance at a training session organized by management constitutes work, but attendance at a wine and cheese party thereafter does not.

Steinberg Inc. (1985), 20 L.A.C. (3d) 289 (Foisy).

▼

CONTRACT TERM Overtime is payable for *time worked* in excess of the regular working day.

ARBITRATOR'S RULING "Time worked" includes time during which employees are under the direction and control of the employer and during which the employees' responsibilities continue even though services are not performed for the employer; hence, lunch period is time worked where employees are required to remain at the workplace in order to be available in case of an emergency.

Religious Hospitallers (1983), 11 L.A.C. (3d) 151 (Saltman).

▼

CONTRACT TERM An employee shall receive 2 hours call time at the straight-time day rate in addition to pay for *time actually worked*.

ARBITRATOR'S RULING Employees are entitled to pay for work including providing information to a supervisor who telephones them at home to inquire about a production error.

Weyerhauser Canada (1983), 9 L.A.C. (3d) 308 (Bird).

▼

CONTRACT TERM	An employee who is requested by the company to work on his regular days off will be paid at the rate of time and one-half for all *time so worked.*
ARBITRATOR'S RULING	"Work" does not require employees to be actually performing their duties. Employees were entitled to be paid for sleeping over at a remote location where they were obliged to remain to finish the job, since they were subject to the direction of management and were thus not free to engage in personal activities of their choice.

Hamilton Street Railway (1981), 1 L.A.C. (3d) 355 (Shime).

TOTAL DISABILITY, see also DISABILITY

CONTRACT TERM	Upon proof that an employee has become *totally disabled,* the company will pay a weekly indemnity benefit; *totally disabled* means wholly or continuously disabled by sickness or an accidental bodily injury which prevents one from working for remuneration or profit.
ARBITRATOR'S RULING	An employee who is unable to work the night shift due to stress reaction, identified and confirmed by physicians, suffers from a permanent disability and is entitled to disability protection in the agreement until he can bump into an available day job.

Hickeson-Lang Supply Co. (1988), 34 L.A.C. (3d) 62 (Mitchnick).

▼

CONTRACT TERM	Employees who are *totally disabled* are entitled to sick pay benefit for the purposes of sick pay; *totally disabled* means a state of bodily injury or disease which prevents the employee from performing the regular duties of the occupation.
ARBITRATOR'S RULING	Participation in an *in vitro* fertilization program involving medical and surgical treatment qualifies an employee for sick leave benefits, since the grievor's absence results from an underlying diseased condition.

Hamilton Civic Hospitals (1988), 32 L.A.C. (3d) 284 (Saltman).

▼

CONTRACT TERM	Sick pay benefits shall be paid if an employee is *totally disabled; totally disabled* means an employee's inability to perform the regular duties pertaining to her occupation due to illness or injury.
ARBITRATOR'S RULING	Participation in an *in vitro* fertilization program, involving medical and surgical procedures to remedy infertility, entitles an employee to short-term sick leave benefits, because it is a recognized medical treatment for a pre-existing abnormal condition, which causes physical incapacity. Infertility itself qualifies as an illness or disease according to worldwide medical standards.

Metropolitan General Hospital (1987), 32 L.A.C. (3d) 10 (H.D. Brown).

▼

CONTRACT TERM	Insurance coverage depends on whether or not employee is *totally disabled.*
ARBITRATOR'S RULING	Clause requires assessment, not just of organic, but also of psychogenic illness.

Dominion Stores (1985), 20 L.A.C. (3d) 97 (Kennedy).

▼

CONTRACT TERM	Long-term disability benefits are available in the event of *total disability,* defined to mean the continuous disability of the employee to engage in each and every gainful occupation or employment for which he is reasonably qualified by education, training or experience.
ARBITRATOR'S RULING	Total disability means inability to perform work reasonably comparable to the work previously performed by the employee even though the employee may be capable of marginal employment.

Dominion Stores (1983), 11 L.A.C. (3d) 221 (M.G. Picher).

TOTAL PAY, *see also* GROSS EARNINGS

CONTRACT TERM	Vacation pay shall be based on 4% of *total pay* for the period between June 1 and May 31.
ARBITRATOR'S RULING	The term includes COLA payments included in wages for work actually done.

Outboard Marine (1982), 4 L.A.C. (3d) 185 (Palmer).

TOTAL WAGES EARNED, *see also* GROSS EARNINGS

CONTRACT TERM
Vacation pay will be calculated on the basis of 6% of *total wages earned* during the 12-month period preceding June 1.

ARBITRATOR'S RULING
Unlike the term "wages paid", the term "total wages earned" includes vacation pay received during vacation year.

Scarborough Centenary Hospital (1984), 13 L.A.C. (3d) 416 (Brown).

TRAINING, *see also* TIME WORKED

CONTRACT TERM
When operational requirements permit, the employer will grant leave without pay to union representatives to undertake *training* related to the duties of a representative.

ARBITRATOR'S RULING
Training includes the receipt of new information, not just the acquisition of practical skills; thus, a one-day union-sponsored seminar on the impact of free-trade qualifies as training.

Treasury Board (Health and Welfare Canada) and Babcock (1989) 5 L.A.C. (4th) 15 (R. Young).

TRANSFER, *see also* SKILL AND ABILITY, *compare* PROMOTION

CONTRACT TERM
In making staff changes, *transfers*, or promotions, appointment shall be made of applicants having the required qualifications and where qualifications are equal, seniority shall be the governing factor. Management rights shall not be exercised in an arbitrary or discriminatory manner.

ARBITRATOR'S RULING
Under this agreement, transfer involves a move outside the bargaining unit, or to another classification, while promotion constitutes either an advancement within a classification or a move to a higher classification. "Staff change" is a broad concept, and includes a reassignment of employees within the same classification to different locations. The employer's decision to make a staff change by reassigning two workers away from their usual stations is arbitrary where it is done without explanation or advance consultation.

Metropolitan Toronto Zoo (1989), 4 L.A.C. (4th) 46 (Swan).

▼

CONTRACT TERM
The union recognizes that the employer has the exclusive right to manage the business including the right to *transfer* employees because of lack of work or for other legitimate reasons.

ARBITRATOR'S RULING
The loss of a major customer by the company is a legitimate reason for reducing production, and therefore for reducing the number of shifts, redistributing the workforce over the remaining shifts, and transferring employees to lower-rated job classifications in accordance with their seniority. Where there is no lack of work, there is no requirement to lay off.

Roxul Co. (1988), 2 L.A.C. (4th) 58 (O'Shea).

▼

CONTRACT TERM
It is the exclusive function of the employer to *transfer* and assign employees provided that a claim for discriminatory transfer may be the subject of a grievance.

ARBITRATOR'S RULING
The term "transfer" means to move from one job to another. The move may be within a classification, or across classification lines. The essential element of a transfer is that the new job and the old must be distinctly different. The term "assign" means the general deployment of the workforce including organization of shift schedules and matters of a similar kind. Here, a move from the recreation department to the custodial shift, in a corrections institution, constitutes a transfer, not an assignment, since the jobs are different. The term "discriminatory" involves drawing a distinction for reasons that are illegal, arbitrary or unreasonable. Here, the transfer was not discriminatory, since the reason was that it was less costly to cover the grievor's absences from work on the custodial shift.

Metropolitan Authority (1983), 10 L.A.C. (3d) 265 (Outhouse).

▼

CONTRACT TERM
Seniority shall be the directing factor, where skills, competency, efficiency and qualifications are relatively equal, with regard to promotions, *transfers* and demotions.

ARBITRATOR'S The term "transfer" does not have a fixed meaning;
RULING depending upon the particular collective agreement, it may or may not be restricted to a move between classifications, and may or may not include a move to a different shift, area, or department within the same classification.
Ottawa General Hospital (1981), 2 L.A.C. (3d) 1 (P.C. Picher).

TRAVEL TIME, see also OVERTIME, TIME WORKED, WORK

CONTRACT An employee will be paid overtime at straight-time
TERM rates for *travel* outside regular hours provided it is essential. Employees will be paid overtime at time and one-half for the first 2 hours of authorized overtime worked in excess of the regular hours, and double time thereafter.

ARBITRATOR'S Travel time outside regular hours is authorized
RULING overtime worked, even though paid at straight-time rates, and should be included in calculating the overtime payable for other overtime work.
Alberta Housing Corp. (1982), 4 L.A.C. (3d) 228 (Taylor).

TRIAL PERIOD

CONTRACT The applicant selected for a job vacancy shall be
TERM given a thirty working day *trial period* to prove his suitability.

ARBITRATOR'S Where a training or trial period is required, the ap-
RULING plicant is to be given a chance, if there is a reasonable likelihood that he could become fully functional within the time provided. A trial period may serve not only to confirm ability but also to provide for a developmental and learning process. While a training period implies a formal system of instruction, with a trial period any development of a candidate is expected to take place in the normal course of events by simply working on the job, without substantial instruction. Not every trial period is of a developmental nature; if it is not, a candidate will be required to possess the necessary present ability; if it is, any appointment must be based on whether it is reasonably likely that the candidate will be able to learn the job in the period provided. The longer the trial period, the more likely it serves a developmental purpose.
Andres Wines (1984), 14 L.A.C. (3d) 238 (Larson).

U

UNFORESEEN EVENTS

CONTRACT
TERM
Longer notice of layoff is required in the event of a scheduled reduction of the workforce due to lack of work, but not where the layoff is due to *unforeseen events*.

ARBITRATOR'S
RULING
The refusal of creditors to continue financial arrangements requiring plant closing constitutes an unforeseen event.

White Farm Equipment (1982), 9 L.A.C. (3d) 366.

UNIFORM/UNIFORM ALLOWANCE

CONTRACT
TERM
Uniforms shall be furnished, cleaned and kept in repair by the employer at no cost to the employees.

ARBITRATOR'S
RULING
Term "uniforms" involves uniformity or sameness and denotes precision or duplication in every way; it does not encompass articles of clothing referred to in the employer's dress code, which allows flexibility as to material and styling.

Westin Hotel (1983), 12 L.A.C. (3d) 193 (Lederman).

▼

CONTRACT
TERM
A clothing maintenance allowance will be paid if the employer requires an employee to supply and/ or maintain *specified clothing in place of a uniform* that would otherwise be supplied and maintained.

ARBITRATOR'S
RULING
A dress code does not constitute the establishment of "specified clothing", so as to attract a uniform allowance, where it does not specify what staff can wear, but is designed simply to ensure that employees are neat, clean and tidy. Only when a dress code extends beyond a minimum standard of dress and serves some productive purpose of the employer does it attract a uniform allowance.

Green Memorial Home Society (1982), 4 L.A.C. (3d) 438 (Ladner).

UNION ACTIVITY

CONTRACT TERM
The parties agree that there shall be no discrimination with respect to terms or conditions of employment on the grounds of *union membership or non-membership or activity or lack of activity.*

ARBITRATOR'S RULING
"Discrimination" for the purposes of the collective agreement refers only to distinctions made in relation to persons covered by the collective agreement, not in relation to excluded personnel. All employees covered by the agreement must be treated equally with regard to benefits under the agreement. The fact that a dental plan is made available to excluded personnel does not violate the agreement.

Major Foods Ltd. (1989), 7 L.A.C. (4th) 129 (Stanley).

▼

CONTRACT TERM
There shall be no discrimination, interference, etc. with respect to an employee by reason of membership or *activity in the union.*

ARBITRATOR'S RULING
A strict and narrow interpretation of the phrase to mean only internal union affairs ignores the context in which collective agreements are signed. Is wearing of union buttons during working hours, communicating the possibility of a strike to the public through the statement "I'm on Strike Alert", protected union activity? Yes, because it is a legitimate expression of the employees' views on union matters, which should be curtailed only where an employer can demonstrate a detrimental effect on its capacity to manage or on its reputation or operations.

Treasury Board (Employment and Immigration Canada) (1989), 6 L.A.C. (4th) 412 (Galipeau).

▼

CONTRACT TERM
The company will provide a bulletin board in the plant for the convenience of the union in posting *notices of its activities.*

ARBITRATOR'S RULING	Only notices concerning union meetings, sports activities, social functions or similar activities organized either for or by the local union are within the article's scope; the employer is not required to give permission to post damaging or defamatory comments (e.g. inflammatory statements imputing to the employer bad faith in negotiations) on the bulletin board, since it is a means of publicizing union activities, not a forum for debate between the union and the employer.

FBI Brands Limited (1987), 29 L.A.C. (3d) 189 (Willes).

▼

CONTRACT TERM	There shall be no discrimination, etc. with respect to an employee by reason of membership or *activity in the union.*
ARBITRATOR'S RULING	Wearing a union button during working hours announcing a day of protest against deregulation of the use of casuals, etc. is protected union activity; the employer cannot interfere with employees' freedom of expression unless an overriding interest is established such as disruption of production or harm to customer relations. In this case, the button contained a simple announcement, and was not provocative, derogatory or offensive.

Canada Post (1986), 26 L.A.C. (3d) 58 (Outhouse).

▼

CONTRACT TERM	The employer shall provide a bulletin board for the purpose of posting *information related to the union's activities.*
ARBITRATOR'S RULING	Information must be factual, not mere propaganda.

Foothills Hospital Board (1985), 23 L.A.C. (3d) 42 (Malone).

▼

CONTRACT TERM	The employer agrees to provide bulletin boards for posting *notices of union activities*; there shall be no posting of political matter on the employer's property.
ARBITRATOR'S RULING	Notice of a Labour Day rally featuring a prominent politician on the day before a federal election is not political matter since it does not support a political party or candidate or espouse a political point of view.

Salvation Army Grace Hospital (1985), 19 L.A.C. (3d) 441 (Burkett).

▼

CONTRACT
TERM

There will be no discrimination, etc. with respect to any employee because of his membership in or connection with the union. The employer will supply a *bulletin board for use by the union* in a mutually satisfactory location.

ARBITRATOR'S
RULING

The union is entitled to post a notice announcing a settlement by the local with another employer since the content does not create strife within the enterprise or compromise the company's public image as neutral in respect of industrial disputes elsewhere, and the wording is tactful and restrained, and not inflammatory, untruthful or malicious.

Plainfield Children's Home (1985), 19 L.A.C. (3d) 412 (Emrich).

▼

CONTRACT
TERM

There shall be no discrimination, etc. against any employee by reason of his membership or *activities on behalf of the union.*

ARBITRATOR'S
RULING

While a union dress button is unobjectionable, wearing a union button during working hours urging a boycott in support of members of the same union striking against another employer (Eaton's) is to import a labour dispute from another employer into the company's store; it is not legitimate union activity, and a company rule ordering removal of such buttons is reasonable.

Dominion Stores (1985), 19 L.A.C. (3d) 269 (O'Shea).

▼

CONTRACT
TERM

No employee will be unlawfully interfered with, restrained, coerced or discriminated against by the company because of *lawful activity on behalf of the union.*

ARBITRATOR'S
RULING

Wearing a union pin to show support during bargaining is lawful union activity.

Air Canada (1985), 19 L.A.C. (3d) 23 (Brent).

▼

CONTRACT
TERM

There shall be no discrimination, etc. with respect to an employee by reason of membership or *activity in the union.*

ARBITRATOR'S RULING
The employer can restrict distribution of a newsletter advocating an unlawful refusal to cross picketlines.

Re Heffernan and White (1981), 3 L.A.C. (3d) 125 (O'Shea).

▼

CONTRACT TERM
No employee will be unlawfully interfered with, restrained, coerced or discriminated against by the company because of *lawful activity on behalf of the union.*

ARBITRATOR'S RULING
Such activity encompasses anything by the union which is lawful and which does not disrupt company operations or interfere with employees' productivity during working hours. The distribution of NDP pamphlets to employees during an election campaign on company premises, which does not affect the employer's control and direction of the workplace, is lawful union activity.

Air Canada (1980), 27 L.A.C. (2d) 289 (Simmons).

UNION BUSINESS

CONTRACT TERM
Leave of absence for *union business* will be granted without pay and without loss of seniority up to a maximum of 3 months.

ARBITRATOR'S RULING
Besides attendance at conventions, preparation for arbitrations, summer school, etc., the term "union business" includes participation by the local president in negotiations between the local and another employer.

City of Kitchener (1982), 5 L.A.C. (3d) 151 (Roberts).

UNION OFFICER

CONTRACT TERM
Union officers are to be retained in employment during their terms of office notwithstanding their position on the seniority list.

ARBITRATOR'S RULING
Having regard for the dictionary definition of an officer as "one who holds an office of trust, authority or command" (Webster's), the term includes officers under the by-laws of the union, including not only the local union's executive officers, but also divisional chairpersons responsible for co-ordinating the activities of the bargaining units which comprise the local.

Dominion Stores Ltd. (1984), 15 L.A.C. (3d) 47 (Yeoman).

UNION PURPOSES

CONTRACT TERM — Bulletin boards are to be used solely for *purposes pertaining to the [union] and its members.*

ARBITRATOR'S RULING — Posting of a notice on the bulletin board urging members to boycott a retail store in support of striking retail employees at Eaton's constitutes a union purpose since it involves communication from the union to its members and does not detrimentally affect the operations of the employer.

Parkwood Hospital (1986), 25 L.A.C. (3d) 125 (Brown).

UNION REPRESENTATION

CONTRACT TERM — The company shall ensure that a *union* steward from the employee's division is *present* when an employee with seniority is being discharged or suspended for a period of 5 days or more.

ARBITRATOR'S RULING — The presence of a union steward beside a representative of the employer who is discharging an employee over the telephone does not satisfy the requirement that a steward be present, since the employee would have no opportunity to consult with and be represented by the steward. As well, the steward would hear only half the conversation, and the fact that the union official was willing to listen did not amount to a waiver of the grievor's rights. A three-way telephone call, through the use of an extension phone or other device, would have satisfied the requirement.

Denison Mines Ltd. (1988), 1 L.A.C. (4th) 391 (Freedman).

▼

CONTRACT TERM — The company agrees that when an employee is to be disciplined *a local union official shall be present.*

ARBITRATOR'S RULING — Discipline is a generic term, and may, depending on the context, include discharge; here, it does, because it would be absurd to require union representation for minor discipline, but not for discharge. Since the right to union representation is a substantive right of basic importance, the absence of a union steward renders the discharge void.

Saville Food Products (1985), 20 L.A.C. (3d) 114 (Brandt).

UNION SCHOOLS AND SEMINARS

CONTRACT
TERM
Time off without pay will be provided to union members who are selected as representatives of the union for attending *union schools and seminars.*

ARBITRATOR'S
RULING
Where union is defined in the collective agreement as Alberta Union of Provincial Employees, then "union schools" refers to schools run by AUPE, not to the Labour College.

Alberta Liquor Control Board (1985), 22 L.A.C. (3d) 445 (Koshman).

UNSAFE WORK, *see also* REASONABLE CAUSE

CONTRACT
TERM
An employee or group of employees who believe they are being required to work under conditions which are *unsafe* or unhealthy beyond the normal hazard inherent in the operation shall have the right to grieve.

ARBITRATOR'S
RULING
Employees must show that they honestly believe the work to be unsafe, and have a reasonable belief, viewed from the perspective of the average employee at the time, that it is unsafe. A collective decision by workers to refuse work because of safety considerations does not constitute a strike.

Eastern Steelcasting (1981), 28 L.A.C. (2d) 310 (Adell).

UPWARD BUMPING, *see* LAYOFF

235

V

VACANCIES, *see also* SKILL AND ABILITY

CONTRACT TERM
When any of the jobs in the employer's premises become vacant on a permanent basis, the employer will post a notice of *vacancy* for a period of 7 consecutive calendar days.

ARBITRATOR'S RULING
A vacancy arises if there is adequate work to justify the filling of that position; an employer cannot decide not to fill the position merely for reasons of scheduling flexibility and cost-saving.

Maplewood Nursing Home (1989), 9 L.A.C. (4th) 115 (Hunter).

▼

CONTRACT TERM
When an employee leaves the company, management will determine whether a *vacancy* exists. A notice of such decision will be posted within 10 days.

ARBITRATOR'S RULING
The company is not under an obligation to post a vacancy at the location where it arose, but may post it at another location, to which it can transfer employees.

Union Gas Ltd. (1988), 1 L.A.C. (4th) 254 (Palmer).

▼

CONTRACT TERM
In making promotions to *vacant jobs* coming within the jurisdiction of the union, the required knowledge and skills contained in the job posting shall be the primary considerations and where two or more applicants are equally qualified to fulfill the duties of the job, seniority shall be the determining factor. Notices of *vacancy* required to be filled shall be immediately posted for a period of seven days.

236

ARBITRATOR'S RULING   A reclassification of an existing position triggers the posting and seniority provisions of the collective agreement. At the instant a new job (i.e. a specific set of duties assigned to one person) is created or an existing job is changed by the employer, it is vacant for the purposes of the agreement; otherwise, the employer could avoid the posting and seniority provisions by reclassifying current employees, even for new jobs.

City of Edmonton (1987), 30 L.A.C. (3d) 353 (Jones).

▼

CONTRACT TERM   A *vacancy* or new job shall be posted.

ARBITRATOR'S RULING   A vacancy or new job is not created merely by alteration of shift hours, work area or days off, and such alteration does not constitute a layoff so as to require re-posting.

Royal Columbian Hospital (1986), 24 L.A.C. (3d) 359 (Kelleher).

▼

CONTRACT TERM   When a *vacancy* occurs the employer shall post notice of the position.

ARBITRATOR'S RULING   Unless the collective agreement provides otherwise, a vacancy is not created by the temporary absence of the incumbent due to illness or vacation.

Disabled and Aged Regional Transit System (1985), 20 L.A.C. (3d) 354 (Solomatenko).

▼

CONTRACT TERM   Those with greatest seniority shall be given preference in job *vacancies* and promotions, provided they possess the ability and the desire to do the work required. Where there are openings, i.e. vacancies within the job classifications covered by the collective agreement, they shall be posted.

ARBITRATOR'S RULING   Employees are entitled to apply for vacancies in the same job classification when they are posted.

Spar Aerospace (1985), 20 L.A.C. (3d) 344 (E.B. Jolliffe). Contrast *City of Victoria*, below.

▼

CONTRACT TERM   When a *vacancy* occurs a notice will be posted.

237

ARBITRATOR'S
RULING

A vacancy exists only where there is adequate work to be done; it does not exist where an employee resigns and work is redistributed to other employees.

Beacon Hill Lodges (1985), 20 L.A.C. (3d) 316 (McLaren).

▼

CONTRACT
TERM

In all cases of promotion, or in filling *vacancies*, etc., notice shall be posted, and the following factors shall be considered: knowledge, efficiency and ability to perform the work; and length of continuous service.

ARBITRATOR'S
RULING

Since an employee has no claim to any particular job within a classification, a lateral move or transfer from one job to another within a classification is not a vacancy requiring posting unless the collective agreement provides otherwise.

City of Victoria (1982), 2 L.A.C. (3d) 368 (R. Brown). Contrast *Spar Aerospace*, above.

▼

CONTRACT
TERM

Notice of a job *vacancy* will be posted; on layoff the least senior employees shall be laid off first and called back last.

ARBITRATOR'S
RULING

A layoff does not create a vacancy because the employer no longer requires the job to be done, but a vacancy does arise where the number of workers to be laid off is reduced because an additional worker is required in a classification. The vacancy exists, and must be posted, even though an employee on layoff may be entitled to fill it under the recall provisions of the collective agreement.

Gray Forging (1981), 30 L.A.C. (2d) 354 (Weatherill).

VACATION/VACATION PAY, *see also* GROSS EARNINGS

CONTRACT
TERM

Employees who have completed 6 months' service shall be entitled to one week's *vacation*, to 2 weeks' *vacation* after 1 year's service, etc.

238

ARBITRATOR'S RULING "Service" includes time spent on disability leave, since vacation entitlement based on length of service should not be affected by involuntary absences, unless there is clear language to the contrary in the collective agreement.

Rahey's Supermarket (1989), 3 L.A.C. (4th) 311 (MacDonald).

▼

CONTRACT TERM Employees with less than one year's service at date of *vacation* shall be paid 6% of gross earnings; employees with one year's service or more shall have 3 weeks' paid *vacation*.

ARBITRATOR'S RULING Service continues to accrue during layoff since periods of layoff do not sever employment so long as recall rights are retained. There is no indication in the language that vacation entitlement is linked to actual performance of work, active employment, or working a specific number of hours or days.

Ron May Pontiac GMC Ltd. (1988), 33 L.A.C. (3d) 129 (MacDougall).

▼

CONTRACT TERM *Vacation pay* shall be paid to laid off employees at the time of layoff.

ARBITRATOR'S RULING While vacation pay entitlement may depend on maintaining status as an employee rather than on actually working throughout the year, an employee who is laid off during the year is not entitled to full vacation pay for the balance of the year, but only to a percentage.

Domglas (1986), 26 L.A.C. (3d) 29 (Kelleher).

▼

CONTRACT TERM Employees will receive *vacation pay* equal to the greater of 4% of their T-4 earnings in the preceding calendar year or 96 hours' pay.

ARBITRATOR'S RULING Term includes vacation pay and holiday pay received in the previous year since these payments are included in the T-4 forms submitted by the company to Revenue Canada.

Canso Seafoods Ltd. (1984), 16 L.A.C. (3d) 253 (Kelly).

▼

CONTRACT TERM	*Vacation* entitlement is based on years of service.
ARBITRATOR'S RULING	Term includes service with previous employer where the business is sold or transferred; otherwise, vacation entitlement would be less than that provided under employment standards legislation, which counts service with the previous employer in calculating minimum vacation entitlement on sale of a business.
	Middlesex-London District Health Unit (1984), 16 L.A.C. (3d) 98 (Saltman).

▼

CONTRACT TERM	*Vacation pay* will be calculated on the basis of 6% of total wages earned during the 12-month period preceding June 1.
ARBITRATOR'S RULING	Unlike the term "wages paid", the term "total wages earned" includes vacation pay received during vacation year.
	Scarborough Centenary Hospital (1984), 13 L.A.C. (3d) 416 (Brown).

▼

CONTRACT TERM	Employees shall receive 11 statutory holidays. *Vacation* shall be based on years of continuous service. Sick leave credits shall accumulate based on months or years worked.
ARBITRATOR'S RULING	Some benefits accrue by virtue of employment, others depend on the employee's presence at the workplace and performance of work. It all depends on the agreement. Here, in the absence of restrictions, employees absent from work because of a compensable disability are entitled to holiday pay and vacations, since continuous service is synonymous with seniority, but sick leave credits do not accumulate since they are based on months or years worked.
	City of Trail (1983), 10 L.A.C. (3d) 251 (Munroe).

▼

CONTRACT TERM	*Vacation pay* shall be based on 4% of total pay for the period between June 1 and May 31.
ARBITRATOR'S RULING	The term includes COLA payments included in wages for work actually done.

Outboard Marine (1982), 4 L.A.C. (3d) 185 (Palmer).

▼

CONTRACT
TERM

Employees are entitled to *vacation with pay.*

ARBITRATOR'S
RULING

A distinction is to be made between clauses which use such language as "total earnings" or "gross earnings" and those clauses which base vacation pay on wages or earnings received for "time worked", "total hours worked", or "all work done". In the absence of a definition in the collective agreement, it is reasonable to look to labour standards legislation, which uses "total wages earned by the employee for the hours worked". Based on this language, vacation pay does not include holiday pay and sick leave pay.

Frelco Limited (1980), 27 L.A.C. (2d) 123 (Thistle).

▼

CONTRACT
TERM

Vacations shall be based on years of service.

ARBITRATOR'S
RULING

Service is not interrupted by period on layoff.

Sola Basic (1976), 11 L.A.C. (2d) 328 (Beck).

W

WAGE-RELATED PREMIUM

CONTRACT
TERM

Contractors or subcontractors engaged by the company shall pay their employees an amount equivalent to the wage rates and *wage rate related premiums* established in the collective agreement. Employees who report for work will receive $10 reporting allowance for each day worked.

ARBITRATOR'S
RULING

The $10 per day reporting allowance does not qualify as a "wage rate related premium", since it is not calculated on an hourly basis, but is a flat amount which is payable to all employees who report to work, whatever their mode of transportation and wherever they live.

Luscar Sterco (1988), 33 L.A.C. (3d) 347 (Jones).

▼

CONTRACT
TERM

In order to qualify for holiday pay, an employee must be *entitled to wages* for at least 12 shifts during the 30 preceding calendar days.

ARBITRATOR'S
RULING

Phrase requires more than continued employment; absence on workers' compensation disqualifies employee from entitlement.

B.C. Railway Co. (1985), 22 L.A.C. (3d) 299 (Hope).

WEEK/WEEKLY SCHEDULE

CONTRACT
TERM

The employer shall post a *weekly schedule* for all employees no later than Friday noon in each *week* for the following *week.*

ARBITRATOR'S
RULING

A weekly schedule is the aggregate number of hours worked in a period of 7 days, normally reckoned from one Sunday to the next. An employer is therefore prevented from changing the work week and schedule from Sunday-to-Saturday, to Thursday-to-Wednesday, since "week" should be given its ordinary meaning Sunday to Saturday.

Inn of the Woods (1989), 7 L.A.C. (4th) 31 (Aggarwal).

WITHOUT DEDUCTION OF PAY

CONTRACT
TERM
Statutory holidays shall be observed *without deduction of pay.*

ARBITRATOR'S
RULING
Term guarantees pay only where an employee is otherwise entitled to it, and thus not where the employee is on layoff anyway.

United Co-Operatives of Ontario (1983), 13 L.A.C. (3d) 376 (Weatherill).

WORK, *see also* TIME WORKED

CONTRACT
TERM
The employer agrees that persons not covered by this agreement will not perform duties normally assigned to persons in the bargaining unit except for purposes of instruction, experimentation, emergency or as may be agreed. In order to provide job security for members of the bargaining unit the employer will not contract out work usually performed by members of the bargaining unit if a layoff follows. Nor will an employee remain on layoff if that employee can perform the normal requirements of the work.

ARBITRATOR'S
RULING
The first clause applies to non-bargaining unit employees, the second to contracting out of bargaining unit work. Where the second clause applies (as here), "work" has a broader meaning than "duties", and is the composite of tasks, duties and activities employees are required to perform. The question is whether the outside contractor is doing similar work for the employer. Where this occurs, and probationary employees are on layoff, a violation of the collective agreement results.

Regional Municipality of Ottawa-Carleton (1989), 9 L.A.C. (4th) 201 (Thorne).

▼

CONTRACT
TERM
Scheduled overtime shall be offered by seniority amongst the employees who normally perform the *work* by department.

ARBITRATOR'S
RULING

"Work" refers to a separate and identifiable task or set of tasks which constitutes a type of job. A classification, on the other hand, is a grouping of the same or similar types of jobs under a single title. Work "normally performed by employees" does not embrace all job functions ever performed by employees in a particular classification, but only work for which an employee is qualified and which he or she has performed on a regular basis.

Strudex Fibres (1989), 6 L.A.C. (4th) 226 (Roberts).

▼

CONTRACT
TERM

For the purposes of calculating vacation pay and vacation bonus, where an employee has been absent on WCB benefits, such time will be considered as time worked, provided that such employee actually *worked* for some period during the vacation eligibility period in question.

ARBITRATOR'S
RULING

An employee absent on WCB who shows up to work on only one day during the year, without authorization by the employer, is not entitled to vacation monies for the year in question. He cannot be said to have actually worked, since he was not directed or assigned work by the employer. One cannot establish a claim to vacation and bonus pay simply by volunteering for work or by assigning oneself to perform work.

Rio Algom Ltd. (1988), 2 L.A.C. (4th) 151 (O'Shea).

▼

CONTRACT
TERM

An employee required to *work* overtime on his first scheduled day of rest shall be paid overtime pay.

ARBITRATOR'S
RULING

Where attendance at a driver education course is voluntary and unrelated to employment in the bargaining unit, it is not "required", and does not constitute "work", even though some benefit may accrue to the employer.

N.S. Civil Service Commission (1986), 25 L.A.C. (3d) 5 (Outhouse).

▼

CONTRACT
TERM

Overtime *work* shall be compensated at time and a half for every hour worked over 40 hours.

ARBITRATOR'S
RULING
Whether travel time is work depends on the circumstances. Authorized travel to and from a professional development conference is work, entitling an employee to overtime pay, even though attendance may not be mandatory.

London Ass'n for Mentally Retarded (1984), 16 L.A.C. (3d) 165 (Saltman).

▼

CONTRACT
TERM
An employee shall receive 2 hours call time at the straight-time day rate in addition to pay for time actually *worked*.

ARBITRATOR'S
RULING
Employees are entitled to pay for work including providing information to a supervisor who telephones them at home to inquire about a production error.

Weyerhauser Canada (1983), 9 L.A.C. (3d) 308 (Bird).

WORK AVAILABLE

CONTRACT
TERM
In all cases of layoff and recall, preference shall be given to employees based on seniority, provided they are able to fill the requirements of the *work available*.

ARBITRATOR'S
RULING
In cases of promotion, it is generally sufficient, depending on the language of the collective agreement, that an employee have the potential to do the job, but on layoff employees must be able to do the work in question without a training period, because otherwise the operation would be severely impaired by the checkerboard move of employees. Indeed, the word "available" is used to indicate that there is a temporal qualification to the work, and that employees must have the present ability to perform it.

Reynolds Aluminum Company of Canada Ltd. (1980), 26 L.A.C. (2d) 266 (Shime).

WORK NORMALLY PERFORMED

CONTRACT
TERM
Persons not covered by this collective agreement shall not do *work normally performed* by clerical employees except in emergencies and for training.

245

ARBITRATOR'S
RULING
Work normally performed by bargaining unit members does not refer to work which is done only by bargaining unit employees, but means work which would have been done by bargaining unit employees if contracting out had not occurred. However, "persons" refers only to other non-bargaining-unit employees of the employer, so that the employer does not violate the collective agreement by having bargaining unit work performed by outside agents if it is contracted out for valid business reasons.

Maritime Telegraph and Telephone Co. Ltd. (1989), 8 L.A.C. (4th) 22 (Archibald).

WORK PERFORMED

CONTRACT
TERM
An employee shall be paid at the rate of time and one-half for all *work performed* in excess of the normal weekly hours of work. An employee who is called in and reports for work outside his regularly scheduled hours of work will be paid a minimum of 4 hours pay.

ARBITRATOR'S
RULING
Employees required to wear paging devices off-duty are not performing work entitling them to overtime by doing so. However, when an employee responds to such a call, he or she is entitled to overtime pay for the period of time spent dealing with the call, if it is in excess of the normal weekly hours of work, since no other reasonable meaning can be attached to the term "work performed". However, the call-in provision applies only to an employee who is called in and then reports for work at the company's premises.

Leco Industries Ltd. (1980), 26 L.A.C. (2d) 80 (Brunner).

WORK SCHEDULES

CONTRACT
TERM
Work schedules, whenever possible, will be determined by mutual agreement between the employer and the employees. *Work schedules* may take the form of either three shift, two shift or single shift rotations.

ARBITRATOR'S RULING The term "work schedules" refers to times of work of employees, the days and hours that an employee may be required to work, and it does not relate to the status of employees as full-time or part-time, or questions of staffing mix; as a result, this clause does not prevent the employer from reducing the number of part-time staff and converting these to a smaller number of full-time positions.

New Vista Care Home (1988), 1 L.A.C. (4th) 227 (Larson).

▼

CONTRACT TERM The employer agrees to hold constructive consultation with the union prior to having the *work usually done* by the employees of the bargaining unit given outside.

ARBITRATOR'S RULING Both the conversion of a subpost office to a franchise, and the establishment of a franchise in an area not previously served by a postal facility, constitute contracting out, where they involve work which would have been done by bargaining unit employees if the contracting out or franchising had not occurred.

Canada Post Corp. (1988), 34 L.A.C. (3d) 28 (Christie).

WORKDAY

CONTRACT TERM New employees will be considered probationary employees for the first 45 *workdays* on the active payroll of the employer. Upon completion of 30 *days worked*, probationary employees shall be entitled to payment for the paid holidays specified.

ARBITRATOR'S RULING Because management needs a reasonable opportunity to assess an employee, paid holidays to which a probationer becomes entitled are not counted in calculating the probationary period; "workdays" and "days worked" are synonymous.

General Coach (1988), 35 L.A.C. (3d) 235 (Roberts).

▼

CONTRACT TERM The *workday* shall be the 24-hour period from the employee's scheduled starting time. The [number of hours in a] *workday* is the 8-hour period at the employee's designated working place.

ARBITRATOR'S
RULING

For overtime purposes, the workday begins at an employee's actual, ultimate, scheduled starting time, not the posted commencement time.

Noranda Metal Ind. Ltd. (1980), 26 L.A.C. (2d) 307 (Gorsky).

WORKING CONDITIONS

CONTRACT
TERM

Any *working conditions* in effect shall continue unless changed during the term of the agreement by mutual consent.

ARBITRATOR'S
RULING

A working condition is a mainstream aspect of the working relationship fixed for a meaningful period of time and regarded by the parties as not within unilateral management control. A total ban on smoking does not violate the prohibition on changing working conditions because the employer had progressively banned smoking from its properties over the years, and therefore the parties could not be said to have regarded the issue as "fixed and not within unilateral management control". However, while it is reasonable to prohibit smoking wherever it is likely that non-smokers will come into significant contact with smoke, the union should have the opportunity to identify designated areas for smokers, if it does not affect non-smokers.

Toronto Transit Commission (1989), 5 L.A.C. (4th) 156 (Samuels).

▼

CONTRACT
TERM

All rights, benefits, privileges and *working conditions* which employees now enjoy, receive or possess, which the employer has knowledge of, shall continue to be enjoyed and possessed insofar as they are consistent with this agreement, but may be modified by mutual agreement between the employer and the union.

ARBITRATOR'S
RULING

The introduction of a requirement that employees punch in and out for paid coffee breaks is not an alteration of a right, benefit or privilege, because these relate to something positive which flows from one person to another, and the employer never by any positive act conferred on employees a right, benefit or privilege of not punching in and out at breaks. However, the change does constitute alteration of a working condition. The existence of a working condition does not necessarily imply a positive act on the part of the employer; it is simply a circumstance under which work is to be performed, or a condition under which employees work.

Glades Lodge Ltd. (1988), 1 L.A.C. (4th) 257 (Veniot).

▼

CONTRACT TERM
All rights, benefits, privileges and *working conditions* which employees enjoy shall be continued, but may be modified by agreement of the parties.

ARBITRATOR'S RULING
A "right" implies an unfettered claim to something, while a privilege or benefit is an advantage enjoyed by one beyond others. An allowance to smoke is not a privilege, and institution of a no-smoking policy does not violate the collective agreement, where there was always a potential, if not actual, control placed on it. The ability to smoke is also not a working condition, where the practice varies from one location to another within the bargaining unit, and it has simply been licensed to a limited degree.

Board of Education for City of Toronto (1988), 33 L.A.C. (3d) 149 (Knopf).

WORKING DAYS

CONTRACT TERM
Statutory holiday pay is conditional upon an employee working the full *working day* preceding and following the holiday.

ARBITRATOR'S RULING
Condition is satisfied where a part-time employee works as required on both qualifying days though less than an eight-hour shift.

Humpty Dumpty Foods (1983), 11 L.A.C. (3d) 385 (Weatherill).

▼

CONTRACT TERM
An employee shall be on probation until he has been actively at work for a total of 65 *working days*.

ARBITRATOR'S RULING
The probation period is not shortened simply because the employee on probation works 11-hour days while most employees work 7 hour days. Sick days and paid statutory holidays not worked do not count, given the purpose of the probationary period.

Metro Toronto Ass'n for the Mentally Retarded (1983), 9 L.A.C. (3d) 58 (Langille).

▼

CONTRACT
TERM

Seniority shall be established after a probationary period of 45 *working days* during a six-month period.

ARBITRATOR'S
RULING

Since the purpose of a probationary period is to give the employer an opportunity to assess an employee, Saturdays and Sundays are included in working days, where they are worked, even though they may be overtime, and not part of the normal workweek.

Edwards, Owen Sound Operations (1981), 2 L.A.C. (3d) 348 (Linden).

▼

CONTRACT
TERM

When a vacancy occurs, the employer shall post a notice for at least 7 *working days.*

ARBITRATOR'S
RULING

In a continuous operation, a working day would mean a calendar day, but where the collective agreement also refers to calendar days in other provisions, a working day excludes Saturdays, Sundays and paid holidays. Since a working day is "the portion of a day assigned for labour", a working day in a continuous operation is a 24-hour period; to be fair to employees on all 3 shifts, the notice should be posted for a full 24 hours on each of the specified 7 days.

Sudbury General Hospital (1981), 2 L.A.C. (3d) 296 (Betcherman).

▼

CONTRACT
TERM

A grievance must be delivered personally to the store manager within seven *working days* of the alleged occurrence said to have caused the grievance.

ARBITRATOR'S
RULING

Where the collective agreement provides for a normal work week of 5 days with 2 consecutive days off, working days are the days that an employee would work (thus, five), not the days of operation of the company (here, six); they do not include the days when the employer is open for business, but the employee is not at work.

Dominion Stores (1981), 1 L.A.C. (3d) 436 (McLaren).

▼

CONTRACT TERM In order to be entitled to payment for a plant holiday an employee must have worked the full *working day* immediately preceding and following the holiday except where management has given permission to be absent on either of these days.

ARBITRATOR'S RULING Because "the" is used, rather than "his", the qualifying days are to be determined objectively for all employees, and not subjectively for individual employees. Where employees are on layoff on the day preceding a holiday, they are not scheduled to work, and are not entitled to holiday pay. A layoff is not synonymous with permission to be absent.

Caravelle Foods (1980), 26 L.A.C. (2d) 1 (O'Shea).

WORKLOAD PERMITS

CONTRACT TERM When *workload permits*, a supernumerary day may be interchanged with a regular day off. Employees who have worked overtime may be granted one hour off for each hour worked provided the *workload permits.*

ARBITRATOR'S RULING In determining whether workload permits the granting of equivalent time off or statutory holiday lieu day exchanges, management need only ascertain whether sufficient regularly-scheduled staff are available; it is not obliged to call in employees on an overtime basis or make other exceptional arrangements in order to grant requests.

Ontario Hydro (1989), 6 L.A.C. (4th) 64 (P.C. Picher).

WORKWEEK

CONTRACT TERM Employees working overtime on Sundays shall receive double time; *workweek* is Monday to Friday starting at 7 a.m. Monday.

ARBITRATOR'S RULING If an employee's regular shift commences late on a particular day and overlaps into a second day, as for example a Friday evening into a Saturday morning, the shift worked is viewed as a "day" corresponding to the day on which the shift commenced. Where a 3-shift operation is in effect, and the collective agreement provides that the workweek begins at 7 a.m. Monday, work between 5 a.m. and 7 a.m. on Monday is to be treated as work on a Sunday, and double time is payable.

Canron Inc. (1987), 27 L.A.C. (3d) 379 (M.G. Picher).

▼

CONTRACT TERM
Overtime at time and a half is payable after 40 hours in a *workweek*; time and a half is payable for work on a holiday.

ARBITRATOR'S RULING
A workweek consists of days and hours spent working within a given time frame, and for purposes of calculating overtime it includes a holiday on which the employee works. No question of pyramiding arises because the purpose of overtime is to compensate for the effort and inconvenience of having to work beyond the normal work schedule, whereas the purpose of holiday pay, an earned benefit, is to ensure enjoyment of a holiday without loss of pay.

J. Xavier Enterprises (1987), 26 L.A.C. (3d) 289 (T.A.B. Jolliffe).

▼

CONTRACT TERM
The standard *work week* shall consist of 40 hours per week comprised of 5 eight-hour days.

ARBITRATOR'S RULING
"Week" may mean a calendar week, Sunday to Saturday, or a period of 7 consecutive days; the reference to hours, rather than particular calendar days, indicates a consecutive day week. The employer violates the agreement when it denies overtime to employees working a continental workweek (7 days on, 2 days off), if they do not work more than 5 days in a calendar week.

Sunny Orange Ltd. (1981), 1 L.A.C. (3d) 381 (McLaren).

XYZ

YEARS WORKED

CONTRACT TERM

Employees shall receive 11 statutory holidays. Vacation shall be based on years of continuous service. Sick leave credits shall accumulate based on months or *years worked*.

ARBITRATOR'S RULING

Some benefits accrue by virtue of employment, others depend on the employee's presence at the workplace and performance of work. It all depends on the agreement. Here, in the absence of restrictions, employees absent from work because of a compensable disability are entitled to holiday pay and vacations, since continuous service is synonymous with seniority, but sick leave credits do not accumulate since they are based on months or years worked.

City of Trail (1983), 10 L.A.C. (3d) 251 (Munroe).

PRINTED IN CANADA